ArtScroll Series®

Rabbi Nosson Scherman / Rabbi Meir Zlotowitz

General Editors

ANGER!

Published by

Mesorah Publications, ltd

The Inner Teacher

A NINE-STEP PROGRAM
TO FREE YOURSELF
FROM ANGER

by Rabbi Zelig Pliskin

FIRST EDITION
First Impression . . . September 1997
Second Impression . . . May 1998
Third Impression . . . January 1999

Published and Distributed by
MESORAH PUBLICATIONS, Ltd.
4401 Second Avenue
Brooklyn, New York 11232

Distributed in Europe by
J. LEHMANN HEBREW BOOKSELLERS
20 Cambridge Terrace
Gateshead, Tyne and Wear
England NE8 1RP

Distributed in Israel by
SIFRIATI / A. GITLER—BOOKS
10 Hashomer Street
Bnei Brak 51361

Distributed in Australia & New Zealand by
GOLDS BOOK & GIFT CO.
36 William Street
Balaclava 3183, Vic., Australia

Distributed in South Africa by
KOLLEL BOOKSHOP
Shop 8A Norwood Hypermarket
Norwood 2196, Johannesburg, South Africa

THE ARTSCROLL SERIES ·
ANGER! THE INNER TEACHER
© Copyright 1997, by MESORAH PUBLICATIONS, Ltd.
4401 Second Avenue / Brooklyn, N.Y. 11232 / (718) 921-9000

No part of this book may be reproduced
in any form without **written** permission from the copyright holder,
except by a reviewer who wishes to quote brief passages in connection with a review
written for inclusion in magazines or newspapers.

THE RIGHTS OF THE COPYRIGHT HOLDER WILL BE STRICTLY ENFORCED.

ISBN:
1-57819-175-0 (hard cover)
1-57819-176-9 (paperback)

Printed in the United States of America by Noble Book Press Corp.
Bound by Sefercraft Quality Bookbinders, Ltd., Brooklyn, N.Y.

Acknowledgments

From the depths of my heart I thank *Hashem Yisborach*, the Father, my King, for all that He has given me.

I thank Rabbi Meir Zlotowitz and Rabbi Nosson Scherman of Artscroll for their positive reactions to the concept of this book.

I deeply appreciate Rabbi Shmuel Blitz's *zrizus* and cheerful encouragement.

I thank Rabbi Yonoson Rosenbloom for his incisive editing.

I thank Mrs. Aviva Rappoport for her insightful editing and feedback. Her work was indispensable.

I am profoundly grateful to my mother for her love and support throughout my life.

I am deeply grateful to my in-laws, Rabbi and Mrs. Simcha Weissman. May you have good health and much *nachas* from your children, grandchildren, and great-grandchildren.

I wish to express deep gratitude to Rabbi Noach Weinberg, Rosh Hayeshiva of Aish Hatorah in Jerusalem who had a major impact on many people, including myself.

I am deeply indebted to all of my teachers throughout my life.

I thank Rabbi Kalman Packouz for his friendship and encouragement.

In retrospect, I am grateful for those who have elicited my anger, for my anger has indeed been my teacher.

I thank all of those who have shared their own first-hand experiences with anger, and those who have attended my anger classes and seminars. Hopefully, what they have told me will serve as an inspiration to others.

Table of Contents

Reflections

Imagine These Scenarios:

You are on a selection committee for a prestigious institution. Two candidates have applied for a job. The person hired will be sharing your office. You have heard that Candidate A publicly humiliated a co-worker and lashes out at subordinates. While Candidate B isn't quite as brilliant or talented as Candidate A, he is competent and qualified and has one outstanding virtue: He is calm and levelheaded under pressure. Both candidates are virtually strangers and this is all you know about them.

Whom would you choose?

You are offered a choice between two computers. One computer system has state-of-the-art technology. The computer, programs, and laser printer work smoothly at lightning speed. The memory capacity is gigantic and the computer can easily run complex, demanding programs. This is a system that would allow you to make the most of your creativity. You

realize that it will take time and effort to master such an intricate system, but once you do, you are assured of a better life.

The other computer is what would now be considered an ancient model. The software you can run on it is inefficient and a source of frustration. The benefit of the old computer system and its software is that you already know how to run it. You won't have to spend any time or effort to learn anything new. While you will be greatly limited when you use it, at least its use is familiar.

In the short term, the old computer system is easier and faster. In the long run, however, you will waste much more time with the old computer and it will be a source of distress. With the new system, the beginning will be difficult, but then for the rest of the computer's life, you will benefit greatly.

Which gift would you choose?

You have been given as a gift a personal mental computer that runs 24 hours a day. You constantly make choices about what programs your brain will run. Unlike an electronic computer, you can't change the hardware, but you can always upgrade the software. The magnificent brain the Creator has given you is perfect for your needs in this world. The content of what you put into it, and what thoughts and images you access, is to a great extent up to you. Some mental programs (i.e., your thoughts and images) which you can choose will be anger-provoking. These are easy and automatic. Even an infant can run them. But there will be an enormous price to pay for using those programs. Other programs will be more spiritual, and will give you greater long-term joy and inner peace. They will enable you to have much more enhanced relationships with other people in the present, and the gain will be eternal.

It is unfortunate that so many people go through life on this planet without learning how to run their brains and minds in the ways that their Creator meant for them. When you know how to use your brain and mind properly, you can experience much joy, inner peace, love, and spiritual elevation.

You have been falsely accused of a serious crime. You may have done a few things wrong, but you are not the one who actually committed that crime. On the day of your trial, you arrive at the courthouse and wait outside until your case is called.

You notice a child running up and down the hall. You realize from his resemblance to the judge inside the courtroom that this child is his son. The child is a bit spoiled and enjoys irritating people. With his father looking on, the boy purposely tries to provoke you.

You know you will soon have to face the judge. You decide not to risk shouting angrily at his son, and instead turn to the boy and say with a smile, "A boy with a father such as yours can surely act better than this."

When you face the Ultimate Judge after 120 years, won't you feel more at ease knowing that He appreciated the way you interacted with His children?

Introduction

ow does my Creator want me to deal with my anger? This should be the first question in our minds when thinking about the subject of anger. Our goal is to internalize a Torah view of reality, other people, and ourselves, for this is what will free us from anger. The goal is to be in control of what we say and do even when we are angry, and to maintain self-respect and respect for others. Even when anger over injustice or evil is justified, the goal is always to think clearly and to act with wisdom.

Our Creator wants us to walk in His ways (*Devarim* 28:9). This is the source of our Torah obligation to conquer anger, as well as to refine all of our character traits. The *Rambam* shows us how high a priority this is by placing *Hilchos De'os* as the second of 83 sections of Torah law in his comprehensive work *Mishneh Torah*. After establishing the fundamental importance of loving and fearing G-d, the next step is to build our character so we can serve Him properly. The Vilna Gaon considers anger one of the two main traits which prevent a person from serving the A–mighty (*Beur HaGra* to *Mishlei* 16:31).

Does an obligation to conquer anger mean that the Torah wants us to cut off our real feelings? Definitely not. Without emotion we cannot experience passion for Torah and prayer, love for our Creator and other people, nor sincere joy in mitzvah performance.

We strive not just to control anger, but to be filled with love for our Creator and His children. When we experience this love, we focus on fulfilling His will. Then all else seems trivial, and very few things get us angry. Our love for other people lets us see their good qualities, either in potential or already expressed, and we judge them favorably and do all we can to help them grow and improve in ways they will appreciate. Angry blaming and condemnation only cause pain and breed resentment and further anger. Love enables understanding and paves the way to motivating and influencing with positive approaches.

As with anything worthwhile, it takes time and effort to change ingrained attitudes towards anger. But by keeping our eyes on our ultimate goal we will accomplish much more than we would have otherwise. It is only to be expected that at first anger will still flare up at times. Yet every mistake gives us vital information on how and what we need to improve. The more time and effort we put into mastering anger, the more expertise we gain.

Rabbi Yosef Leib Bloch of Telz emphasizes in *Shiurei Da'as* (Essay: *Al Yechsar HaMezeg*) that our Creator created us to experience each feeling honestly and intensely. To be a complete person, one needs to experience anger at times. It would be wrong to try to completely eradicate any quality bestowed upon us by our Creator. As the *Rambam* comments: "Don't be a bad-tempered person who becomes angry easily. Neither should you be like a corpse that doesn't feel anything. Rather, be in the middle. Don't become angry except over a serious matter in order to prevent a person from acting similarly another time (*Hilchos De'os* 1:4). The *Rambam* also states that ideally parents and other leaders should feign anger when they must rebuke while inwardly remaining calm (ibid. 2:3).

Rav Tzadok HaKohen tells us that "all that the Creator has created, He has made for a meaningful purpose" (*Tzidkas HaTzadik*, no. 103). Anger can signal us that an injustice is being committed and motivate us to speak up and take action to right the wrong. An angry person has added physical strength, crucial for survival or rescue efforts when lives are endangered. Interactions with a tough, mean person might demand an angry defense to ward off an attack. When a dishonest person knows that an angry response might come his way, he will be more likely to act with greater integrity. When a physical task, such as opening a jar, is difficult, a little bit of anger increases the adrenaline level, providing added strength. Anger is like salt — in small amounts it enhances; too much can spoil (*Imrai Haskel*, p. 64).

While anger does have its positive aspects, it is such a powerful emotion that it can easily be the source of much distress, harm, pain, and destruction to ourselves and others. In most daily interactions, brute physical strength is not needed while clear thinking always is. Calm, clear thought cuts through difficulties and solves problems more effectively and efficiently than does anger. Self-respecting and other-respecting communication gets the point across much better than an angry outburst.

Even people who are seriously motivated to conquer anger often fall into the trap of denying that their angry feelings exist. Denying anger can cause muscular aches and pains or other psychosomatic problems; holding back denied anger often causes blowups when the pressure builds up to the bursting point. STEP 2 discusses the importance of recognizing and acknowledging anger, and STEPS 6, 8, and 9 supply tension-releasing tools.

Many of us who are sincerely concerned with conquering anger feel guilty when we experience normal feelings that we wish we didn't have. A lot of people's anger might be understandable, even justified. Time is precious, so people who waste our time cause a loss. Our dignity is valuable, so anyone who attacks it is acting wrongly and should be told to stop. Rudeness can be irritating; delays and slowness can be frustrating. We have a right to privacy and rightfully expect others to respect our borders. Unfairness and injustice is unacceptable. In all of these situations one needs to think clearly and choose the wisest course of action. Angry feelings are, by their nature, often out of our control, yet our choice of words and actions are always under our control. The *Rambam* tells us that when another person wrongs us, it is improper to just remain silent and feel animosity (*Hilchos De'os* 7:4,5). We are instead supposed to speak up and talk to the person, but we need to do so with dignity and respect. If we haven't learned to control our anger, we won't be able to fulfill this mitzvah properly; if we train ourselves to look for solutions, rather than either suffering silently or blowing up and becoming enraged, we will find them. STEPS 4 and 5 elaborate on this.

Anger brings untold suffering in its wake. Control over anger is a skill that can be learned. Many, many people, some of whose vignettes are presented throughout this book, have found that controlling their anger was not only possible, but that it benefited their life much more than they could have ever imagined.

> My marriage has changed from being a place of constant friction and quarrels to a peaceful haven. In the

old days I would come home and no sooner than a few minutes had passed before I was angry about one thing or another. It was like having strong static on the line every time you tried to speak on the telephone, or like sleeping in a bed full of sand. Now that I focus on what I can appreciate rather than on what is wrong, I feel a sense of gratitude whenever I come home. An anger-free home is like having a symphony orchestra. There is a beautiful sense of harmony.

For me Shabbos is now a true day of rest. Anger used to ruin my Shabbos. When the children sat at the same table, I was constantly angry about what they said or did. Looking back I see how I focused on trivialities, letting petty issues spoil the most precious day of the week. Now I create a joyous and peaceful atmosphere at home for my family and look forward to the wonderful spiritual experience of appreciating the creation of the world. The Shabbos table is one of the highlights of my life and that of the entire family.

My daughter's telling me, "I love you, Mommy, for the way you act so nice to me," made all the efforts I put into conquering anger worthwhile. She revealed that she used to cringe every time I would ask her to do anything because she knew that if she made a mistake, I would scold her angrily. Now that I calmly, with love and respect in my voice, point out ways to do things better, she looks forward to hearing my advice and suggestions. I even overheard her say to

*her brother, "When I have children of my own, I hope
that I will speak to them the way Mommy speaks to
me." If I won the lottery, I wouldn't have felt any
more joy.*

*Driving without anger is a totally different experience
than driving with anger. I frequently wave and smile
to other drivers, and they smile back. When I used to
get angry at other drivers, I would get angry looks and
stares in return. The negative energy sent my way just
increased my anger and I would get into frequent
shouting matches. Now I wish others a great day, and
that's the kind of messages I hear in return. Driving in
traffic has become almost fun.*

What is so wrong with anger? Anger prevents clear thinking and leads to many mistakes, at times serious ones. Anger
provokes impulsive behavior, getting people to say and do
things they later regret. For this reason Yaakov, our forefather,
cursed the anger of his sons Shimon and Levi. Their anger led
to bloodshed. Yaakov also took away the rights of the first-
born from his oldest son Reuven because of his impulsivity.

Anger is harmful to everyone — physically, emotionally,
and spiritually. Anger makes it hard to think straight, hard to
pray properly, and difficult to study Torah. An angry person is
likely to cause distress and suffering to other people, either
verbally or physically, violating many Torah commandments
along the way. Anger in its many forms — such as excessive
frustration, smoldering resentment, grudge-bearing, and rage
— is harmful to one's health. Anger destroys peace of mind
and blocks feelings of happiness and joy.

Anger begets anger and harms relationships with other
people. In any shouting match tempers flare like a forest fire.
No one wins and everyone loses. Anger in marriage can

transform a dream into a nightmare. Anger at children can make their childhood a source of painful memories for a lifetime. Anger at friends can destroy the friendship. Even anger at a stranger can cause much unpleasantness for all parties concerned.

Anger can easily lead to bitter arguments and quarrels. Many people have left good jobs in a fit of anger. Pushing and shoving others, hitting, kicking, and even biting are all products of anger. The injuries and damage caused by anger are both physical and emotional. Physical wounds eventually heal; many emotional wounds never do.

The stories of people who caused themselves and others pain with anger speak for themselves:

My mother lost her temper at me quite frequently. When my own children were growing up, I followed my mother's example, even though I thought I never would.

Once when my daughter came home after being a Shabbos guest at a friend's house, her first comment to me was, "It was amazing that on Friday afternoon there was no screaming and shouting. I thought that everyone would act as crazy as in our house." Hearing this was the shock that woke me up and made me decide to try to do something about my anger. I still have a long way to go. But I am committed to do all I can to create a more peaceful environment.

I ruined my marriage with my anger. I got angry at my wife over such minor matters that it causes me embarrassment every time I think about it. The divorce was painful. My loneliness and distance from my children is a constant reminder to me of how

much my anger cost me. I used to blame my anger on my wife. Now I realize it was mostly my own fault. True, if she hadn't responded to my anger with her own anger, our marriage could have been saved. But I was the one who started the angry quarrels. I wish I could begin my marriage over from the beginning. Now that I know how dangerous and harmful anger is, I would do all I could to conquer it, instead of feeling justified in letting off steam whenever I was upset.

I always wanted to be a teacher. I love to learn and I enjoy imparting my knowledge to others. But at the end of the first year of teaching, the principal told me that because of my anger I had alienated a number of important parents. He said I would have to look somewhere else if I wanted to teach.

I once became so angry at one of my children that I hit him way too hard, to the point where he needed stitches. The doctor warned me that if this ever happened again, he would be obligated by law to report me. I don't consider myself an abusive parent, but what can I say? I called up a counselor and scheduled a series of regular appointments. It was worth paying someone to monitor my progress. I never want to repeat what I have done.

What about a person who easily loses his temper — won't it be hard for him to control his anger? It certainly will be. Yet that is our task: to do the difficult. Shlomo HaMelech said about anger, "He who is slow to anger is better than a strong man, and a master of his passions is better than a conqueror of a city" (*Mishlei* 16:32). This clearly tells us that being slow to anger takes effort, and that once someone is angry and is in a fit of passion, it is even more difficult for him to restrain himself. But someone who is driven by visions of greatness can master noble qualities and can heroically accomplish the magnificent. Seeing the conquering of anger as a royal achievement can motivate us to make the necessary effort. A world-champion boxer or a mighty warrior only becomes that way because of his regular program of exercises and practice over a long period of time. By consistently working on conquering anger, it is possible to gain an inner spiritual and emotional strength that is very powerful.

The Vilna Gaon notes that "overcoming negative character traits is the essence and purpose of life" (*Beur HaGra* to *Mishlei* 4:13). Even very great people need to work on conquering anger: "Rabbi Moshe Feinstein was extremely mild-mannered. In the most tense and provocative situations he would not show a trace of anger. In reference to this, he once remarked, 'Do you think I was always like this? By nature, I have a fierce temper, but I have worked to overcome it.'" (*Reb Moshe*, Mesorah Publications).

The secret is to remain unafraid of our anger and to learn from it. Anger is our inner teacher (*Eruvin* 65b). It teaches us about our subjective needs and what it is that we truly consider important. What we consider trivial will not arouse our anger. The occurrence of anger as well as its intensity, frequency, and duration teach us about our self-esteem. A person who has internalized a rock-solid sense of personal worth will find that fewer things arouse his anger and that any anger he may experience lasts only for a relatively short time.

Anger and what we say and do when angry teach us about our level of self-mastery and the extent of our virtues, such as patience, unconditional love, judging people favorably, humility, and joy.

Anger or freedom from anger teaches us about our relationship with our Creator and our willingness to accept His will. A person with a profound love for the Creator and a total acceptance of His will experiences elevated emotional states and maintains an awareness that everything in his life is part of the Divine plan and is for his ultimate benefit. In this context, there is no place for counterproductive anger. When every encounter with a "difficult" person is seen as a Creator-sent challenge and opportunity for spiritual elevation, it becomes easier to act in more dignified and refined ways.

Each person experiences various levels of control over his anger, depending on the situation. And, of course, we don't stay in one place. At times we are more elevated and spiritual, and at times less; at times we are more patient and resourceful, and at times less; at times we feel better about ourselves and other people, and at times we feel worse. Anger teaches us that we are imperfect and consistently need to improve and grow. A decrease in anger teaches us that we are making progress.

This book is a practical guide offering underlying concepts and practical hands-on tools for decreasing and preventing anger. The step-by-step program is for anyone wishing to gain greater mastery over his emotions, and also provides a useful model for those in the helping professions.

In addition, certain people will find this book of particular benefit:

- Parents who frequently lose their tempers with their children
- Children who often become angry at their parents for making demands on them
- Husbands and wives struggling to break the cycle of criticism and blame
- Teachers who easily become angry at their students
- Brothers and sisters who fight and argue

- Employers who feel frustrated by their employees
- Employees who feel irritated with their co-workers
- Roommates whose disagreements end up in disputes
- Anyone who deals with the public

Each reader will find certain ideas and concepts that are more relevant to them than others. Experiment with the tools and techniques gathered from many sources and see which ones work best for you. Hopefully you will be able to pick and choose from the available menu and create your own personal program.

While you are reading this book it is impossible to know which ideas will prove the most useful and effective. Some people are more motivated by realizing the harm of anger, while others find their motivation in seeing the benefits of greater amounts of patience, unconditional love, and joy. Some people find it easy to hear a new idea and are able to integrate it immediately; others need to review an idea many times before it becomes their personal perspective. Some people find that tools such as slow, deep breathing work best for them; others benefit greatly from visualizations and creative imagery. Try each tool to see if it works for you. For instance, many people are amazed that by emotionally detaching themselves from a difficult situation — such as by "going to the balcony" and becoming an objective observer — they become calm. Yet only by testing this out yourself can you see if it is an effective technique for you.

As you continue on your life's journey and mission, you will see which ideas you remember when you need them the most. Even if at first you don't feel that a specific idea or tool will work for you, you might be pleasantly surprised that it does.

Bear in mind that the STEPS are meant to be seen as a comprehensive approach. Viewing any single idea or tool out of that context could cause misconceptions that will limit the benefits of the entire program.

We will never totally complete all the work that needs to be done with *tikkun hamiddos,* developing our character traits. There is always more to do, more to fix, for character development is a lifetime process. We will always encounter new situations and new life tests. Focus on improvement, not on perfection. Perfectionism causes counterproductive guilt and anxiety. As the Chazon Ish tells us, "The wise person will feel great joy in improving his character traits" (*Emunah U'Bitachon* 4:15). Be wise and feel this joy whenever you see progress, for it is this joy that will prevent discouragement and will keep you motivated to continue improving.

Step 1

Commit Yourself to Conquering Anger

Step 1

Commit Yourself to Conquering Anger

ongratulations! The fact that you are presently reading this book shows that you are motivated to gain mastery over anger. You have taken the most important first step: making the commitment to conquer anger.

The intensity of your commitment is a key element in how successful you will be. The stronger your commitment, the more likely it is that you will conquer anger. When you are totally committed to mastering this trait, you will discover the ways and means that are best for you. It will take trial and error, you will make mistakes and have relapses. But eventually you will be successful. Our Father, our King, helps those who strive to elevate themselves.

One source of encouragement is hearing from people who succeeded even though they initially did not think they would:

> I did not think I would ever be able to conquer my anger. I have an extremely intense nature, and I grew up in a family where everyone became angry easily. I felt it was in my genes and environment. I thought that living with powerful anger was natural and normal. I lost my temper frequently, and this became part of my identity.
>
> I wanted to get married, and I began to realize the harm anger had caused other members of my family. Their marriages were problematic. They yelled frequently at their children. I said to myself, "I'm not going to let anger control me and ruin my life." My commitment was stronger than my anger, which I have to admit was quite strong.
>
> I have been married now 40 years and am blessed with wonderful children and grandchildren. I have many friends and am professionally successful. I consider the one major factor that has made my life a blessing instead of a curse: my total commitment to conquering anger.

1. The more difficult it is for you to conquer anger, the greater you become

Some people are by nature more emotionally intense. They can experience profound joy and even ecstasy at times. At other times, this same intense nature creates deep feelings of sadness and existential loneliness. Someone with such a nature will usually have more difficulty dealing with anger than a person with a more phlegmatic nature.

The *Rambam* begins *Hilchos De'os* (1:1) by noting that people are born with very different natures. About anger, the first character trait that he discusses, the *Rambam* writes: "There are those who have a bad temper and are always angry. And there are those whose minds are always calm, and who never become angry. And if such a person does become angry, he will only become angry to a small degree and even then only once every few years."

Why did the *Rambam* start with this observation and not with the statement that developing one's character is a Torah commandment? The *Rambam* is making a general point about the task of character development. Unlike mitzvos such as eating *matzah* that are generally the same for every person, the development of our character presents unique challenges for each person. With respect to perfecting any particular character trait, some people will face a much more difficult challenge.

Let us look at two extremes. One person has an intense and irritable nature. He grew up in a dysfunctional or abusive family, witnessing much anger, and he was constantly screamed at and insulted. He now finds himself in an environment with people who are aggressive and insensitive to his feelings and needs.

Another person was blessed with a serene nature and grew up in a calm and peaceful home with loving, understanding parents. Presently he is surrounded by people who respect the feelings and needs of others.

These two people have very different emotional natures and life histories. Their approach to anger will be completely different. And so it is with everyone. Your view of anger is uniquely yours.

Your nature and upbringing determine the starting point of your *avodas Hashem* (Divine service) in conquering anger. The more prone you are to anger, the greater your reward for conquering it. As Rabbi Tzadok HaKohen stresses, "The area of a person's fault and deficiency is that with the greatest potential for merit" (*Tzidkas HaTzadik*, no. 70).

Rabbi Avraham, the son of the *Rambam*, writes in *HaMaspik L'Ovdai Hashem*, "The highest level of being slow to anger is when a person's intellect is the master of his emotions. Such a person has his emotions work for him according to the requirements of the Torah. A person who has a naturally cold personality or lacks a tendency towards anger has not reached the level of the person who has a natural tendency to become angry but gains controls over his temper."

You did not choose your emotional makeup, you did not choose your family, and you have only limited choice as to how other people will react towards you. But you can choose how you will respond to your anger.

A friend of mine told me:

> I have a bad temper and continuously need to hold it in check. Even as a toddler I became much angrier than my siblings. I started out in life with a low tolerance for frustration.
>
> I used to envy people with calmer natures. I felt that they were so much luckier than me. Why couldn't I have been given a serene nature?
>
> I complained to my rabbi and said it wasn't fair that I wasn't given an easier nature. His response was very helpful. He quoted to me a well-known letter of Rabbi Yitzchak Hutner. Rav Hutner wrote to a student that exactly in the place where he has to fight battles with himself, there he will find his greatness. One serves the A–mighty precisely to the degree he has to overcome difficulties.

After this talk, I began to view each battle with anger as an opportunity to express my love for my Creator. I felt a profound sense of victory every time I won a battle. Whenever I made a mistake, I resolved to learn from it and to use it as a means of teaching others to conquer their anger. Since I have had to fight anger, I feel better equipped to help other people than someone who never had an issue with anger.

2. Believe in your ability to conquer anger

The biggest obstacle to conquering anger is the feeling, "I'm naturally an angry person and nothing will change it." If you believe that, your entire life will be a constant process of "proving" that you cannot control your temper. Every explosion of anger will reinforce this false belief. But losing one's temper only proves that one has not conquered anger. It does not prove that he cannot conquer anger.

Our Father, our King, has given us free will. Believe in your ability to remain silent when that is the most appropriate response. Believe in your ability to speak respectfully even when you are frustrated, irritated, or angry. Believe in your ability to walk away from a situation if that is necessary to calm down. Believe in your ability to learn alternative ways of interpreting situations. Believe in your ability to learn to remain calmer or more centered and balanced in situations that used to get you angry. All of these are learnable skills.

The A–mighty leads each person along the path he decides to travel (*Makkos* 10b). Sincerely deciding to conquer anger assures you the Divine assistance that you will need for your journey. In your own words, ask G-d to help you succeed. Even before reading further, try saying, "My Father, my King, Creator and Sustainer of the entire universe, please give me the strength, wisdom, patience, and perseverance to conquer anger." Repeating this short yet powerful prayer frequently works wonders.

I guarantee you that anyone who is sincerely motivated to improve in these areas will be able to do so. I know many people who have succeeded, and I have interviewed many who have shared with me their stories about how they learned to control their anger. You do not need to be a totally righteous person to succeed, nor do you need superhuman qualities. But you do need perseverance.

How can you gain a greater belief in your power to overcome anger? Remember times in the past when you controlled your anger. Remember situations in which you did not become angry, even though you often do in similar situations. Remember instances in which you changed the way you viewed a particular situation and this enabled you to calm down. Remember times when you had the courage and patience to work out a practical solution with someone who was annoying you. By focusing on your successes, you will increase your belief in your ability to have greater self-mastery in the future.

Remember a time when you began to feel angry, but something suddenly enabled you to gain control. Perhaps you realized that the person irritating you was much stronger and it would not pay to show your anger. Or perhaps someone you wanted to impress entered the room and you immediately calmed down. Almost everyone will calm down in the middle of an angry outburst if the telephone rings when they are expecting an important call, or if there is a loud knock on the front door.

A friend of mine shared with me an incident that left an indelible impression on him. He had a job working for a tall, husky fellow who was very well known and financially successful. The man was a tyrant. He was highly critical of everyone and everything, and had a terrible temper. He would scream at anyone who offended him in any way.

One day my friend saw a little old lady drive her car straight into his employer's expensive antique car. My friend's first thoughts were, "Oh no! The little old lady has had it."

The employer was furious. He jumped out of his car, slamming the door with a powerful bang. He angrily approached the elderly woman's car and pulled the front door open with tremendous force. And then, just as he was about to punch this defenseless old lady, he recognized her.

His anger melted away as he meekly said, "Hi Mom, I sure hope that you weren't hurt or shaken up."

What about the damage to his car? What about his fury and rage? As soon as he recognized the object of his wrath, *Key* his anger disappeared. In its place was care and compassion.

The most important requisite for success is to keep striving. Don't allow mistakes to derail you. A person who has a history of frequently getting angry will fall back into old patterns until the new pattern becomes second nature. Three elements of anger are: frequency, duration, and intensity. As you continue to work on anger you will find that you become angry less frequently. Your anger will pass more quickly. And if you do become angry, your anger will not be as intense as formerly.

Don't expect an instant transformation. Unrealistic expectations can cause needless discouragement. A pattern of many years will take time to change. Don't allow setbacks to discourage you. If you think that because you want to overcome anger, you will never get angry again, you are dooming yourself to great disappointment when you realize that your wish has not magically caused all anger to disappear.

Even after implementing the suggestions in this book a number of times, you might still become angry. If you do, be resolved to begin again. You never really go back to square one when you work on yourself. Each victory empowers you. View any loss of temper as a learning experience.

If you were ever angry in the past and are not presently angered in similar situations, you have proof that you can overcome anger. Regardless of how long it took you to reach your present degree of self-control, your inner mind now knows that you have the power to switch from being angry to letting go of your anger. It is just a question of proficiency. The mental process involved in overcoming anger can eventually become almost automatic.

Each of us can go from a state of not being angry to becoming angry in just a few seconds. Fewer people, however, have learned to reverse the process. By gaining greater mastery over your mind, you will be able to go both ways with equal speed. When you realize that you have easy access to joy, love, or serenity in place of anger, you will choose the former states. This skill takes practice over time, and not everyone spends enough time practicing. Those who do, have acquired the ultimate skill for living a rewarding life. Utilize every time you become angry to learn more about your response patterns and to discover what works for you in overcoming them.

3. Learn from other people

"Who is wise? He who learns from every person" (*Pirkei Avos* 4:1). Telshe Rosh Yeshivah Rabbi Chaim Mordechai Katz used to say, "Be resolved to learn from all the people in your immediate surroundings. When you see someone with positive character traits, learn from him how to develop those traits. And when you see someone with negative traits, reflect on the harm done by those traits."

Ask people what attitudes have helped them remain calm or in control in situations that make you angry. Ask people for the tools and techniques they find effective. By using thought patterns and behaviors of people who have greater control over anger as models, you yourself will eventually serve as a model for others. Those who have seen you become angry will now see that you have conquered anger, and they will learn from you.

Rabbi Nosson Tzvi Finkel, the Alter of Slobodka, who educated an entire generation of Torah giants, used to relate:

> *When I was a young man I observed how even very simple people can overcome their anger when they are truly motivated. Two peasant women set up separate booths to sell beans in the Vilna marketplace. They soon started arguing over territorial rights. The anger escalated, and one woman loudly cursed her competitor. It appeared she would not soon be calmed. But, when someone came to her booth to purchase a few pennies worth of beans, it was amazing how this peasant woman immediately regained control over herself and smiled a sincere smile. With extreme politeness, she gave the customer what he requested.*

The lesson the Alter learned was that a few pennies have the power to change a person's state from one extreme to the other. In the midst of her anger, she calmed down in a split second and showered her customer with heartfelt blessings.

Someone once asked me, "True, this incident shows that a person can put his anger aside. But the bean seller was angry at her competitor, not at the customer."

The distinction is valid. But this story still demonstrates that when we are motivated to change our emotional state, we can. It is more difficult to overcome anger towards the cause of that anger, but it is still possible. Anger is an inner state. The other person is only a catalyst. Whether you remain angry is up to you. Overcoming anger is a skill that is learnable.

We all have great resources for self-control at our disposal. Even criminal lawyers all agree that when their clients are motivated to stay out of jail, they can control their actions, and this includes hardened criminals with long police records.

Imagine this scene: A witness is testifying against someone who had helped him in many ways. His testimony is filled with half-truths, exaggerations, and outright lies. With his testimony, the witness is buying his own freedom. As the accused hears the witness testifying, he is enraged. He feels like standing up in the courtroom and threatening to kill the witness. But before he lets go with an angry outburst, his attorney whispers to him, "Cool it fast or you'll lose the case. If you intimidate the witness, I'm walking out of here." In such circumstances, the most hardened criminal will have the control to remain silent. He is furious at the person testifying. But he knows the negative consequences of an angry outburst, and he remains quiet. Learn from him.

> *I was fired from my job. I went to my boss and complained that I had been doing a good job. He agreed I was doing a good job, but told me the rest of the staff could not work with me because they were always afraid of my blowing up at them for not doing things my way. He felt bad about firing me, but he had no choice.*
>
> *After two weeks of looking for a new job without success, I went back to my employer. "I'm asking you for one more chance," I told him. "I am totally*

committed to be more accepting of the rest of the staff. If I lose my temper at anyone, I will leave on my own."

He agreed to give me a chance. Fear of losing my job gives me the self-discipline I need not to speak to the rest of the staff in anger. This has helped me at home also. I see that I can do it.

I used to get angry at my children for all sorts of reasons. I felt they were holding me back from really making good use of my time. I began to feel resentment if they caused me even a few moments of "wasted time." This resentment caused me to become angry at my husband, my children, and anyone else I viewed as wasting my time. I was highly irritable most of the time.

Then I heard a talk about child-raising that transformed me. The time you spend with your children is time you are emulating our Creator. Your children need your love, your compassion, and your empathy. Developing these qualities in yourself and in your children is the highest level of creativity. Child-raising is an art form that is greater than any other form of art. This takes patience. But so do most masterpieces. The more difficult it is for you to be loving and patient with your children, the greater "you" that is being created. Time spent calmly with your children is more creative than any painting. You are teaching them qualities that they will pass on to future generations. I repeat these thoughts to myself each day, and I feel like a new person. I enjoy my children so much more than I used to, and while kids will be kids, they act much better than they previously did.

❖ ❖ ❖

I used to look at teaching as entering a battlefield. The young boys I teach have a lot of energy and consistently did things that got me angry. I came home exhausted and did not know if I should continue teaching. Then I started mastering a positive attitude towards the children in my classroom. I started looking at their energy as a positive force that I would utilize for developing within them a love for learning. Now I am much more lenient in enforcing minor details of discipline. I look at the big picture. Now I am happy to see the smiling faces of my students as they greet me in a friendly way. They used to be afraid of me and I thought that what I did was working. When I compare that with how my days go now, I see that it's two different worlds.

I am a bus driver. Passengers used to get me angry. They would ask stupid questions. They would blame me for being late when heavy traffic slowed me down. They would ask me to stop for them in the middle of a street, even though it is illegal and could have cost me my job. Every day I came home exhausted. The stress caused me many near accidents. When a friend of mine who also drives a bus died of a heart attack at a young age, I realized I would either have to develop a calmer attitude or change jobs. I spoke to a few bus drivers in the same city who drove in a relaxed manner. I learned from them how they viewed passengers as the source of their livelihood and felt gratitude to them. Driving with feelings of gratitude made all the difference. Now I actually enjoy my job.

Even Haman can teach us something about anger

In *Megillas Esther* we find an instance of Haman controlling his anger. Yes, the very same Haman who because of his anger at Mordechai for not bowing down before him planned to destroy the entire Jewish people, was able to hold himself back from acting in anger.

We read in the Megillah (5:9,10), "That day Haman went out joyful and exuberant. But when Haman noticed Mordechai in the king's gate and that he did not stand up and did not stir before him, Haman was filled with wrath at Mordechai. [Nevertheless,] Haman restrained himself and went home. He sent and summoned his friends and his wife, Zeresh." *Rashi* comments that Haman strengthened himself to control his anger because he was afraid to take revenge without the king's explicit permission.

Note that Haman was "filled with wrath"; his whole being felt the anger. Yet, out of fear of negative consequences, he was able to refrain from acting impulsively. Even one of the most evil people in history was able to control his reactions when motivated to do so.

---

4. Don't blame others — take the responsibility yourself

Take responsibility for conquering your anger. It's very easy to blame others for angering you. People who get angry easily frequently say to others, "It's all your fault!"

No one can "make" us angry. Other people can be annoying or inconsiderate, but only we can make ourselves angry. Anger is an inner process occurring within the mind, nervous system, and our bio-chemistry. Regardless of what others say and do there is no law of nature that says that we must become angry.

Of course, if the people in our environment were all sincere, honest, understanding, loyal, trustworthy, intelligent, efficient, logical, reasonable, dependable, considerate, reliable, warm, and kind, and did whatever we asked them to the first time we asked, we probably would not become angry very often.

But the reality is that we all come in contact with people who are rude, argumentative, unreasonable, irrational, selfish, incompetent, inefficient, wasteful, dishonest, obnoxious, inconsiderate, stubborn, inflexible, lazy, or unreliable. Getting angry at them will not move them from the second category to the first. Remaining calm and thinking clearly will, however, give us a far better chance of becoming a member of the first group ourselves.

> *My husband and I were on the verge of divorce. We fought all the time and each of us blamed the other for the ugly arguments. Finally, we came to the same conclusion: We were both responsible. We decided to give the marriage another chance and committed ourselves to conquering our anger.*
>
> *We viewed conquering our anger as a joint project. We became partners and worked as a team. Even if one of us did not like something the other one said or did, we agreed that we would resolve our differences in a mutually respectful manner. Today we both feel fortunate that we have saved our family from being torn apart. Our new way of interacting brings out the best in both of us, and we are like completely different people.*

> *Ever since I conquered my anger, my married children visit me much more often. I used to spend their*

whole visit complaining that they did not come often enough. I did not consider myself as having a problem with anger. In my mind, the only problem was their inconsiderateness in not visiting more often. Then I heard a lecture on anger and tried to take a more objective view of the situation and my part in it. I came to the conclusion that it would be wiser for me to tell my children how much I enjoy their visits rather than complaining about their infrequency. Not only do I enjoy their visits much more now, they visit me much more frequently.

5. Anger prevents clear thinking

It is a fact that when we are angry, we do not think as clearly as when we're calm: "When a person becomes angry, he forgets what he has learned, and he increases foolishness" (*Nedarim* 22b).

Moshe, our Teacher, became angry three times and each time his anger caused him to err (see *Vayikra* 10:16; *Bamidbar* 20:10 and 31:14). In each case Moshe became angry because of what he viewed as violations of important principles. Yet even so, one of the greatest men who ever lived erred because of his anger. Some people convince themselves that they still think clearly when they are angry. But if this was not true of Moshe Rabbeinu, how much less true is it of us.

Orchos Tzadikim, (ch. 12, *The Gate of Anger*), defines anger as "an illness of the soul" and states: "Observe and you will see that when people become angry and maintain their anger, they are not aware of what they are doing. They do many things that they would never do when they are not angry. Anger takes away a person's clarity of thought, and he says many things that just lead to arguments and quarrels. Therefore it is impossible for a person with a bad temper to escape committing major transgressions. This is why Eliyahu HaNavi said to Rav Yehudah (*Berachos* 29b), 'Don't become angry and you won't sin.'"

When we are in the throes of anger, we cannot see the entire picture. Why is this so?

The purpose of anger is to protect us when we are in physical danger. When we experience anger, many physiological changes take place in our circulatory system. Blood flows to where it is needed the most to defend ourselves from injury. The biochemistry system produces more adrenaline to give us greater strength to fight or take flight. At the same time, less blood flows to our brain. Since our brain receives less oxygen from our blood when we are angry, our thinking is not as clear. We tend to react impulsively and say things we regret. We do not take into account how much we stand to lose by our actions. In anger, people quit good jobs, and break off the most precious friendships and relationships. If we were calmer and thought more clearly, we would see that the other person really did not cause us any actual loss or harm, or that the loss is minor and inconsequential. We would see that the target of our anger did not do anything wrong or improper, that he was just acting in his own best interests, just as we try to act in ways we feel are in our own best interests.

One easy-to-apply tool to decrease anger and enhance clarity of thought is to breathe slowly and deeply. The extra oxygen calms our muscle system and enables more oxygen to reach the thinking center of our brain. As soon as you are aware that you are angry, make it a habit to start breathing slowly and deeply. If possible, take 10 slow, deep breaths. This slow breathing works best when you repeat to yourself the words "calm and relaxed" over and over again.

Try this out right now. Breathe slowly and deeply 10 times. Repeat the words "calm and relaxed" each time you breathe out. You might want to imagine a relaxing scene such as a waterfall, lake, forest, or beautiful garden. This alone can have a soothing effect on your emotional state and enable you to think more clearly.

My business was in deep trouble. We were losing money, and I did not have a clear plan how to turn things around. The financial stress was getting to me. I was edgy in the office and even worse at home. I shouted at my wife and children way out of proportion to anything they did.

Things hit rock bottom when I became furious at my business partner for making a decision that caused us a loss. "I should never have gone into business with you," I said with venom. "It was the worst mistake I ever made. The day I decided to make you my partner was the beginning of the end of my career." I went on and on for some time.

My partner remained calm. He told me, "The present loss is minor. I understand that you are under pressure, and what you said to me is only an expression of your frustration and worry. I have some ideas to improve our financial situation. If you want to separate, I will respect your decision. But please give my ideas a chance. We share a common fate and there is the saying, 'If we do not hang together, we will surely hang separately.' If in two months, my plan has not made a positive difference, I will make it easy for you to dissolve our partnership. Your friendship is important to me, and I want to maintain it whether or not we remain business partners."

Fortunately, my friend's ideas worked, and we began making a profit. I am forever grateful for his sensitive way of speaking to me. I can see now that when I was angry, my thinking was wrong. My friend is highly competent and talented. I have gained tremendously in the past from his astuteness and foresight. My anger blinded me from seeing his strengths. I was focusing only on his mistakes. I have resolved never to make an important decision if I am angry.

6. Anger prevents clear speaking

"Death and life are in the power of the tongue" (*Mishlei* 18:21)

Words are powerful. They can build and they can destroy. With words you can give encouragement. You can motivate and influence in many positive ways. Words are a vehicle for many acts of kindness. Your words can change someone's entire life for the better. They can give hope. They can be the foundation for many accomplishments and can bring happiness and joy. Your entire life will be full of happiness as you continuously bring happiness to others.

Since words are so powerful, they can destroy. Words can cause pain and distress. The Torah (*Vayikra* 25:17) forbids us to say words that cause needless pain.

The Vilna Gaon wrote: "Speaking hurtfully to someone is worse than hitting him. When you hit someone, you affect his body. Words go much deeper. Moreover, bruises eventually heal. But the negative effect of words may never be healed" (*Beur HaGra* to *Mishlei* 15:1 and 14:30).

In discussing the prohibition against *ona'as devarim* (causing pain with words), the *Sefer HaChinuch* (338) writes:

"The Torah takes a very strict stance on *ona'as devarim* because it causes so much suffering. Many people care more about verbal insults than they would about a financial loss, as the Sages have said, 'Causing pain with words is worse than cheating others financially.' It is impossible to list all the potential ways that one can cause pain to others. Each person must be as careful as possible in this matter."

The *Chinuch* adds: "We must be careful not to cause even young children any pain with words unless it is absolutely necessary to teach them proper ways to behave. This applies even to one's own sons and daughters. A person who is careful in these matters will live a long life full of blessing and honor."

The *Chinuch* concludes by telling us that: "This prohibition does not apply in those instances where someone starts up with you by insulting you. The Torah does not obligate a person to be like a stone and remain silent when someone curses and insults him. Rather, the Torah commandment is that we should keep a distance from *ona'as devarim* and we should not start up with others by insulting them. As a rule, a person who does not insult others will be saved from many quarrels. When you are extremely careful not to cause others pain with words, the only people who will insult you are idiots, and one need not pay attention to what an idiot says. Even if someone's insulting you does cause you to reply, a wise person will be careful to reply with cleverness and as pleasantly as possible. He will not become very angry, because anger is for fools. We can learn that we are permitted to reply to insults from the law that we are permitted to protect our lives and property. When your life is in danger, you are permitted to kill a person who is trying to kill you. We are not obligated to allow others to cause us damage and harm. We are permitted to do what is necessary to protect our property. Similarly, we are permitted to say things to others to protect our dignity. Nevertheless, there are elevated people who are able to remain silent even though others insult them. The Sages have praised them highly for their elevated level."

In the *Pele Yoetz* we find the following: "Causing pain with words is worse then cheating others financially. The A–mighty gives strong retribution for *ona'as devarim*. Many people are guilty of violating this prohibition because they do not realize what constitutes *ona'as devarim*. The general rule is that anything you say that will cause someone pain is considered *ona'as devarim*. In order to remember what is included in this prohibition, keep in mind the statement of Hillel (*Shabbos* 31a), 'Whatever you would dislike someone to do to you, do not do to your fellow man.'

"There are people who cause others pain in the form of jokes and humor. This is similar to someone who shoots an arrow at another person and claims that he is only joking. The punishment for such an offense is so severe that the humor will turn into a misfortune. Because this prohibition is so serious one must be very careful not to violate it especially since people are very sensitive and feel pain even over slight statements of others. Some people rationalize and claim that they have a right to insult someone because of what the other person has done to them. They also mistakenly think that when someone insults another person as a joke it is not a violation of this prohibition. Because they lack awareness of their transgressions, they do not regret their wrongs in this area.

"It is important to know that you have no right to cause pain with words to another person even if that person wronged you. It is appropriate to try to correct that person, but this should be done with inner feelings of sincere concern for that person's welfare. If your intention is for revenge, it is a violation of the Torah prohibition against taking revenge. When the Torah commanded us not to insult other people, it is obvious that it did not have to warn us not to insult people who seek to help us. Rather, the Torah was warning us not to insult even those people who distress us. If you insult someone as a joke, you are finding humor at the expense of the blood of another person. A husband should be especially careful not to cause his wife pain with words since women tend to cry more easily than men (*Bava Metzia* 59a). A person should constantly strive to have other people feel positive about his behavior towards them, and this way the A–mighty will be pleased with him" (*Pele Yoetz*: section *ona'ah*).

7. The four levels of angry people

The Sages (*Pirkei Avos* 5:14) list four levels of anger:

- There is a person who becomes angry easily, but is easily appeased.
- There is a person who is slow to anger, but slow to calm down once angered.
- The lowest level is someone who becomes angry easily and is difficult to appease. The *Mishnah* calls such a person evil. Even if he has not yet done anything seriously wrong, his bad temper can easily lead to serious offenses.
- The highest level is someone who is slow to anger, and easily appeased.

Notice what is missing: The *Mishnah* does not mention a fifth possibility: a person who never gets angry at all. The highest level that can be expected is someone who is difficult to anger and easy to appease. Such a person does not automatically let go of the anger on those rare occasions when he does become angry. Yet he is still considered to be righteous. By setting this level as your goal rather than total perfection, it will be easier for you to continuously improve. You will have more realistic expectations and therefore a greater chance of succeeding.

Let us take a closer look at the four levels mentioned.

The person who gets angry easily, but finds it easy to calm down, is someone whom minor and trivial matters rankle and frustrate. The small irritants of life upset him. Such a person might become angry about delays, interruptions, poor service, all forms of rudeness, slights to his honor, someone forgetting a special occasion or an anniversary, being asked to do things when he or she is busy, bureaucratic snags, the mistakes and stupidity of others, being accused of making a mistake or doing something wrong, a lack of gratitude or appreciation, not being invited by others, and similar common occurrences.

Even though this person becomes angry easily, he either overcomes it himself or is quick to accept an apology.

The next level is someone who becomes angry only when under unusual stress or when seriously provoked. Once he becomes angry, though, he does not easily let go of his anger. He will insist on an explicit apology, and even then may force his antagonist to seek his forgiveness many times. Included in this category are people who eat themselves up over something someone said or did to them years ago.

The worst pattern is to become angry easily and to maintain that anger for a long time. Such a person ruins his life by filling it with bitterness and resentment. About such a person, the *Gemara* (*Pesachim* 113b) comments succinctly, "The life of a person who angers easily is not considered a life."

Rabbi Yosef Leib Bloch (*Shiurei Da'as*, Essay: *HaAdam U'Tshukosav*) describes the life of a person who becomes angry easily: "At times we see a person who walks around gloomy and sullen. His heart is full of anger and resentment — not because of anything major, but because small things bother him excessively. He is constantly involved in trivial squabbles. Anyone who observes this person will look on in wonder. He could live a life of financial abundance and emotional happiness. Why does he need to make himself so miserable over such inconsequential details? He destroys the entire quality of his life. Anger causes people to want to harm themselves. We see this in young children who in a temper tantrum will bang their heads against a wall."

No person would choose such a life. But we all know people who fit Rabbi Bloch's description. Instead of enjoying life and feeling grateful for what is going well, an angry person focuses on what goes wrong. He not only suffers the actual loss of not having things go his way, his anger increases his distress many times over.

Instead of enjoying the food and meals his Father, his King, has given him, an angry person will think about what is not as he would like it to be. Instead of enjoying his children, he will consistently focus on how they displease him. An angry person ruins holidays, vacations, and celebrations for himself and others. Shabbos, which was meant to be a day of rest and inner peace, can become a day of stress and tension. Anger is so powerful that it can destroy in a moment what would take a lifetime to build.

Some people hold onto their anger for many years. Wouldn't it be wonderful if those same people could hold onto joy, gratitude, and serenity the same way?

Have you ever heard an elderly person complain with great bitterness of how others wronged him 50 or 60 years ago? Carrying that resentment for so many years has multiplied the pain and loss many times over. This is like a debt on which the interest is constantly compounded. This long-lasting resentment accrues much suffering for oneself and others.

The ideal pattern is being slow to anger and letting your anger pass quickly. Qualities that will help you reach this ideal are: internalized *emunah* and *bitachon* (awareness of the Creator and His benevolence), patience, humility, judging people favorably, seeing the good in events and situations, healthy self-esteem, joy and enthusiasm for life, a sense of perspective, compassion for others, the ability to forgive, unconditional love, the ability to ignore trivialities, flexibility, and a Torah sense of priorities. Even if you are not yet on this level, integrating the concepts in this book and applying the tools and techniques it provides can eventually enable you to reach it.

8. The six key principles of motivation

To reach a goal, especially a difficult one, takes a strong degree of motivation. There are six key elements that play a major role in what we are motivated to do or to stop doing. They are:

- Right
- Wrong
- Gain
- Loss
- Pleasure
- Pain

When you do something, why do you do it? Analyzing the reasons behind your behavior and actions and looking at why you refrain from doing the things you do not do, you will find various combinations of these six factors.

You do things because:
- they are the right things to do
- it is wrong not to do them

- you gain by doing them
- you would lose out by not doing them
- they are pleasurable
- you will suffer pain if you do not do them

You do not do things because:
- it is right not to do them
- they are wrong to do
- you will gain by not doing them
- you will lose by doing them
- you have more pleasure doing something else or more pleasure in not doing them than if you were to do them
- you will suffer pain if you do them

Let's see how these six motivating factors apply to working on anger, or failure to do so. (There is certainly the possibility that a person is not aware of his anger. Recognizing our anger is a prerequisite for doing something about it, and this issue will be addressed in STEP 2.)

First let's take a look at the motivations of someone who loses his temper and doesn't try to do anything about it:

- He might feel that he has a right to get angry and that his anger is justified.

  ❏ *I have a right to show people how I really feel.*

  ❏ *I want others to suffer for making me suffer.*

- He might not think that anything is wrong with getting angry, that it is harmful to repress anger and even healthy to "let off steam," or that he cannot help it and therefore isn't really doing anything wrong.

  ❏ *Anger is a natural emotion, and if it's natural it must be okay.*

  ❏ *I've always been this way and there is nothing I can do about it. Others will just have to live with my anger.*

- He might feel that he gains more from his anger than he loses.

  ❑ *If I do not get angry, no one will listen to me.*

  ❑ *When I get angry, people leave me alone, and I do not have to do what they ask.*

Anger is manipulative. People tend to give in to the requests and demands of someone who is angry. People who are not highly skilled at influencing others with positive methods find it much easier to scream, yell, shout, and insult. Their anger helps them manipulate others to do what they want or to refrain from what they tell them to stop doing. Since an angry person can look like a crazed maniac, others find it safer to give in to their requests. While in the long run a person loses out greatly with this pattern, the immediate payoff increases its use.

For instance, if someone is too lazy to help another person, getting angry at the person who asks for help is one way of avoiding the necessity of doing something he finds unpleasant. And, that person will think twice before asking the angry individual for help again. If you get angry at someone for insulting you, he is more likely to stop now and be careful in the future. Some people use anger like a porcupine uses its stiff, sharp bristles — as a weapon to keep others away.

- He might not be aware of how much he loses out by becoming angry.

  ❑ *I do not see any great loss to myself from becoming angry. If others do not like my anger, that's their problem.*

  ❑ *Very few people have ever told me that they purposely avoid me because of my temper, so I'm not certain that I lose too much from being the way I am.*

The Vilna Gaon (*Beur HaGra* to *Mishlei* 11:12) comments about the loss caused by insults, "When you focus on the eventual outcome of your words, you will be careful not to insult others. The only way you can insult someone is by failing to see the harm you are causing yourself by turning the person against you. Practically speaking, you can never know when you will need this person's goodwill."

A habitually angry person may be blind to the resentment he causes. He may not be aware of how people speak about him behind his back (even though they are wrong to do so). A single person may not realize how many people are afraid to marry him or to suggest a possible match because of his anger. An angry parent might not be aware that there are people who would not want to marry his children because they are afraid of his anger. A person looking for a job might not be aware that his temper has caused prospective employers not to hire him. An employer might not be aware how many highly talented employees have left his company because of his anger, or a person might not be aware of who avoids him to spare themselves from having to deal with his anger.

One director of a large company took a special leadership-training course where he was told to interview eight of his employees for feedback on his strengths and weakness from their point of view. He scored very high in many areas. But the employees all said that they could not trust him. He was puzzled by this since he valued integrity and was very honest in his relationships with all his employees. He asked them what they meant by this.

"Someone in the company," they explained, "once told you some bad news about a loss we incurred. You were furious and berated someone who was blameless. Since then, we have all avoided providing you with negative information."

This man said that not having vital information when things went wrong prevented him from taking the steps necessary to correct a problem and caused him major financial losses.

• He might feel that the pain of trying to do something about anger is too great.

❑ *Working on anger is hard work. Do you mean I have to think constantly about how I react and what I say? That's too difficult for me.*

❑ *I've tried to control my temper, and I have been successful at times. But after I pat myself on the back and think that I've finally made it, I find myself caught off-balance again and lose my temper. Since I see that even after all my efforts I still get angry, what's the use of trying again?*

• He might not derive any pleasure from working on his character traits, and might find pleasure in causing others who have annoyed him to suffer.

There is an emotional release when you scream and shout in anger or insult someone. Tantrums enable a person to let off steam and release tension building up inside. There is pleasure in taking revenge or "seeking justice" against someone who insulted you or caused you a loss.

Do you enjoy being angry? Some people enjoy the appearance of power and strength that anger gives them. But the sense of power that comes from anger is illusory. Real power is self-mastery (*Pirkei Avos* 4:1). Real power is knowing how to express yourself in a way that does not demean yourself and is respectful of others. Real power is having so much self-esteem that nothing anyone says or does can take it away from you. Real power is being so secure and balanced that you do not lose your temper.

How to become motivated

It takes a strong degree of motivation to do all you can to overcome anger. How will you get yourself motivated? The first step is to recognize the following points:

A. It is right to work on anger. The *Rambam* (*Hilchos De'os* 1:5) states that this a Torah obligation (*Devarim* 28:10).

When reflecting on anger, keep in mind that "The A–mighty loves people who control their temper" (*Pesachim* 113b). Recognition of this fact alone can be a powerful motivating factor in conquering anger. When you work on overcoming anger, you are working on a trait that will make you beloved in the eyes of your Creator. While He loves all of us all the time — "And I have loved you with an eternal love" — (*Yirmiyahu* 31:2) — by our working on our anger we become closer to Him. Winning the A–mighty's love should be on the top of our list of priorities.

The Chofetz Chaim writes about guarding one's tongue:

> The Sages have taught that when you refrain from transgressing, you thereby fulfill a mitzvah and you will be rewarded as if you actively performed a good deed. Every day you can fulfill many good deeds by guarding your tongue (*Chovas HaShemirah*, ch. 1).

When you conquer anger, inevitably you will refrain from much *lashon hara* that you would otherwise have spoken. This is the fulfillment of a major mitzvah. It is a mistake to view refraining from angry or derogatory remarks as merely passive: You are fulfilling a mitzvah every time you are provoked and don't respond.

B. It is wrong not to control your temper. If you speak to someone in anger when other people are around, you can easily cause him embarrassment and humiliation. Even if no one else is present, scolding or shouting in anger causes the victim great distress.

Every normal person considers it wrong to hurt another human being. But it is easy to overlook the pain you cause others with your anger. When we get angry we do not think objectively. We are so intensely involved with our own feelings that we fail to think about the suffering we are causing.

In Hebrew the word for a cruel person is *achzar*, which derives from the word *zar* — stranger. Only our failure to identify with our victim as a fellow human being allows us to treat him with cruelty.

Rabbi Yisrael Salanter said that most violations of the Torah commandments relating to our dealings with other people are the consequence of anger (*Tenuas HaMussar*, vol. 1, p. 338). And in his comprehensive work on anger, *Erech Apayim*, Rabbi Avraham Yellin lists some of the likely sins that result from anger: (a) taking revenge and bearing a grudge; (b) lying to justify one's anger; (c) speaking *lashon hara* against the person who is the object of one's anger and enjoying hearing other people speak *lashon hara* about them; (d) refusing to do acts of kindness, which will lead to many violations of Torah law; (e) harming an animal that angers us.

Anger frequently leads to *ona'as devarim*, the prohibition against causing pain with words. Even kind and respectable people will say things in anger that they would not think of saying when they are calm. When a person "loses" himself in anger he doesn't pay attention to what he is saying, how he says it, and where he says it. Screaming at someone in public or otherwise embarrassing him publicly is equated by our Sages with murder.

My older sister frequently treated me meanly. Afterwards she always excused herself by saying, "I was just in a bad mood." Her attitude seemed to be: "Whenever I am in a bad mood I can act towards you any way I please and cannot be held responsible."

Years later many of the things she said and did still haunt me, especially when I am feeling insecure. It would have made a major difference in both our lives if she had had the self-discipline to control herself when she was in a bad mood. If she had shown some sincere regret after she felt better, and apologized, my entire childhood would have been much more enjoyable and less painful.

A student once said, "I do not allow myself to become angry because if I do, I know my anger terrifies everyone around. One of the last times I became really angry at someone, as opposed to ranting and raving in private, that person locked himself in a room and did not come out for hours. I realized it wasn't worth turning my whole family against me."

When a person who lives a Torah way of life is calm and patient with others, it is a *kiddush Hashem*. People see how pleasant and elevated are the ways of someone who lives according to Torah. Conversely, anger causes a *chillul Hashem* (see *Yoma 86*).

Before I was observant, I was at the home of some religious relatives of mine for Shabbos. The mother kept getting angry at her children for not sitting quietly at the table. I said to myself, "If this is what it's like to be religious, I do not want any part of it." Her anger almost prevented me from finding a Torah way of life. Fortunately, I was later the guest of various other religious families and was amazed at the wonderful atmosphere in their homes on Shabbos. I am now observant.

Unfortunately, not everyone will overcome a first impression. People who are considering becoming Torah observant notice the emotional reactions of Torah observers. If someone sees a Torah observant couple insulting one another, they will later be skeptical of discussions about the harmony of a Torah home.

I once had a non-observant physician as a guest in my home for Shabbos. He needed a lot of attention, and I didn't give the children as much attention as I should have. As a consequence, they left the table a number of times, and the younger ones made a lot of noise. I kept thinking that this highly intelligent person would view the lack of perfect behavior on the part of my children as reflecting negatively on my child-raising skills. To my great relief, at the end of the meal he thanked me profusely for inviting him over. "What I enjoyed most," he said, "was that you did not get angry at your children even once. My father was highly authoritarian, and at times tyrannical. I would have been smacked for not behaving perfectly when guests were present. I really admired the way you were patient and loving with your children the entire time."

C. By conquering anger you gain spiritually and emotionally.
Spiritually, you are fulfilling the Torah commandment to walk in the A–mighty's ways and freeing yourself from all of the

Torah violations caused by anger. Emotionally, you will experience more joy and inner peace. This decreases the stress caused by anger and ultimately enables a person's immune system to work better. Your relationships with other people, especially with family members, will be smoother and more enjoyable. People will like you more, and this will help you financially, socially, and even spiritually.

The wife of a reformed angry man had this to say:
"The difference between before and after is night and day. Living with an angry spouse is darkness. A person who blows up frequently puts everyone in the house constantly on edge. If you make a mistake, he shouts. If you say the wrong thing, he insults you. If you get in his way, his anger informs you of his displeasure. When you conquer your anger, everyone in the house can enjoy your presence."

> *I was so used to my outbursts that I never contemplated what life would be like without them. Now, however, I see that the way I was living was not really living. I used to become irritated and upset over any trivial thing that was not precisely to my fancy. I cannot remember any experience that was ever totally enjoyable since I could always imagine it being even better than the present reality. Even if I stayed in the most expensive hotels, some service was inevitably imperfect. Whenever I interacted with someone, I always focused on what the person was doing wrong. No meal I ate was ever as good as my mother's cooking. I viewed the world through judgmental, angry lenses. Every day I succeeded in finding something to be irritated about.*
>
> *What was the turning point in my life? Someone whom I could tell sincerely cared about me told me*

that he would like to tell me something, but wasn't sure if I was prepared to listen. I told him to go ahead.

He spoke to me for two straight hours. He told me at length how I was ruining my own life and making everyone with whom I came into contact miserable. Yet with just a change in perspective, he told me, I could transform my world.

What was that little change? Instead of asking about every thing, person, or situation, "What is wrong here?" he told me to ask, "What is good about this?" In the beginning, what was wrong always came to my mind first. At times, I had to think for a minute or two to find the good in a situation. I wasn't sure I could do it, but eventually I changed my entire perspective. After a few days of effort, it became easier to notice what was good with things. I've been doing this now for over five years. I frequently have people who knew me before tell me that I am a totally new person and much more enjoyable to be around. I can now differentiate between something that is a real problem and something that is illusory.

I find that my entire relationship with the Creator is at a different level. I enjoy my life to an extent that I didn't believe was possible before.

D. You can make working on self-improvement a pleasurable experience. Making progress provides you with a wonderful feeling.

I used to feel that getting angry gave me power over others. But the power of self-mastery that I have now makes whatever power I had then pale in comparison.

Whenever I feel an urge to say something to some-one who has irritated me, I think first about what would be the most respectful and considerate way to say it. I love these editing experiences. An editor who works for a major publisher will focus on grammar, correct word usage, and the flow of sentences. He will keep the chief editor's criteria in mind. I edit my speech with the A–mighty's criteria in mind. The reward for this is way beyond what any human could ever pay.

E. Keep in mind the debit side to losing your temper. In 1990, *The New York Times* reported that researchers had gathered a wealth of data suggesting that chronic anger is so damaging to one's body that it ranks with, or above, cigarette smoking, overweight, and a high-fat diet as a cause of early death!

Even when anger is justified, the long-term consequences of how it is expressed must be taken into consideration. Just because you are right, doesn't mean that it is wise to say whatever pops into your head.

How much vital energy do we waste by wanting someone else to know that we are resentful? Holding onto resentment creates many forms of psychosomatic problems. Rabbi Abraham J. Twerski, M.D., writes in his insightful commen-tary on *Mesillas Yesharim*: "All we will accomplish by bear-ing a grudge is letting the resentment fester within us, possi-bly causing depression, migraine headaches, and high blood pressure. Does it make any sense to harm ourselves because we are angry at someone else? This is why King Solomon says (*Koheles* 7:9), 'Anger rests in the bosom of fools'" (*Lights Along the Way*, p. 170).

"A person who has a bad temper will be hated by others" (*Orchos Tzadikim*, ch. 12). Someone who had overcome a bad temper once said, "Not only did other people feel neg-atively towards me when I become angry, I detested myself. I felt so awful every time I did or said something I shouldn't have. I finally said to myself, 'It's not worth torturing yourself just to ventilate your anger!' As I started gaining more con-trol over what I said, I also developed tools and techniques that have enabled me to live a much more peaceful and enjoyable life."

> *A car bumped very lightly into my car. There was no real damage, but I was furious. After all, that driver could have caused me a major loss. I let him know in no uncertain terms that he was a menace on the roads. He became defensive and insulted me. Then he pushed me, and I pushed him back. Before I knew it, we were in the middle of a real fist fight. A num-ber of bystanders pulled us apart. In the end, I need-ed x-rays to make sure I had no broken bones. My health is more important to me than being able to tell someone off. Reflecting on this, I made a powerful commitment to be more careful with what I say, even when I am upset.*

In a recent incident, a motorist's unchecked anger almost cost him a large financial loss. He was driving from one state to the other. In his home state radar detectors are legal, but in the neighboring state, not far from where he lives, they are illegal. While driving in the neighboring state, he was stopped by a policeman and told that radar-detection devices are illegal in that state. Rather than just apologizing and telling the policeman that he did not know they were illegal, he told the policeman that he had done nothing wrong and would soon be leaving the state anyway. His wife followed suit and started verbally abusing the policeman.

The policeman proceeded to write out a ticket. But while writing out the ticket, the policeman thought he recognized this couple's name and asked the driver what he did for a living. He replied that he owned a certain business. At the mention of the company name, the policeman smiled and said, "I do business with your company, and So-and-so is the salesman I deal with."

The now friendly policeman then gave the driver and his wife a valuable piece of advice. "At first I didn't think I was going to give you a ticket," he said. "You are from a state where radar-detection devices are legal and I was going to let you off with a warning. But when you both spoke so angrily, I vowed to teach you a lesson by writing a ticket that carries a large fine. In the future, be more careful how you speak."

These situations happen to everyone. Our anger causes us losses we don't even know about.

Make a list of the damage caused to yourself and others by your anger. Regardless of the size of your list, you will see that your monetary losses were certainly much greater than you thought. As you write the list, appreciate the inner strength and courage that you are showing by being honest with yourself.

One of the losses of angry people is that others will be afraid to give them advice or point out their failings. And if someone does try to guide them, they will not accept anything that carries a trace of criticism. An angry person will neither accept criticism nor be able to correct others.

Reproving others is a positive commandment: "You shall reprove your fellow, and do not bear a sin because of him" (*Vayikra* 19:17). To qualify as a mitzvah, however, reproof must be given properly. This means using a pleasant tone of voice and giving the critical remarks in private. And, it is essential that the person on the receiving end feel that the rebuke is solely for his benefit. If, however, you rebuke someone in a loud and angry voice and embarrass him, then what you are doing is a transgression, and has no chance of success (*Orchos Tzadikim*, ch. 12).

Awareness of the damage and distress caused by your anger will motivate you to do whatever it takes to gain greater emotional self-control. The best way to ascertain the actual effects of your anger on others is to ask them. Think about the people you get angry at the most. Give them permission to tell you the truth about how they feel when you speak to them in anger. The answers you receive will be eye-opening.

> *I used to yell at my children quite frequently, even though I knew that it was a mistake. I told myself that all the nice things I do for them far outweighed any negative effects of my anger. I received a tremendous shock when I asked them to describe in detail how they felt. They told me they were terrified of me when I was angry and feared that I would physically harm them. At times, they had frightening nightmares. When they woke up in the middle of the night, they couldn't fall back asleep and just lay in bed crying to themselves. I love my children and don't want to cause them pain. The shock of what I was doing to them has motivated me to be extremely careful with what I say and how I say it.*

Think about the distress and unpleasantness you have experienced in the past when you were on the receiving end of an angry outburst. Observe how ugly a person looks when he is angry. Do you want to look ugly and ridiculous to others? Look at an angry child's contorted features, his screams of rage, and how he tries to attack the source of his anger. Adults become angry over different things, but the picture is similar.

Interview people and find out from them how much they have suffered from the anger of others. You might want to ask them, "How do you feel towards the people who get angry at you?"

Ask anyone in the field of counseling about the tragedies caused by anger. Verbal and physical abuse cause intense suffering for many years. Anger breaks up families. It is at the root of many divorces. My experience as a counselor is that a large number of couples who go for counseling ultimately do so because of anger. Anger prevents them from finding peaceful solutions when disagreements arise. If two people are able to discuss matters thoroughly without anger, they often can come to a mutually acceptable agreement without a third party.

There are always issues that might require some outside intervention to find creative solutions, but in an emotionally peaceful atmosphere most issues can be resolved. The whole process of finding solutions with a third person can be enjoyable when both parties are free from anger and resentment.

Angry parents destroy the self-esteem of their children. Memories of a parent's anger can last a lifetime. Children of chronically angry parents live in constant fear. Home life is associated with stress and tension, and they will flee the home at every opportunity. Some children of angry parents have even been known to silently rejoice at their parents deaths. That too can lead to unbearable guilt on the part of their children.

Angry teachers take away their students' natural love of learning and teach their students lessons far different than they think.

"A teacher who easily becomes angry causes much damage," writes the *Chazon Ish.* "Such a teacher frequently becomes angry over the wrong things or inconsequential matters. Because he rebukes his students in anger, they will not accept his criticism on important matters. Moreover, his students will learn more from his faulty behavior than from his lessons and lectures. Students use their teachers as role models and emulate even their negative character traits. A teacher with negative traits who considers himself an almost perfect person will find ways to rationalize all his faults and improper behavior. Following his example, his students will likewise do things which are improper yet consider them to be elevated acts. Such an educator will keep reproducing offspring in his image" (*Emunah U'Bitachon* 4:16).

Angry employers rob employees of self-confidence and the motivation to work hard. Who wants to work hard for the benefit of a boss who is a slave driver? Who can take any initiative if every mistake produces fury? If an employer screams at his employee, the employee might not respond to his employer, but he is likely to take out his anger on a customer. Eventually the employer will lose out because of the bad will he has caused.

A young couple came to speak to me about anger. They were expecting their first child and were looking forward to becoming parents. The young man, however, had a strong fear. His father had an awful temper and beat his son, frequently with a belt, when angry. Since it is easy to revert to the patterns of our childhood, the young man wanted to work on his own temper even before his first child was born. His foresight is admirable.

9. Don't be a perfectionist — focus on improvement

In my experience, it is possible for a person who becomes concerned about his anger to find himself becoming angry even more frequently than before. If you try to control your anger in a way that is not appropriate for you and your unique temperament and life situation, you might become more tense than you were. And that tension can lead to new explosions of anger.

This is less likely to happen when you use approaches that are right for you. You might have to experiment to see what works and what doesn't. For some people the awareness that anger is wrong and harmful to themselves and others is sufficient. Others feel so guilty over their anger that their guilt causes stress that makes them lose their temper more frequently. Some people need to think more about their anger, while others are better off if they think about it less and instead focus on joy and other positive emotions. Some people need to think more about their emotions in general, and others need to think less about them. If one approach doesn't work for you, try a different one.

It is also likely that what is perceived as more anger is simply greater awareness. Before, you didn't notice when you were angry; now you do.

Don't be a perfectionist. Perfection, as they say, is the enemy of the good. A perfectionist views anger as all or nothing. If he gets angry once, he views himself as a total failure at mastering his anger. This discouragement will prevent him from further attempts at gaining control. Trying to eliminate anger all at once will cause tension leading to angry outbursts. Rather than perfection — complete elimination of all anger — make your goal that of our Sages: slow to anger and quick to be appeased.

Focus on improvement, no matter how incremental. Keep working on decreasing anger. View any increase in control over what you say and do as a concrete achievement. Respect your progress, for it is that respect which will enable you to continue improving.

---

10. *Teshuvah* for anger — apologize and ask forgiveness

Every time we speak to someone in anger, we cause him distress or pain. Sometimes that pain will be intense, and at other times minor. But in either case we have an obligation to ask forgiveness (see *Rambam, Hilchos Teshuvah*, ch. 2). Make apologizing and asking for forgiveness from anyone you have spoken to in anger a part of your program to combat anger. Not only is this part of the *teshuvah* process for causing pain to others, but the knowledge that you will have to ask for forgiveness will help deter future outbursts.

Even very great people become angry at times. A lesser person might deny that he did anything wrong, or he might be too embarrassed to ask someone for forgiveness. The greater the person, the quicker he will be to admit his mistakes and correct their harmful effects.

There are two aspects of *teshuvah* (repentance): rectifying past errors and determining never to repeat them. Think of the people you have hurt with your anger in the past. Sincerely ask them for forgiveness. If you have caused great distress, you will have to show the person whose forgiveness you seek that you deeply regret the pain you have caused.

Sincere regret is powerful. When you sincerely ask another person for forgiveness, he will be more open to accept responsibility for his part in the angry interaction. Be prepared, though, for varying responses. The other person might say, "You caused me so much pain it is difficult for me to forgive you." Be willing to return to the person even a number of times until your sincere efforts show the person how deeply you regret the pain you had caused.

Other times you will be told, "You've asked me to forgive you many times already, yet you still keep losing your temper. I don't trust you." Hopefully, you will be able to respond, "I can understand why you don't trust me, but I still ask your forgiveness for the way I acted in the past. I am not asking you to trust me on blind faith. I sincerely want to conquer my anger and have begun a program to do so. I will do all I can to control myself in the future. I plan to show you over time that I have really made changes in the way I react."

If someone asks you for forgiveness for their anger towards you, be quick to forgive (*Hilchos Teshuvah* 2:10). This person has made himself vulnerable. Have the nobility of spirit to forgive when you see that he regrets what he said or did in anger.

11. Be totally committed

A slave's thoughts are focused on gaining his freedom. If you are a slave to your anger, the time has come for you to make a choice. Choose freedom. Liberate yourself from anger.

The ideas in this book are not cold facts to be momentarily considered and then forgotten. Review is what will integrate these new ways of handling anger into your personality. Repetition is necessary, too, for these thoughts to become automatic even in times of stress, when someone says or does something that is distressing, irritating, or even infuriating. Review works by strengthening the neural connections which form the physical basis of memory. For greatest effectiveness, the antidote to anger must be linked to the actual experience of anger. This association will naturally occur through repeated review of the material presented in this book. The visualization tools in particular will improve your ability to react appropriately in difficult situations and with difficult people, as Rabbi Wolbe explains:

> A foul-tempered person's natural mental reaction is that he *should* become angry if someone behaves in a manner that goes against his will or if someone insults him. That immediate reaction is accompanied by mental imagery. He has pictures in his mind of how he will react in expressing his anger. We have to work on ourselves so that our immediate reaction will be based on Torah law as it applies to that particular situation. When a person is angry, he is likely to react in a self-defeating manner. When you use your intellect to choose the proper reaction, you will determine the most effective way to behave. The more you think in terms of what is sensible, the more it becomes part of your mental imagery and this will be your immediate reaction in future situations (*Alai Shur*, vol. 1, p. 144).

The effort you put into overcoming anger is a wise investment. Rabbi Yisrael Salanter taught, "It is worthwhile for a person to study *mussar* his entire life even if it only helps him to refrain from speaking *lashon hara* just once" (*Ohr HaMussar*, vol. 1, p. 55). This certainly applies to anger as well. A good way to prepare yourself for the challenge is to emphatically declare at least 10 times: "I am totally committed to conquering my anger." The first few times may sound less than enthusiastic, but don't let that stop you.

Keep repeating it with greater intensity and eventually you will be able to say it with complete sincerity. The verbal repetitions are giving a strong message to your subconscious that you mean business.

Any public declaration of commitment makes us more likely to keep that commitment. Tell your family, friends, fellow students, and co-workers that you are committed to conquering your anger. If you have the courage, put up a sign in your home, office or dorm room saying, "I hereby declare that I am committed to conquering my anger. I will be grateful to anyone who assists me."

Step 2

Be Aware Of Your Angry Feelings When You Are Angry, And Recognize What Makes You Angry

Step 2

Be Aware Of Your Angry Feelings When You Are Angry, And Recognize What Makes You Angry

1. Anger is an insightful teacher

No knowledge is more crucial to us than knowledge of ourselves. And it is precisely that knowledge that anger provides.

Anger is a powerful teacher (see Eruvin 65b), and if we are wise we will learn from it. Anger gives us an unmistakable message about ourselves. As students of anger, we must be prepared to listen, for even the best teacher in the world cannot succeed if the student refuses to pay attention.

Anger teaches us what we really consider our true priorities in life. If you want to know whether a particular person places a higher value on material or spiritual attainments, observe what makes him angry. What does he value more, the dignity of others or money? His anger will reveal the answer. Rabbi Yosef Leib Bloch of Telshe noted that the very same people who preach moderation in religious and spiritual matters are easily incensed at any affront to their personal honor. This shows clearly that their own honor ranks above that of Hashem on their scale of values.

> I used to be very upset when my young children became angry at one another for breaking a toy. I would point out that the mitzvah of loving one another should be so great in their eyes that they should forgive each other even for breaking a favorite toy.
>
> Then one day, a neighbor used my computer and broke a piece that I needed to have repaired. I was outraged and muttered out loud, "See what happens when you do a person a favor."
>
> One of my children overheard me and asked innocently, "Dad, shouldn't our love for others outweigh the loss of even a favorite toy?" She was right, of course. My anger taught me that it was easier for me to tell something to my children than to internalize it myself. My embarrassment was mitigated only by my happiness that my daughter had taken my lesson to heart.

Anger also lets us know which qualities we have already developed and which need further work. Do we rejoice in the opportunity to help others, or do we resent every intrusion on our time? Our response to others' requests will hold the answer.

I was visiting someone in his apartment. Over the course of a few hours, there was continuous knocking on the door as neighbors came to borrow various items. My host responded to every request with a big smile that wordlessly proclaimed, "I'm delighted to help you. Please ask me anytime you need something."

As I was about to leave, I asked him, "Isn't there a limit to your patience? People bother you constantly, yet you are not the slightest bit upset."

"Nobody is bothering me," he told me. "They are giving me the opportunity to do chesed. If every knock on the door brought a visitor bearing gifts, I would eagerly answer the door. Those who come to borrow are similarly affording me an opportunity to do something priceless."

I began to think how I would have reacted in his place. By the third knock, I would have been annoyed. Where I live people don't borrow something unless it's an absolute necessity. I was genuinely inspired to see someone who was enthusiastic about every act of chesed.

The way we speak when we are angry reveals a great deal about our spiritual level. Whenever the Chofetz Chaim, for instance, was upset, the students could look forward to hearing some profound insight from him (*Alai Shur,* vol. 2, p. 223). Other people are careful to begin every rebuke, "Zei gezunt." For many of us, though, anger brings out the worst in us.

I am usually careful about my language, but when I get very angry, the curses that come out of my mouth shock even me. Once I got into an argument with a taxi driver, who I felt had tried to cheat me. He was a gentle person and responded to my tirade by telling me, "I feel that what I asked for was fair. You have a right to disagree with me. But you look like a religious person. I can't believe that someone who considers himself religious could talk like that. You should be ashamed of yourself." I was. From then on I made up my mind to watch what I say even when I'm angry.

Loss of control can lead to the worst crimes. Our Sages say, "Someone who tears his garments, breaks his possessions, or throws away his money in anger is considered as if he worshiped idols. That is the way of the evil inclination: Today he tells you to do this, and tomorrow he tells you to do that, until finally he tells you to worship idols" (*Shabbos* 105b). How you react when you are angry is a strong indication of whether your intellect or your baser instincts control your life.

Anger teaches us about our awareness of G-d and His supervision of the world. Anger teaches us about our level of love and compassion for others. Anger teaches us about our level of humility and patience. Anger teaches us about our need to control others. Anger provides important clues about our level of self-esteem. Anger teaches us about our ability to judge others favorably. Anger teaches us about our level of communication. Anger reveals our level of impulsiveness. Anger teaches us whether we view others with a "good eye" or a "bad eye," whether we tend to focus more on the positive or negative. Anger teaches us if we tend to blame others for matters beyond their control or for those that are actually our own fault. Anger shows how considerate we are with the dignity and feelings of others.

Anger teaches us how easy or difficult it is for us to forgive others.

Anger also teaches us when you are making progress in all of these areas.

2. Have the courage to confront anger

The clarity of vision into ourselves that anger provides can be frightening. Shutting our eyes might often seem the safer course. But the benefits of self-knowledge are so overwhelming that any momentary discomfort is a small price to pay.

It takes courage to confront our fears. Courage does not mean being unafraid. It takes no courage to confront something which does not frighten you. A person who loves dogs does not require courage to walk past a dog. Courage is the ability to overcome our initial intimidation. Anger is a frightening force. Even acknowledging its presence takes an act of courage. Yet there is no choice, because unacknowledged anger is like a vicious dog without a leash. Only acknowledged anger can be controlled.

People often deny unpleasant emotions because they feel they reflect badly on them. This is a mistake. It is important to recognize that Hashem created us in such a way that every normal person experiences nervousness, guilt, and embarrassment. Envy is a test for all of us. So is anger, desire, and the need for the approval of others. While the particular mix will vary from person to person, everyone will experience the entire range of emotions. Recognizing this will make it easier for you to acknowledge your own emotions.

Many years ago, I heard my Rebbe, Rabbi Mordechai Gifter, describe how aware Rabbi Yosef Leib Bloch, the Telshe Rosh Yeshivah, was of his impulses. One day, Rabbi

Bloch was out walking with another person. As they passed some pottery lying by the roadside, Rabbi Bloch commented, "I feel a sudden impulse to smash that pottery with my walking stick." This total awareness of his impulses was coupled with the self-discipline to withstand those impulses. This is a mark of greatness.

"Have you seen a man who is wise in his own eyes?" asks King Solomon, the wisest of all men. "There is more hope for a fool than for him" (*Mishlei* 26:12). The Vilna Gaon comments on this verse that one who is wise in his own eyes is unaware of his negative behavior. Without such an awareness there is no hope that he will correct himself.

Feeling bad about your anger is, in fact, positive: It shows that you are aware of your problem and eager to do something about it. My Rosh Yeshivah, Rabbi Chaim Mordechai Katz, used to say that there is no bigger blessing for a person than having one's faults pointed out. Thus we find among Yaakov's blessings to his children, criticism of Reuven for his impulsiveness and of Shimon and Levi for their anger. The criticism was a blessing, Reb Mottel pointed out, because it enabled them to focus on what needed improvement.

If you view awareness of your anger as a blessing, it will be easier for you to acknowledge it. Feeling bad for the wrongs that you have done is part of the purification process (*Tzidkas HaTzadik,* no. 57). So if you feel bad about your anger, feel good that you feel bad!

The only blessing and acquisition a person can accrue in this world is the improvement of his character. The *middos* we attain through working on ourselves truly become part of us, unlike material possessions, which cannot be integrated into our being. Every action you take to conquer anger is thus an integral part of a mitzvah that only you can do for yourself, and thus the source of incalculable joy. Any initial pain felt as you confront your anger will seem, in hindsight, as a positive turning point in your life.

3. It is easy to deny anger

It is very easy to deny anger. Many people react to their own anger with denial and insist that they are not angry when they clearly are. Their jaw is clenched, their muscles are tight, and their expression is that of a fire-breathing dragon, yet they demand to know, "How can you possibly think that I'm angry?"

Some people deny their anger by calling it a different name: "frustration," "irritation," "being upset." They take the stance that until someone is throwing things in a temper tantrum, he is not really angry. Very often people mean that as long as they have even a modicum of control over word and deed, they are not really angry.

But anger comes in many flavors. If you feel aggressive, annoyed, argumentative, bitter, bothered, defiant, disgusted, enraged, frustrated, furious, hatred, hostile, impatient, incensed, indignant, inflamed, irate, irritated, livid, mad, malicious, offended, outraged, rebellious, resentful, spiteful, sullen, vengeful, venomous, vicious, or violent — that's called anger.

A person is considered angry, writes Rabbi Moshe Chaim Luzzatto in *Mesillas Yesharim,* any time he is influenced or affected by anger. From a Torah viewpoint, even slight anger is anger. And any time anger affects us we have an obligation to do what we can to decrease the effects.

Vital step forward

There is a positive aspect to our tendency to deny anger. It reflects a recognition that it is wrong to get angry and that anger is negative. But just as denying an illness will not make it go away, so too denying anger will not make it disappear.

Overcoming anger is difficult. But it is even more difficult if you deny it. Only when you have acknowledged your anger, are you in a position to deal with it.

Whether or not you are angry right now, try saying, "Yes, I am angry" five times. This will take the sting out of admitting that you are angry when you actually do feel mad. Then, when you actually do become angry and are able to admit, "Yes, I am angry," you will find that this admission provides a slight sense of release. You are no longer repressing your feelings and trying to convince yourself that you are not angry. This emotional honesty is itself liberating and leads to better ways of handling your anger. Now you are in a position to concentrate on achieving a more relaxed state of mind and to work out the underlying problem.

Suppressing anger

Many people confuse learning to control and reduce anger with suppressing it. They then worry that this suppression of such a powerful emotion will have adverse consequences. And they are right to worry. Suppressed anger can eventually explode in angry outbursts. Or it can cause a person to act out his anger in passive-aggressive ways. Bottled-up rage can also damage health.

But expressing anger the wrong way is even more destructive. Wrongly expressed anger leads to both physical and emotional abuse. One public figure who advocated expressing one's anger rather than repressing it was not even invited to his own children's weddings. Ultimately, "letting off steam" and "venting" in inappropriate ways causes more damage to the angry person than repression does.

Far better than suppression is finding solutions to the

aggravating problem (STEP 5), learning to communicate displeasure in a self-respecting manner (STEP 4), reframing the situation in a Torah-consistent manner (STEP 3), or utilizing tools and techniques to decrease or eliminate the anger (STEP 6). These are all valid and healthy ways to handle anger.

---

4. Denial of anger because you think, "I shouldn't be angry."

Some people deny that they are angry because they feel that it is wrong to be angry. Sometimes this is coupled with guilt over feeling angry with someone who had done so much for them. But whatever the reason for the denial, it won't work.

Anger is a natural emotion, part of being human, that we all experience from early childhood on. As we grow older, we develop spiritually and emotionally in ways that hopefully help us reduce our anger. But we all began life experiencing frustration and anger.

Even as adults, we cannot always control the initial momentary response of anger. But we can control what we say, what we do, and the tools we choose to overcome anger. Having the courage, honesty, and humility to admit to a human frailty offers us greater hope for spiritual growth than denying reality.

Sometimes people deny their anger because they themselves realize that the cause of their anger is too trivial to merit the type of response they are experiencing. For example, someone kept you waiting for 15 minutes more than the agreed-upon time. The 15 minutes made no difference at all, but you take it as an indication that the other person does not consider you important enough to be on time. Or someone fails to respond to your request, and you interpret that failure as a lack of respect.

Whenever your response seems out of proportion to the provocation, ask yourself, "What is involved here that I am reacting like this?" Sometimes you are already irritated and the slightest additional provocation triggers an explosion. Or you might be under a lot of tension and stress. When we are tired or under pressure even little matters can loom large.

Other times a particular incident automatically reminds you of an intense past experience. There are techniques (presented in STEP 6) for desensitizing ourselves to memories of past events.

Lack of sleep or food makes us more susceptible to anger. For some people, changes in hormonal balance can have a similar effect, as can certain medications. (If you suddenly find yourself more irritable than usual, check your medications.) Others have food allergies that can affect their hormonal state. These are possibilities that should be taken into consideration if someone is having an especially difficult time with anger.

Some people who frequently have sudden and unpredictable explosions of angry rage triggered by trivial events might have an undiagnosed neurological disorder, chemical imbalance, or other physical ailment. It is important to first rule out such contributing factors.

5. Be open to feedback from other people

We experience ourselves differently than others experience us. Our own experience of anger is an internal feeling. Other people observe us from the outside. They see our facial expressions, the tightening of our jaw, or a clenched fist. These reactions are clear to everyone but ourselves (unless we are looking in a mirror). If others remark on your frequent or intense anger, believe them. They are usually right. It can happen that someone will misread your expression as one of anger when it isn't. But if a number of people comment on your anger or someone who is close to you comments frequently, take what you hear seriously.

Sometimes you may be accused of yelling when you perceive yourself as operating in a normal tone of voice. What has usually happened in such circumstances is that the other person perceives your underlying anger, even if you have not dramatically raised your voice. What they call yelling is a subjective perception of how your real emotion feels to them.

> *When people used to tell me that I was angry, my initial response was "You're wrong; I'm not angry. I know my feelings better than you do."*
>
> *Finally, someone suggested that I carefully observe instances where two people disagree over whether one of them was angry. I witnessed five such instances and each time I agreed with the accuser and not the person denying that he was angry. These observations made me think that perhaps I might be wrong too when I deny others' accusations of anger.*
>
> *The next time someone pointed out that I was angry, I stopped in the middle of my usual denial to ask myself if I was being honest about my feelings. I had to admit that I was feeling a bit frustrated, which is just a less intense form of anger.*

6. How to recognize your own angry feelings

Some people are very aware of their feelings. Others are not. To gain greater sensitivity to your feelings of anger, you need to be aware of the tension in your muscles when you become angry, your tone of voice, your pattern of talking, and even changes in your breathing.

Consider two questions:

The first is: How do you know that you are angry when you are angry? Think about this for a moment.

The second question is: How do you know you are calm when you are calm?

Sometimes it's quite obvious that you are angry. You are shouting or insulting another person. You might even throw something, kick something, slam a door, bang your hands against the wall or on a table. All of these actions convey a clear message: "I'm furious right now. I need to do something to release the unbearable tension."

Then there are passive-aggressive forms of anger. You are angry at someone but do not feel up to confronting him directly. Perhaps you are afraid of an angry counterattack or are worried that he will take revenge later. Or you may hesitate because you know in advance that he will shift the focus from his actions to your reaction, telling you, "The only reason you are irritated is because of your own issues." And of course he is partially correct: The issues that are important to you will determine the degree of your reaction. But he is failing to acknowledge that being upset is usually subjective and that you still have a right to discuss the matter.

Depression is at times anger turned inward. When we feel angry but try to bury those feelings under the rug, usually because we do not have effective tools for resolving conflicts, the burden is enormous. At the first sign of depression, look for the underlying anger. One way suppressed anger surfaces in disguise is in passive-aggressive responses, such as: "forgetting" to do something you were asked to do, procrastinating, performing your task inefficiently, stubborn insistence on having others do things your way, etc. Even though you are not openly hostile, a closer look will tell you that you are irritated with the person and that you are acting differently than you would otherwise.

At other times, it is not obvious at all that you are angry. Your words and behavior are controlled. Nevertheless, if you were completely self-aware, you would find a number of indications that you really are angry, because an angry person thinks differently. He blames others more readily, and might even wish someone harm or feel happy if he suffers some loss or pain.

When you are angry, your tone of voice is different. The throat muscles constrict and anyone can hear the difference in the way you sound, even though you are not shouting or screaming. Your tense, controlled tone of voice conveys suppressed rage. In the future, pay attention to the way you sound when you are joyous, calm and relaxed, versus the way you sound when you are angry, irritated, or upset.

Our muscles are a highly sensitive biofeedback system. When we are angry, our muscles become tense. As soon as our mind perceives something as irritating or stressful, our muscles instantly react. Even if our conscious mind does not acknowledge the frustration or anger, our muscle system will do so automatically. The next time you become angry focus your mind on the different muscles throughout your body. Be aware of the muscle tension in your stomach, in your jaws, in your neck and throat, in your arms and hands. Mentally check your body from head to toe.

This process of muscular awareness will allow you to recognize anger as soon as it starts. In addition, by allowing you to experience your anger in a concrete fashion, awareness of muscle tension helps you avoid expressing it in other ways.

Many people fuel their anger by thinking angry thoughts

and thereby prolong what might otherwise have been a momentary reaction. They might think obsessively about the incident that triggered their reaction or talk about it to others. If they react angrily to the person who has irritated them, his or her response may only provoke them further. The next time you are angry try to do the opposite. Quiet your mind and just experience your anger. Try to stop thinking in words as you just experience your anger physically. This can take a bit of practice, but it is worth the effort. It will enable you to better understand the nature of your anger and to release it in Torah consistent ways.

7. At times you might be angry at yourself

Much anger stems from a sense of failure or disappointment with oneself. At times, this is expressed as anger at others who have triggered this sense of failure by pointing out a mistake or fault. You know that they are right and you are upset with yourself. For some, this feeling of anger is translated positively in a resolve to correct the fault. But often, it is expressed negatively as discouragement or self-pity, along with anger at the person who provoked these negative feelings. This is counterproductive and harmful.

Rabbi Shlomo Wolbe, one of the great *mussar* personalities of our generation, advises the students in his *mussar* groups to be patient with themselves because impatience only leads to discouragement and giving up.

When you become aware of a fault in yourself, look at the positive side: Your new awareness offers the possibility of self-improvement and nothing so elevates a person as correcting a negative trait.

8. Become aware of the chain reaction of your thoughts

We often intensify our anger by projecting a particular incident way beyond its present context. Recognizing the chain reaction that certain types of situations trigger is a crucial step in gaining control of our anger. For example, your child does not obey you. Immediately you start thinking, "If he ignores me about little things, he surely will not listen to me about bigger things. If he won't listen to his parent, he'll never have any respect for any person in authority. He'll grow up to be a rebellious, wild person who will cause me intense embarrassment." Most of your anger has nothing to do with the present minor incident that has just taken place, but is a result of your fantasies about the future.

> A friend of mine was recently in a small town and started jaywalking against the light. Just then he noticed a nearby police car heading in his direction. In anticipation of a ticket, he became angrier and angrier at the unknown policeman. "What chutzpah to give me a ticket," he thought. "Everybody jaywalks. Why is he picking on me?"
>
> As the police car drew alongside him, the policeman called out, "Hey, Joe, I thought it was you. I'm thrilled to see you. How have you been, old pal?"

> A messenger who brought me a note saying that the boss wanted to talk to me had a grave look on his face. My first reaction was, "The boss must be angry about the terms of the last deal I negotiated." Then I

told myself: "I tried my best. I researched the deal thoroughly and think the result was a good one. If he comes on too hard, maybe I should think of finding another job." I walked into the boss' office already upset over his ingratitude.

He took my hand and shook it warmly. "I want to congratulate you for the great job you did and let you know there is a big bonus in it for you."

Later, I asked the messenger why he had had such a serious look on his face. He had no idea what I was talking about. The boss handed him a note, without saying a word, and told him to deliver it to me. Imagine what a fool I would have felt like if I had spoken angrily to the boss.

Awareness of these patterns is itself the surest cure. As soon as you recognize that fantasy is at the root of your panic and anger, they will subside. Be on the alert for such patterns in your thinking. You will soon find your own humorous story to illustrate how far our minds can carry us from reality in a matter of seconds.

---

9. Anger in the present is frequently related to past events

The brain is a remarkable data base containing memories of an entire lifetime. All our joys, every moment of inspiration, everything we have read or heard, is stored in our amazing brain. So, too, is every incident of anger.

What happens in the present is associated in the brain with what happened in the past. That is fortunate — even lifesaving. When you cross a busy street, your brain processes, on the basis of past experience, a massive amount of information about cars — their power, speed, the effect of being hit by one. All this takes no more than a fraction of a second. Likewise, when you feel happy, your brain is making subconscious associations with other such occasions. Similarly, when some incident in the present reminds you of an unpleasant past memory, your brain makes the association and some of the past emotions return.

If you find yourself overreacting to what is happening in the present, ask yourself: "Does this remind me of something that happened in the past?" Awareness of how past events can trigger your anger in the present will help you overcome this anger. The mere act of recognizing that you are overreacting to what just occurred will help you put the immediate event in perspective. Also, by understanding the power of past memories you become able to deal with those memories and reduce their negative hold over the present. In STEP 6 you will find an effective technique for doing this.

I told someone an amazing story to which he responded, "You're kidding." I became furious and told him, "How dare you call me a liar!"

He was taken completely aback by my reaction. "I never called you a liar," he said. "Whenever I hear anything unusual, my standard response is, 'You're kidding.' No one has ever taken offense by that expression before."

Then I remembered being told as a child, "If someone tells you, 'You're kidding,' he's calling you a liar." When I thought about it, I realized that this was ridiculous. I wonder how many other similar responses trigger anger that is totally unrelated to reality.

I heard someone humming a song, and all of a sudden I felt a surge of anger. At first, I couldn't understand why. Then I remembered that in the fourth grade the teacher called on me, and I didn't know the answer. One of the other children in the class started humming that song to make fun of me. My mind associated that song with being humiliated.

10. Special issues that can cause anger

A. Religious *yetzer hara*

Rabbi Simchah Bunim of P'shischa used to say, "Even what you do for the sake of Heaven must be for the sake of Heaven." If you are angered by someone interrupting or interfering with your mitzvah observance or because they are careless about a particular *halachah*, your rebuke must be expressed in a manner that is consistent with Torah. The first and foremost criteria is to feel a deep love for the other person. When you pray, you are talking to your Father, your King, and when you talk to another person, you are talking to one of His children. Your love for your Father, your King, must be expressed in the way you speak to His children. Losing your temper at someone for not doing what he should, usually helps neither of you.

Losing your temper at someone for disturbing your prayers is not the proper Torah response. Hashem has sent this person to test you. Thank Him for this opportunity to elevate yourself. Speak to the person who interrupted you with the respect due to one created in the Creator's image.

Anger reveals to what extent we have integrated Torah concepts. There are many stories of great Torah scholars who didn't become angry when someone dropped their *esrog,* and thereby rendered it invalid. They prized their *esrogim* as a means to do the will of the Creator. They realized that it made no sense for that same *esrog* to be the source of anger, which is against Hashem's will.

The *yetzer hara* often tricks us into thinking that our anger over *halachic* violations is an expression of our religious sensitivity. And indeed it is sometimes necessary to show outward anger — e.g., to children or students — to prevent the repetition of sins. But these instances should be the exception. In general, the only kosher anger is that which is expressed outwardly while inwardly you feel calm.

> *When I was a young yeshivah student, one of the boys wanted to use the key to the yeshivah's Torah library outside of regular hours. When the person in charge of the key refused to give it to him, he became enraged, and told him that he would suffer eternal punishment for causing bitul Torah.*

Contrast that incident with the following.

> *I once had a roommate who was such a serious learner that his only yetzer hara was not to think Torah thoughts before reciting the morning blessing on the study of Torah.*
>
> *One day he was locked in his room because someone had forgotten to fix the lock as they should have. As a result, he missed learning with a chavrusa that afternoon. He neither became agitated nor did he recriminate the guilty party. When I asked him why he wasn't angry he replied, "I study Torah to do the A-mighty's will. If it is His will that I am in this room now instead of the yeshivah, I accept His will wholeheartedly."*

I used to become furious when anyone spoke lashon hara around me. I felt as if they were trying to pour poison down my throat. I was once at a large banquet when someone at the table started to talk about someone we both knew. Thinking she was about to speak lashon hara, I cried out, "That's lashon hara, I don't want to hear it." Everyone turned around. The person turned red and in a choked voice, told me, "I was just going to say that our friend had surgery recently and would appreciate visitors." With tears in her eyes, she got up and walked out.

I called her a number of times the next day to ask forgiveness. At first she was too hurt to talk to me. Finally she forgave me, but only on condition that I never embarrass anyone like that again.

B. Money issues

Money plays a major role in our lives, and, not surprisingly, is the cause of much anger. Frequently the amounts involved are small, but they still raise issues of control, insecurity, fear of deprivation, or being taken advantage of.

Our anger over monetary matters teaches us how high a priority we place on money and how high a priority we place on the honor of others. Someone who blows up repeatedly over trivial losses, for instance, is far from the Torah view that material things can never be the source of true happiness.

I was going to my brother's wedding in a strange city. On the way from the airport, I mentioned to the driver that I was from out of town. When we reached our destination, the fare seemed quite high, and I saw that it had taken 30 minutes instead of the 15 I had been told to expect.

I was furious at the taxi driver and accused him of taking advantage of me by taking a circuitous route. He insisted that the traffic was heavier than usual.

The exchange took only a few moments, but I was highly agitated and repeated the story over many, many times in the course of the celebration. Instead of enjoying my brother's wedding, I spent the entire time venting my anger over a few dollars which didn't make a drop of a difference.

Whenever I felt I was being overcharged, I would accuse the store owner of being greedy. Some storekeepers replied matter of factly, "That's my price. Take it or leave it." Others insisted I was getting a real bargain.

But one took great offense. "Please, never come back into my store again," he told me in a very hurt tone of voice.

His reaction forced me to confront my own quickness to accuse others of greediness. I realized that I had a deep emotional fear of being considered a sucker. When I thought about it, I saw that this was ridiculous. I will be judged by how I treat others, not by how others treat me. From then on I was resolved to negotiate in a respectful tone of voice.

I had an elderly uncle who never became upset over the loss of money. He once explained to me that as a

young boy, his grandfather told him the Talmudic state-
ment that a person's character is judged by his behavior
in three situations: when he is dealing with money, when
he is drunk, and when he is angry. "My grandfather told
me," he said, "that I should always view money as a
means to serve the Creator and not to turn it into a form
of idolatry." Then he blessed me that I should always
react calmly to the loss of money, for that is a sign of
great character. You are truly wealthy when no amount of
financial loss can cause you to lose your peace of mind.

My grandfather died a month later and I always
considered this talk of his as his personal ethical will
to me. Looking back, I see that I didn't suffer any
financial loss by adopting this attitude, and I have
had a great emotional gain.

11. Discovering your pattern

By considering the questions that follow, you will gain
greater insight into when and why you get angry. The time it
takes to clarify these issues are well worth it.

A. Write a list of times you became angry

Think of at least five to ten times when you became angry
to any degree, even if you controlled what you said and did.
It will be helpful to write them down.

When you are angry, it is easier to recall other instances
of anger. If you have a hard time recalling specific instances
of anger, you might have to wait until you feel angry again
to do so. The list of anger-provoking situations given in the
appendix may also help you remember situations that have
gotten you angry in the past.

Ask those closest to you for examples of your anger. They, unfortunately, will be more likely to have a number of clear memories.

Think of how you reacted to frustration as a child. Did you throw tantrums, or did you sulk alone? In adulthood many people repeat childhood patterns.

Awareness of a childhood pattern allows you to change it. Don't let your childhood self set automatic patterns to rule the rest of your life. Through your choices of words and actions you are free to create new patterns.

Once you start compiling a list, you are likely to remember many more instances of anger. Your patterns will become clearer the greater the number of memories.

B. Questions to clarify your patterns

Here are some questions that will make it easier for you to pinpoint your personal pattern of anger:

• Is there a specific person who angers you frequently? What does he or she say or do that arouses your anger? Is it the basic message he conveys, or the way he says it? Is he or she patronizing or condescending? Does this person try to control you? Do you make more demands on this person or have greater expectations from them? Does this person's facial expression bother you?

Someone once described how he threw a chair at a person who had infuriated him. That person made a certain facial expression that reminded him of his father's when he criticized him. He had suffered a great deal from his father's criticisms and took the other person's use of that facial expression as a deliberate taunt.

If you dislike someone, you might get angry at what he says or does even though someone else doing the same thing would have no effect. At times, it is people's failure to honor your requests that irritates you. Perhaps their refusal calls into question your authority or perhaps you feel they owe you something for past favors.

- Are there particular situations when you become angry more easily than usual? What about those situations makes you angry?
- What type of pressure leads to your becoming angry? Are you more likely to become angry when:
    - (a) tired
    - (b) hungry
    - (c) in a rush
    - (d) preparing for Shabbos or other holidays
    - (e) at the Shabbos table
    - (f) it is before a wedding or other special occasion
    - (g) you have just experienced a disappointment or failure
    - (h) you have a headache or feel ill
    - (i) it is very hot or raining
- Are you taking any medication that causes irritability?
- Does your self-esteem fluctuate, and with it your levels of anger? What are the key factors that raise and lower your feelings of self-esteem?
- Do you become angry more easily at family members or at strangers?
- Do you get angry more easily at work or at home?
- When does someone else's anger get you angry and when doesn't it?
- Do you get angry when someone disagrees with you, or only in specific situations?
- What type of corrections do you appreciate and what type irritates you?
- When do insults make you angry and when are you able to ignore them?

- When you become angry, do you prefer to retreat to a quiet place or to discuss it with the person who has provoked your anger?
- Do you tend to blow up and shout when you become angry or do you quietly seethe?
- With which people do you never or rarely get angry? Why do you think that is?
- Is there a particular tone of voice or facial expression that gets you angry?
- Do you become angry at inanimate objects such as a stuck drawer?
- Do you tend to blame others for your anger or do you take responsibility for it yourself?
- What faults of yours are at the root of your anger? Rabbi Chaim of Volozhin writes in *Ruach Chaim* (2:1) that whenever a person observes a fault in someone else, he should check himself for that fault, since we have a strong tendency to notice our faults in others (see *Kiddushin* 70b). This provides us with an important clue to our anger.

12. There are different types of angry people

Not all anger is the same. It differs both in its genesis and the way it is expressed. There is no one model for anger but rather a variety of patterns. Gaining awareness of your pattern will make it easier to develop appropriate control. Awareness of other possible patterns will also help you deal with the anger of others.

Whatever your pattern, it is important to remember that your particular personality is exactly what you need for your unique *avodas Hashem* (service of G-d). The qualities that cause your anger are the very same qualities that offer you the greatest possibility of spiritual greatness. Rabbi Tzadok HaKohen reiterates this a number of times. In *Tzidkas HaTzadik* (no. 44) he writes, "A person with the quality of passion, whose passion has previously led him to forbidden desires, should not feel that he is deficient because of that quality. By directing that passion in the right direction, he will find an intense love and passion for seeking truth."

Your temperament is not an accident. It is the raw material Hashem has given you to work with. "A person cannot break his basic personality," writes the Vilna Gaon (commentary to *Mishlei* 22:6). "But everyone has free will to choose how he will act within the basic structure of that personality. Whether a person will be righteous, or evil, or average is up to him."

A person who never experiences anger will not be rewarded for not expressing anger. He feels no impulse to do so, and is therefore not tested in this regard. A person who tends to become angry and masters that anger, elevates himself.

People who have major struggles with anger frequently have strong or intense natures. Such natures have many positive sides as well. A strong-willed person with a lot of drive will likely accomplish more than a more passive person. On the other hand, he will be more frustrated and impatient as he confronts obstacles. He must work on balancing positive drive with patience and humility.

A person with an intense emotional nature can develop a passionate spiritual relationship with Hashem. Such a person can pray with fervor, be empathetic and compassionate towards other people, and sensitive to what words and actions will cause others distress. At the same time, such a person is more vulnerable and is easily hurt.

A person who is very exact and proper will be meticulous about details. Honesty seemingly comes naturally to him. But such a person is easily irritated by others who are not so meticulous or honest. He needs to appreciate the positive side of this trait while developing more understanding of others.

See if you can discover your own pattern(s) among the following types:

≈⌐ Rarely angry, easy to appease

This type of person never becomes angry over trivial matters. He is free of the arrogance and conceit that are at the root of much anger (see *Mesillas Yesharim,* ch. 22). He only becomes angry over issues dealing with serious losses or injustice. Even when he is angry, he is in control of what he says and does, and easily accepts a sincere apology.

Some of those who have reached this lofty level, once had bad tempers. Only long and arduous work on their thoughts and actions brought them to their current level.

≈⌐ Worst form of anger

The worst type of angry person is compared to an atheist. Such a person, as described by Rabbi Moshe Chaim Luzzatto, "is easily filled with rage. His ability to think clearly is grossly impaired because of his anger. A person of this type would destroy an entire world if it were possible for him to do so. His rational intellect is not in control. He is as unthinking as a wild animal, and would violate every transgression in his state of rage. He is led in the direction his anger takes him" (*Mesillas Yesharim,* ch. 11)

This type of person is highly narcissistic. Only he exists. No one else counts. He is usually preoccupied with fantasies of success, power, wealth, and brilliance. He requires constant attention and admiration. He will respond with intense rage to being criticized or being defeated in any way. He feels entitled to make any demands on others, and reacts angrily if those demands are not met. He lacks empathy for others and doesn't care how much suffering he causes.

Most of us have some aspects of this type within us. That is why the Sages refer to anger as a false god within man (*Shabbos* 105b).

ᕦᕤ Impatient person

Impatience is the source of much anger. The impatient person is always in a rush. Therefore, delays and inefficiency upset him greatly. We live in a period of proliferating timesaving devices. Messages that once took weeks to reach their destination, now arrive in seconds. But instead of making life more tranquil, these devices have only made it more hurried. The faster things go, the less tolerant the impatient person is of delays.

ᕦᕤ Low tolerance for frustration

Some people are born with a low tolerance for frustration. Whenever things do not go as hoped, or they do not get what they wished, they become frustrated and lose their temper. Even petty matters upset them although they may not explode.

ᕦᕤ Intense nature

There are those who have very emotionally intense natures. When such a person is joyous, he is intensely joyous. But when he becomes angry, he has a fiery temper.

Two intense people can have a wonderful relationship when all is going well, but when either one is angry, the other one is likely to be as well, and their anger will escalate rapidly.

If both parties work together to conquer anger, they can maintain their relationship. Indeed, even if only one party is committed to do all he or she can to conquer anger, he or she can do much to improve the relationship.

✑ The authoritarian personality

The authoritarian personality who is authoritative and even dictatorial uses anger to intimidate and coerce. Such a person will blame others for his anger, accusing them of failing to respond rapidly enough to his commands. He is capable of using physical violence to discipline. Some authoritarians are perfectly pleasant to most people, but are tyrants with their children and others they perceive as weak.

✑ The sensitive soul

Some people are inordinately sensitive to words and even to the tone of voice others use when speaking to them. The sensitive soul is poorly equipped to deal with aggressive people and often overreacts to perceived injustice.

✑ The injustice collector

There are those who collect injustices. They are always on the lookout for unfairness and are quick to feel that others are being favored over them. When anyone has anything they lack, they see unfairness. Complaining about the unfairness of life is this type of person's favorite conversation. He experiences a certain pleasure every time he finds an injustice to complain about.

Yes, there are many injustices deserving our strong condemnation, and we are obligated to right wrongs. But one who reacts angrily to everything he perceives as unjust will find himself perpetually angry. He will not, however, be effective in remedying the causes of that injustice.

≈≈ Complain and blame

The Chofetz Chaim describes a type of person who complains and blames easily. Such a person typically judges others negatively, and is highly suspicious that others do not like him (*Shemiras HaLashon,* vol. 1, *Shaar HaTevunah,* ch. 16).

In this category are all those who are perpetually suspicious that others are talking or acting against them. In some, those suspicions result in perpetual anxiety, and in others in openly expressed anger at those who are suspected.

> *I used to think I was too smart to judge people favorably. I did not want to be considered a sucker. Then I read in the name of the Vilna Gaon that "Hashem loves those who constantly find merit in others." I decided that having Hashem love me was better than always assuming the worst of others. After a few weeks, I realized that my former negative judgments were frequently mistaken. Now I enjoy the challenge of finding favorable or mitigating explanations for others' behavior.*

≈≈ Chip on the shoulder

"There are people," Rabbi Gershon Chanoch of Rudzhin said, "who wake up in the morning already full of anger. They go around looking for another human being upon whom they can pour their wrath" (*MiMayanos HaNetzach,* p. 270).

≈≈ Out to get what he wants

Some parents inadvertently raise their children to think that they can get what they want only through temper tantrums. Such children learn that if they stay angry long enough and loudly enough they will eventually get what they want. The more this anger is reinforced the greater chance that this pattern will persist into adulthood. Those who believe that they can get what they want by tantrums may occasionally be short-term winners, but they will be long-term losers.

∼⌢ Histrionic

Those with histrionic personalities react dramatically to even the most trivial events. They are prone to scream easily and to have frequent irrational outbursts, which often leave others puzzled about what could have set them off. Frequently, the triggering agent turns out to be associated in their minds with some past painful situation.

∼⌢ Overwhelmed

Sometimes the cause of anger is the feeling of being overwhelmed. Accumulating debts or a high-pressured job, with which one is never caught up, are just two possibilities. Over-committing is also another common cause of feeling overwhelmed. Some people who are normally quite pleasant become angry easily when tired, hungry, or under stress.

∼⌢ Affected by the states of others

Some people are unusually sensitive to the emotional states of those around them. That quality can be very positive: Such people are naturally compassionate and empathetic. But they also have to learn to protect themselves from the negative energies of angry people.

∼⌢ Cold anger

Not all anger is expressed in violent outbursts. There are those who never blow up. Rather, their face and tone of voice become icy. Those whose anger is expressed glacially often don't recognize that they have a problem with anger at all.

⇒⇐ Passive anger

Some people are too timid to explicitly express anger. Rather, they try to get back at the cause of their anger passively: They will perform inefficiently, come late, find excuses, etc.

⇒⇐ Sustains resentment

Some people are capable of sustaining resentment over incidents that took place 30 and 40 years ago, keeping them as fresh as if they happened yesterday.

⇒⇐ Anger over mistakes

Some people become excessively irritable over any mistake. They are the ones who angrily correct the Torah reader if he makes a mistake. You can literally hear the anger in their voice.

⇒⇐ Idealist

The idealist becomes angry at others for not living up to his ideals. While his ideals might be exemplary, his anger isn't. He needs to develop a more tolerant attitude towards others.

⇒⇐ Dissatisfaction with oneself

Someone who is dissatisfied with himself might let out his deep frustration at others. This dissatisfaction could be in various areas: spiritual, financial, social, and in one's professional or personal life. Many people today find their work empty and alienating, even though to the outside observer they may appear highly successful. Unable to vent these feelings at work, they do so at home.

⇒⇐ Grew up in angry environment

Those who had parents who were frequently angry are more likely to repeat this pattern, even though they know intellectually how destructive anger can be.

☙ Victim of abuse

Childhood abuse is much more common than previously thought. Abuse can be verbal — e.g., constantly belittled or humiliated — or even physical. A defenseless child is terrorized when giant adults are angry, all the more so if he is grossly mistreated as a result. When victims of childhood abuse are told as adults to control their anger, they may become furious at the one advising them for not being sensitive to all that they have suffered.

When memories of past abuse have been suppressed, or not entirely acknowledged, the victim is unlikely to find healthy ways to release pent-up rage. He is prone to angry outbursts that seem exaggerated in relation to the triggering event.

Studies of victims of childhood abuse have found that adults who confront the pain of their past are less likely to mistreat their own children.

☙ When others insist he is angry

Some people have a naturally serious mien which others mistake for an angry countenance. When others insist that he is angry, he insists that he is not. When they insist enough, he gets angry.

☙ Inner resentment

There are those who show no external signs of anger, but their inner resentment keeps festering and feeding on itself. Many who fall into this category were not permitted to express their anger in constructive ways when they were children. They were told that any form of anger is not permissible, and that they shouldn't get angry. Children should not be told to will their anger out of existence. Rather children should be taught how to reduce displeasure and express what remains in productive ways.

⤜⤙ Doesn't recognize it at all

There are those who neither recognize their own anger nor express it. Their anger harms no one but themselves. While they may be fooled about their anger, their nervous system is not. One common result is psychosomatic ailments.

⤜⤙ Apathetic

The last type of person who has a problem with anger is someone who doesn't become upset over anything. He is apathetic to injustice and the wrongs that people perpetrate against one another. The desecration of G-d's Name or defilement of His world leave him unmoved, and he will counsel anyone moved to righteous indignation to take it easy.

13. Gain awareness of your needs

Everyone has certain needs. In the proper balance, these needs are important for a normal fulfilled life. Yet not all needs will be met. The needs that are met are opportunities to be grateful to our Creator for giving them to us. The needs that are not met are opportunities to accept His will. When other people don't meet our needs, we are likely to feel resentment and anger. When we make excessive demands, these wishes have even less of a chance of being met. It is often the failure to have these excessive demands met that is a root cause of anger.

The more expectations we have of others, the more likely we are to be angry when those expectations aren't met. Conversely, the fewer expectations we have of others, the less chance we will become angry.

One man who never becomes angry revealed his secret: "I have no expectations. I try to make things happen. But if they don't, I focus on what I can do, and not on what I can't. I am grateful for any favor anyone does for me. But I never expect anything."

Below is a list of some of the needs and desires that are at the root of your becoming angry.

ᗖᗗ The desire to control others

Some people have a strong desire to control others. A controlling person constantly makes demands on others. If they fail to meet those demands, he becomes frustrated and angry. Issues of control can cause major battles in a marriage, especially if both parties have a strong need to control.

A controlling person creates resentment everywhere he goes, and many people will go to great lengths to avoid him.

ᗖᗗ The desire for independence

Some people have an excessively strong desire for independence. Anything they perceive as an attempt at control, even something as innocuous as being asked to pass the salt, will enrage them.

ᗖᗗ The desire to have others live up to their standards

Some idealists are easily irritated by people who do not measure up to their standards and quick to condemn others for not behaving as the idealists think they should. When they overreact, other people develop negative attitudes towards them and their ideals.

One of the ideals of an idealist should include the virtue of being careful with the feelings of other people. Developing sensitive ways to influence others will help spread the idealist's ideals much more effectively than anger.

Rabbi Moshe Feinstein had this to say about idealists: "There are world movements that speak of humanitarianism, but are willing to kill those who oppose them. The proper Torah attitude is demonstrated by Avraham's having prayed for the welfare of Sodom, even though they behaved in a manner diametrically opposed to Avraham's ideals. We should not hate those who reject our idealistic values. Rather, our inner wish should be that our opponents should improve their ways" (*Darash Moshe*, p. 13).

∾ The desire to appear right

A person who has a strong desire to always appear to be right will get angry at others who question his accuracy or point out that he made a mistake. If you want to convince someone of the rightness of your position, losing your temper is one of the worst ways to try to do it. If you are right, prove it in a rational, logical way. Explain your reasons. Show your evidence. Cite your authorities. Loss of temper is an expression of lack of convincing proof.

A person who wants to be right will appreciate challenges to his position. Those challenges will help sharpen his own clarity.

∾ The desire to appear competent

A person who has a strong need to appear competent will get angry at anyone who questions his competency. (By contrast, a person who really wants to be competent, not just appear to be, will appreciate it when others point out ways to improve.)

A parent who has an excessive need to be seen as a good parent will react with fury if his children's behavior embarrasses him in public.

∾ The desire for appreciation

A person who has a strong need for appreciation resents it when others are not as grateful as he would like. Needless to say, his resentment rarely elicits greater respect.

A sincerely giving person, on the other hand, appreciates gratitude but is not upset when it is not forthcoming. They view lack of gratitude as the problem of the recipient of the beneficence, not theirs.

☙ The desire to be understood

A person who has a strong need to be understood is likely to become angry if he feels misunderstood. Another person's understanding, however, cannot be demanded. Becoming angry at someone for misunderstanding you is pointless: He probably will misunderstand your anger as well.

If being understood is important to you, find an insightful individual who has a deep understanding of personality and the uniqueness of each individual, in whom to confide. By remaining calm and explaining yourself to the best of your ability, your chances of being understood are much greater.

☙ The desire to be taken care of

A person who has a strong need to be taken care of by others will have many unmet expectations that lead to anger. Such a person views every failure of others to meet his expectations as a sign that they do not care about him at all. His anger only makes it harder for others to want to meet his expectations.

☙ The desire to be free from frustration

Our anger is an indication of our level of tolerance for frustration. We all have our limits. Some people are easily overwhelmed. Others can tolerate a great deal of frustration over a long period of time.

All frustration depends upon the way you view a situation. Once you adopt the Torah perspective, you will be able to deal with situations calmly.

↘↙ The desire to be loved

Everyone needs to be loved. Some of us had this need met to a significant degree when we were younger; some of us did not. Early deprivation in this regard can have lasting consequences, and in fact much inter-familial strife has its roots in childhood needs for love not being met.

The ultimate solution to feelings of being unloved is to internalize the awareness of Hashem's love. A person who experiences this love will not react so strongly if he feels unloved by another human being. This is, of course, a high level of spiritual attainment.

The best way to make oneself beloved by others is to love them. When you experience unconditional love for others, most people reciprocate your love (see *Mishlei* 27:19). By focusing on increasing your positive feelings towards others, you will both lessen your anger and take a major step towards meeting your need to be loved.

↘↙ The desire not to be deprived

Some people have particularly strong material needs, and will tend to see others as competitors for scarce material goods. Strong material needs are an expression of spiritual emptiness and can never be satisfied even by attaining the objects of one's desire. Spiritual achievements are the only cure for this inner emptiness.

↘↙ The desire to feel important

Everyone has a need to feel important. A person who did not grow up in a nurturing environment is likely to feel insecure, and thus be more vulnerable to exaggerating slights and insults. Innocent statements and actions may be perceived by an insecure person as attacks. On the other hand, a person whose self-esteem is intact is not subject to such feelings of being threatened. Internalizing the Torah awareness of each person's intrinsic worth is a solid foundation upon which to base feelings of importance.

ᗡᗢ The desire to feel that one is a good person

A person who doesn't feel that he is basically a good person is likely to become angry at anyone who makes him feel guilty. A person who is confident of his basic goodness, on the other hand, will not be destroyed by guilt. He will repent the wrongs that he does, and if he is spiritually elevated, he will be grateful to those who point out his failings and thus afford him an opportunity to improve.

ᗡᗢ The desire not to appear foolish

No one likes to appear stupid or foolish. Those who have a particularly strong need never to be thought stupid, will react strongly to anyone they perceive as trying to deceive them.

No one else can make a fool of you except yourself. And the surest way to be thought a fool is to get angry.

ᗡᗢ The desire for respect

There are those with a strong desire for social recognition and prestige. They crave all signs of deference and social privileges.

The better you feel about yourself, the less angry you will become at others for not showing you respect. Self-respect is something that no one else can ever take away from you. Your anger is a litmus test of your self-esteem.

ᗡᗢ The desire for perfection

Perfectionists dread finding flaws in themselves or anything they do. They place themselves under constant pressure in their quest for perfection, and the pressure is likely to breed anger.

ᗒᗕ The desire to be treated fairly

Everyone wants to be treated fairly and justly, but some people have an excessively strong need for things to be fair and just. Such people are prone to stressing that "it's the principle that counts." Given that unfairness is common, such people are likely to blow up quite often.

If you want things to be fairer, think of positive ways to motivate and influence. But eating yourself up with resentment over injustices to you or others will just cause you indigestion.

You are not being fair to yourself if you deprive yourself of joy and serenity because someone has acted unfairly. Right the wrongs you can. Do what you can to prevent future wrongs. But don't allow what you can't change to prevent you from appreciating the rest of your life.

ᗒᗕ The desire for privacy

Some people have a strong need for privacy. When others encroach on their privacy, they become irritated and angry. Since we all feel differently about the level of privacy we want, it is impossible for others to know our limits unless we indicate this to them. Getting angry will only confuse the issue.

---

14. The next step: "What did this teach me?"

After you have calmed down from a bout of anger (the sooner the better) ask yourself, "What did this incident teach me about myself?" Listen carefully to the answers you give yourself. After analyzing the lessons to be learned from your anger, you are ready to answer the next three questions:

- "What can I say and do when I am angry to resolve a problem instead of creating an even bigger problem for myself?"
- "What can I do to overcome my anger after I become angry?"
- "What can I do to prevent becoming angry in the future?"

Answers to these questions will be dealt with in later steps.

Step 3

Focus on Controlling Your Own Reactions

Step 3 11-25-00

Focus on Controlling Your Own Reactions

Part A: Focus on controlling your own reactions

1. Desire for control leads to anger

ngry feelings often flare up when other people don't act the way we would like them to or events don't conform to our agenda. The irony is that in our quest for control over these externals, we lose control over ourselves.

I used to be a very controlling person. I had a major need to feel totally organized and in control over all aspects of my life. This created tremendous tension and

I frequently became angry. Eventually, the constant stress brought on a mild heart attack at an early age.

In the end, this crisis turned out to be a blessing in disguise. During the first few days in intensive care I had no control at all over my life — I was totally dependent on others. My recuperation in the hospital gave me plenty of time to think. I came to the conclusion that I had to let go. I realized that if I wanted to lead a healthy life, I'd have to make my desire for organization and control over externals much less of a priority than it had been.

The stronger a person's need to control others, the angrier he will become when those people don't submit to his demands. Reducing the desire to exercise control over others will make it easier to avoid anger. Viewing anger from this perspective — as stemming from a need for control — is a valuable tool to help you gain mastery over anger.

- If you feel angry about what another person said to you ...
- If you feel angry about the quality of service or work provided ...
- If you feel angry about noise or traffic levels ...
- If you feel angry about disorder created by others around you ...
- If you feel angry about demands made on your time ...
- If you feel angry over the behavior of your spouse, children, employees, or students ...

... recognize that a desire for control is the underlying cause of your anger. Remind yourself that the behavior of other people is beyond your power to control. Give up trying to control others, and concentrate on increasing control over yourself.

Each one of us is the master of his own inner kingdom. While total sovereignty over others is an impossibility, it is possible for us to control our own responses and reactions to people and events. Throughout the day, instead of reacting automatically, make it a habit to first ask yourself, "What would be the best thing for me to say or do right now?" An effective way to internalize this tool is to repeat the previous sentence until it becomes a part of your mental outlook.

There are, of course, many instances when we need to motivate and influence others, but this can be accomplished much more effectively and efficiently without anger.

> As manager of a large store, I took my job seriously and did all I could to create an efficient organization. The negative side to my sense of responsibility was that I took it personally if an employee didn't accomplish all he was supposed to. When that happened, I wouldn't hesitate to reprimand the delinquent party in the strongest terms. The net result was that the employees made a pretense of efficiency whenever I made an appearance, but only went through the motions the minute I left. They worked for a paycheck and nothing more.
>
> I read about strategic management approaches and realized I needed to create a different atmosphere in our business. My goal became one of getting all of us to feel like we were one big happy family. To develop a strategy, I asked myself this question: "How can I motivate the workers to adopt the approach I want them to?"
>
> I visited a few successful, well-run stores that were known for their excellent record of employee satisfaction. I discovered that in none of these stores was anger a part of the motivational strategy. I realized I couldn't just pretend to care about my employees — I would have to feel real concern for their total welfare. I clarified for myself, point by point, ways to enhance

my daily interactions with them in the workplace. Then each day on the way to work I spent a few minutes repeating to myself, "I truly care about my employees."

I was amazed to see how fast the entire atmosphere in the store changed for the better. My anger had been preventing me from using more effective management tools.

2. Anger operates in a vacuum

A life centered around wish-fulfillment is doomed to be full of anxiety, disappointment, and anger. A person living such a life chains himself to the fallacy: "I will be happy only if all my wishes are fulfilled." Yet, as our Sages say, "Whoever has 100 wants 200; whoever has 200 wants 400." Obtaining everything our hearts desire is an impossibility — yet we know that it is a mitzvah to be happy. It stands to reason, then, that happiness need not be dependent on gratification of our desires. In fact, a joyous, happy life comes from feeling gratitude and appreciation for what we have and experiencing joy for the mitzvos that we do.

The many thousands of thoughts that go through our minds each day affect our emotional state at any given moment. This will work for us or against us, and we have the free will to choose which one it will be. When our mind focuses on thoughts that are conducive to happiness or joy, that is the state we will be in. As someone once said, "The city of happiness is in the state of mind. Only if we look in the right place will we find the city."

On the other hand, when our mind focuses on thoughts that are conducive to anxiety, depression, or anger, that is the state we will be in. This is measurable on biofeedback machines. For example, the readout on an EMG, electromyograph, which measures electricity generated by muscles, changes instantaneously when thoughts change. It has been proven that when a person thinks anger-producing thoughts — such as memories of disappointment, unfairness, insults, or being on the receiving end of someone else's anger — his measurable stress level will go up. On the other end of the spectrum, thoughts of a relaxing scene — such as a peaceful lake or waterfall, a kindness given or received, or one of life's beautiful moments — will show a lowered stress level. These changes in muscle energy occur in a fraction of a second.

R' Yosef Leib Bloch notes this phenomenon. "The nature of a person is that when he thinks and talks about the distress and suffering he experienced in the past, even though right now his entire life situation is a fortunate one, he will actually feel some of that pain" (*Shiurei Da'as*, Essay: *Emor Me'at, VaAsai Harbai*).

When we keep thinking about times in the past when people made us mad, we will reexperience the anger we felt at the time. The present rerunning of those mental films and tapes increases the distress, pain, and harm, multiplying the original anguish. If anyone else would insist on showing us such a film, we would ask him to turn it off. Take charge of your internal movie projector. Turn off the films that irritate and anger you, and play the ones that will fill you with happiness. Many people find this difficult and even impossible to do at first, but once they make it a top priority to live a joyous life, they find themselves able to make the necessary effort to replay happy scenes of moments that filled them with appreciation and gratitude. Gradually, their lives were transformed.

The questions to keep asking oneself are:
- "What do I appreciate?"
- "What do I feel grateful for?"
- "What is going right in my life?"

All of these questions will enable you to focus on joyous and happy thoughts.

People who are full of anger keep their main focus on the negative: what people are doing wrong in the present, what they did wrong in the past, and how they might do something wrong in the future. People who are full of joy keep their main focus on what is right and on what they can do in the present and future to enhance their lives.

If you are awake 16 hours a day, you have 57,600 wakeful seconds in your day. By keeping your main focus during these seconds on the type of thoughts you wish to think, your life will be joyous. As it states in *Mishlei* 15:15: "The life of a person who consistently thinks positive thoughts is like a constant party" (see *Consulting the Wise,* p. 17). Controlling what we think throughout the day is the key to the quality of our life; trying to consistently control others and the environment is not.

A truly joyous person automatically feels less of a desire to control others. His joy comes from within, freeing him from the need to change something outside of himself in order to be happier. By keeping our focus on controlling and mastering our inner emotional states, rather than on trying to control what other people say and do, we will gradually build greater control over our frame of mind and be able to experience more happiness.

Each and every one of us would like to go through the day feeling happy and enthusiastic. Who doesn't want to feel calm and relaxed when tackling life's challenges? Positive feelings of patience, compassion, empowerment, and love are too precious for us to allow them to be dependent on external factors. A person who does not exercise control over his own mental and emotional states leaves himself a victim to what others say and do to control him. If there was a machine that controlled our emotions, we definitely would not give control over the buttons of that machine to anyone else. If you let other people "make" you angry, you're giving them power and control over you. It's as if you're letting them push your buttons.

It takes time to develop emotional self-mastery. But it's worth it. Control over our own state of mind puts the buttons to the happiness machine in our hands. When we are filled with happiness, anger is left out in the cold.

3. Sincere humility decreases anger

Because anger often has its roots in a desire to control, a sincerely humble person will not get angry often. As the *Rambam's* son writes, "Anger and arrogance are partners. Inner feelings of conceit lead a person to become angry. Conversely, humility leads to forgiveness" (*HaMaspik LeOvdai Hashem*, p. 44). Moreover, the issues that arouse a humble person's anger will be different from those that infuriate a person whose anger stems from ego, arrogance, and conceit. Helping others and not causing anyone pain, rather than trying to control others, will be a high priority for the person with humility. Any anger he feels will be coming from a deep concern for the welfare of other people. A person like this will be careful about what he says and does, and anger will not be a problem for him.

An arrogant person feels that he is the only one who counts and that other people exist solely to serve him and meet his needs. In its extreme form, as when a person sees himself as the center of the universe, arrogance is an aspect of idol worship. Such self-centeredness easily spills over into anger and insensitivity to other people.

The virtue of humility, arrogance's opposite, is an awareness that everything we have is a gift from our Creator, Who sustains the entire universe (*Mesillas Yesharim*, ch. 22).

Humility has nothing to do with feeling inferior. It is rather an accurate perception of reality. It is an awareness of one's own smallness and limitations in comparison to the vastness of the Creator's creation. At the same time, humility contains an awareness of our own intrinsic worth as well as the inherent worth of every other person on the planet. A humble person has his eyes turned Heavenward and becomes G-d-centered instead of self-centered.

How can we develop greater humility? Firstly, by reflecting on the infinite vastness of the universe compared with a human being. Picture your city or town as part of a larger country. Then imagine how that country looks to someone standing on the moon. Planet earth is a relatively small planet in our galaxy, and it is estimated that there are between 100 billion and a trillion galaxies, with over 100 billion suns in each galaxy! The size of the universe is so great that no matter how large we think it is, our minds cannot grasp its immensity. Seeing ourselves in this context gives us a sense of proportion. This sense of proportion will decrease anger.

A person without a sense of proportion will get just as angry over some spilled milk, a minor delay, or poor service as he will over a major loss. With a sense of proportion, we can remain calm in situations that cause those without this perspective to lose their temper.

Thinking about our human frailty opens us to reflect on the greatness and awesome power of our Father, our King. Each of us began life as a tiny infant, helpless and dependent, and we are destined, after 120 years, to return to being a soul without a body. Everything we are able to do, accomplish, experience, and know is only because our Creator has given us that particular gift. Rather than denying our strengths, virtues, and achievements, we should gratefully acknowledge these gifts. We openly admit that everything we have has only been given on loan so that we will be able to fulfill our mission in this world. Isn't this cause for humility?

Internalizing this awareness renders conceit and arrogance obsolete. The only way to sustain arrogance is to blind oneself to reality. Arrogance is possible only if one is unaware of the total picture. Since this is the case, arrogance itself is proof that there's no reason to be arrogant!

> *I never considered myself arrogant — but when I started to think about how many times I lost my temper, I realized that someone who really lacked arrogance wouldn't have become angry in many of the instances I did. I felt terrible about seeing this in myself and spoke to my Rabbi about it. He told me that while it would be unfair and inaccurate to consider myself an arrogant person, there were aspects of arrogance in my reactions. My newfound awareness can give me the positive feeling of knowing that I am working on improving myself in this area. People who are totally arrogant have a tendency to deny it. My awareness is in itself the beginning of humility.*

True humility is relaxing. It frees us from the need to seem perfect, to be a person who never makes mistakes. With humility, we can calmly say, "I was wrong," or, "Yes, I made a mistake." Humility is the awareness that we are fallible human beings with no claim to perfection.

True humility and a life of joy go hand in hand. With humility we are able to appreciate and enjoy all that our Father, our King, has given us. With humility, we give up expectations which are at the root of much disappointment and feelings of deprivation. We stop paying attention to what we don't have. The more joyous we are, the less anger we experience in life.

True humility frees us from approval-seeking. A humble person treats others with respect and finds that most people reciprocate. He doesn't waste time, energy, and money trying to impress others. He does not feel a need to appear stronger, wiser, wealthier, or better than others in any way, or to win their admiration purely to bolster his own ego. Humility frees us from needless worry about how other people see us. It frees us from the need to pretend to be different than we actually are, in order to fit some preconceived ideal image. This freedom to be ourselves will allow us to enjoy life more. We will no longer fear making mistakes, which will make us more open to acquiring more knowledge and skills. We are free to enjoy the learning process without feeling worried about how long it takes us to grasp and master the new material.

A person who feels sincere humility will be liked and respected by others. Their admiration will be an automatic byproduct of his lack of arrogance.

Life is filled with opportunities to gain humility. This is for our own spiritual good. When we anticipate these opportunities and view them in a positive light, our emotional reactions to them will also be positive. Often challenges to grow in humility come when we least expect them. It is worthwhile to develop the habit of saying, "I can use this opportunity to gain greater humility."

- When success eludes us ...
- When we are spoken to disrespectfully ...
- When we feel disparaged ...
- When we see our own flaws (or have them pointed out to us) ...

... we can use the opportunity as a springboard to develop greater humility. We can say to ourselves, "This is a wonderful opportunity to gain greater humility."

The next time you find yourself getting angry, try this simple test: Ask yourself, "If I had a greater amount of humility right now, would I still feel angry?"

> *Someone once quoted me out of context in such a way that anyone hearing the remarks would think I said something ridiculously stupid. I felt humiliated and angry — humiliated at the thought that people would think I was stupid enough to make such a statement, and angry at the person for misrepresenting me publicly. I spent a disproportionate amount of time dwelling on this incident, far more time than it was worth.*
>
> *Then I started to think of it in terms of humility. I asked myself, "If I really felt humble, how much would this actually bother me?" My answer surprised even me: "Not very much." I realized that any actual loss was minimal or non-existent. I also decided to use this painful incident to try to be more careful not to believe as absolute truth statements that reflect negatively on others. It gave me a stronger awareness of how easy it is to take a person's remarks or actions out of context.*

Even with a greater sense of humility, there will be times of stress, times when fatigue or hunger defeat our efforts at self-control. But with humility, our tolerance for frustration will be greater. And even when we do become annoyed, our reactions will be more moderate and under control.

Even with a greater sense of humility, we will encounter situations, such as injustice, that make us angry. But with a greater sense of humility, the words we say and the actions we take will be thought out and under our control with an eye on the outcome

4. Contemplating "Nothingness" and "Oneness" decreases anger

Contemplating two seemingly opposite concepts — "Nothingness" and "Oneness" — can help us connect with our Father, our King, on a deep level, thus increasing our level of humility and freeing us from anger.

The Torah (*Devarim* 4:35) states, "*Ein od milvado* — nothing else exists besides Him.*" There is nothing beyond or outside of our Creator; all of creation is a manifestation of His will. Human beings, in and of themselves, are nothing. The awareness of this nothingness is humility.

At the same time, the Torah concept of nothingness includes an appreciation of our tremendous value and worth, for each one of us is a manifestation of the Divine will. Keeping this in mind on a deep level will automatically decrease, and often even eliminate, anger.

If someone does or says something that would have gotten you angry in the past, repeat to yourself, "*Ein od milvado* — nothing else exists besides Him.*"

The concept of "Oneness," which we repeat daily in the *Shema,* is that the Almighty is One (*Devarim* 6:4). That is, all that exists in His creation is part of Him. Realizing this also builds humility. We are all an integral part of the Divine Oneness, sharing a common bond and reality with everything else in the entire universe. All human beings and all matter are part of our Creator's creation. The idea of this "Oneness" is so important that it is one of the six constant mitzvos that we are to keep in mind at all times (Chofetz Chaim in *Beur Halachah, Orach Chaim* 1). Not only is there only one G-d, but all that exists has its source in His Oneness.

Contemplating the Oneness of the Creator will free you from anger. Repeat the word "*Echad*" or "Oneness." As you repeat this, think about the size of the universe and how our

Father and King is the Creator and Sustainer of this Oneness. Experience the elevating spiritual feelings associated with this concept. Again, as you keep this in mind on a deep level, you will experience anger decreasing and even disappearing. Let every *mezuzah* you pass remind you to connect with the Creator. This will serve as a tool to commit yourself to do His will and to conquer anger.

Part B: View yourself as valuable

---

1. Internalizing the Torah view of your worth will free you from anger

---

Low self-esteem and feelings of inferiority distort a person's view of reality. He will misinterpret even minor slights and ordinary mistakes as concrete evidence that others think little of him. Feeling attacked and diminished, he then looks for ways to bolster his fragile ego. Often his insecurity is irrationally expressed as angry outbursts targeted at those he views as a threat. In reality, those people have nothing against him. They might even view him favorably if he wouldn't get angry at them.

> *I couldn't get a dial tone on my home phone so I called the phone company from a pay phone. The person I spoke to told me they would fix the problem within a few hours.*
>
> *Over four hours later, the phone still wasn't working. I called the service department a second time to ask why my telephone hadn't yet been fixed. When I gave my name and number, the company representative on the other end of the line informed me that my request was not listed.*

"Are you accusing me of lying?" I fumed, my frustration boiling over.

Later in the day, the line was eventually reconnected. When I thought back to my angry outburst at the anonymous person who took my call at the phone company, I felt slightly ashamed. Now it was easy to see that she was only trying to explain that they hadn't yet fixed the phone because somehow it wasn't on their list. She was only trying to defend the service department — but I took it the wrong way, as a personal attack on my integrity.

A healthy, realistic, and comprehensive Torah view of our inherent self-worth frees us from the need to prove to ourselves and others that we are important.

In the entire universe, we humans are the only beings created in the image of our Creator. This incomparable, prestigious value is ours from the moment of birth and stays with us a lifetime. We are told that each person should say and strongly believe, "The entire world was created for me" (*Sanhedrin* 37a). Internalizing the awareness that the entire world was created for you — a human being, who is the crowning glory of Creation — will give you an invincible self-image. And when self-esteem is high, anger is less likely.

If we are important and valuable, it is only because we have been imbued by our Creator with essential worth and are beloved by Him. There is no need to prove this over and over again, nor can anyone ever take this away from us.

Try repeating to yourself, "My essential being is valuable at all times. Nothing anyone says or does can decrease my intrinsic value. Even if I make mistakes, my value is infinite. My beloved Father and powerful King loves me, and I will do all that is in my power to reciprocate His love."

Each time we recite a *berachah* (blessing) we have an opportunity to upgrade our self-image. With it, we express our awareness that G-d is *Melech HaOlam,* King and Ruler of the entire world. Each connection with our Creator as Father and King reminds us that we are His child and therefore a person of infinite value and worth.

2. Decide to view yourself as 10 out of 10

If you feel that you are not yet able to internalize the Torah awareness of your true value, at least decide to view yourself as a "10 out of 10" — the tops. Why? Because you decided to, that's why. After all, there's no law that says you can't.

Imagine the following scenario: A young fellow walks by and we ask him what his self-image is. He says, "I'm 10 out of 10." We are interested in hearing more about his life history. A dismal picture of one failure after another emerges: He never even graduated elementary school, has never held a steady job, and is penniless; he lacks even basic social skills and has no close friends; his appearance is unkempt. Why, we wonder in amazement, does this ne'er-do-well think he deserves a 10! The only thing going for him is that he is a basically good person and seems happy to be alive.

We ask this apparent failure, "How can you view yourself as a 10 out of 10 when you are not intelligent and don't know very much?" He replies, "Yes, I am lacking in this area, but my total value as a person is 10 out of 10."

"But you don't have money," we probe further.

"True, I am poor. That is my financial situation. But my self-image is dependent on how I view myself and I view myself as a 10 out of 10."

"But you aren't popular or handsome," we insist.

"You're right, but those are only technical problems. My value as a person is what I decide it will be, and I've decided it is 10 out of 10. After all, why in the world should I decide that

I am any less than that? Sure, I would like to have more knowledge, more money, more friends, better looks and so on. But even before I figure out a way to do this, I will maintain my decision to view myself as a 10 out of 10."

Most of us have encountered people whom we might see as less than a resounding success in many areas, yet they seem to have high levels of self-esteem. The secret is: Self-image is how we decide to view ourselves.

As children, we were given messages, both subtle and not so subtle, about our self-worth — from our parents, siblings, teachers and fellow students, friends and relatives. Some of those messages were positive ones while others were negative. We weren't old enough to winnow out the negative ones, and took them all in, more or less, at face value. We believed these messages to be the total reality. Now that we are more mature, we can reevaluate our old conclusions and decide for ourselves who we really are.

Choose the Torah outlook of who you are. You are created in the image of the Creator, you are a child of our Father, our King, and the entire world was created for you! Make the decision to view yourself as a 10 out of 10 — because that's what you really are. The decision is in your hands.

3. Don't give anyone else control over your self-image

Making our self-esteem dependent on what others do or say is ridiculous. Our sense of worth is far too precious for that. Reminding ourselves that we have intrinsic worth whether or not anyone listens to us, whether or not anyone respects or honors us, whether people praise us or insult us, will free us from slavery to others — and slavery to anger.

Anger when used to control and dominate other people creates a momentary illusion of importance. It is as if the person is telling himself, "If I can control another person, then I am a superior human being." But does this really make sense? Is this rational?

If you find that your self-image goes up and down depending on the way someone speaks to you, you are giving that person the power to control you. If you become angry at a person for lowering your self-image, realize that the only way he was able to do so was because you decided to allow him to do it. Why be an accomplice to this crime of robbing you of your birthright?

On a practical level this means that even if someone makes an insulting remark, talks to you in a way you don't like, or otherwise tries to chip away at your self-esteem, you can still control your reaction. Develop the self-mastery to consider yourself a valuable person regardless of how anyone speaks or acts towards you. View the other person's insensitivity, aggressiveness, or one-upmanship as his problem. If someone slights you in any way, it is his problem. It has nothing to do with your true value as a person. Internalizing this will free you from much anger.

A person with ideal inner strength and emotional independence will be able to ignore the negative remarks of anyone who spitefully wants to cause distress. This is the goal to strive for.

> I used to feel like less of a person whenever someone spoke to me condescendingly. All the more so if someone actually insulted me. The motto running through my mind was, "You are only valuable if other people think well of you." When I analyzed this as an adult, I realized that my attitude was arbitrary and false. I grew up in a home where the opinions of other people were taken much too seriously.

I was impressed at how a mentor of mine was able to remain calm even when verbally attacked, and I asked him how he did it. He told me his major focus was on truth. "If I keep truth as my guide, then the disapproval of other people who are wrong doesn't really affect me. My value as a person is independent of what any mortal thinks of me."

I see how this has helped him live a great life. What is fascinating is that he is respected and well-liked by others much more than people who consistently seek the approval of others.

---

4. Make your self-image independent of your emotional state

Our emotional states have a tendency to go up and down, and many people find that their feelings of self-worth fluctuate right along with them. When they are successful and things are going well, their self-image goes up. They feel buoyant, filled with self-confidence, and are willing to overlook and forgive. But when things don't seem to be going the way they had hoped and planned, when they make mistakes, their self-image takes a tailspin. That's when anger is likely to be more of a problem.

Lately it's been particularly infuriating to me when opinionated people spout their personal viewpoint as if they were infallible and omniscient. "What a nerve!" I think. "How can they be so certain they're right?"

The other day a close friend challenged this attitude of mine. "So what if a person feels that his arbitrary, subjective opinions are the final word?" he asked. "Why should that bother you so much?"

"You know," I told him, "that's a very good question. I wonder why I get so angry about it."

The next time I heard someone state his personal opinion as absolute truth in what seemed to me a pompous, arrogant manner and I felt my blood pressure rise, the answer suddenly hit me.

I've been out of work and job hunting for the past several months. People tell me that the job market is tight, but I still feel unsure of myself — especially around people who sound so confident and self-assured. It was a real eye-opener to realize that my anger was due to my own insecurity at this time. After a few more similar experiences, I found that another person's self-confidence no longer bothered me.

By learning to separate our emotions from our sense of worth, we can keep our level of self-esteem more constant. Even when experiencing emotional ups and downs, we can still think of ourselves as a 10 out of 10. With a stable self-image, it becomes easier to climb up out of an emotional slump. This consistency of self-image has wide-reaching effects on a person's ability to remain calm and centered instead of angry.

5. Appreciating your worth empowers you to improve

Awareness of our weaknesses, negative patterns, and limitations can make us think less of ourselves. But that is exactly when it is so important to remember our intrinsic worth, because a person who feels good about himself will be willing, and even eager, to improve. As Shlomo HaMelech said, "Do not rebuke a fool lest he hate you for doing so; rebuke a wise person and he will love you" (*Mishlei* 9:8).

Our Creator gives each of us a unique nature and unique life tests. Your own nature is exactly what you need to serve the A–mighty. Many people find that when they list their main strengths and positive qualities side by side with their worst faults and negative traits, both lists are just opposite sides of the same picture. Very often the source of our greatest strengths lies in our areas of weakness. Knowing this can help us pinpoint our areas of potential.

For instance, a person who gets angry quickly might be a person who is very intense. This same intensity enables him to relate to ideas and other people on a deeper level. Similarly, a person whose feelings are easily hurt will often have a sensitivity to the feelings of others, too, and be kind, empathetic, and compassionate. Impatient people are very often those who have a strong inner capacity to get things done. Every nook and cranny of our personality should be explored, appreciated, and utilized to the fullest. Awareness of our inner potential will automatically make us feel better about ourselves, which will in turn motivate us to reach even higher levels of character improvement.

Often excessive, unproductive guilt over past wrongdoings prevents a person from viewing himself in a positive light. It is very important to remember that repentance out of love for Hashem transforms any wrongs we may have done into mitzvos. This is an extraordinary concept that is crucial to keep in mind.

6. Find someone who believes in you

If you find it difficult to transform a negative self-image into a positive one, you will gain by finding a teacher, mentor, family member, or friend who believes in you and your abilities. A reinforcing influence from someone with a positive view of people in general and you in particular can be a great help, particularly if you have been subject to constant disparagement. At the same time, remember that you really don't need another human being's approval to feel positive about yourself. You already have the approval of your loving Father and powerful King. Add to this your own self-approval and belief in yourself and you have all you need to see yourself positively.

I used to get good marks in school, but I definitely wasn't brilliant. My entire family is very creative but I didn't see myself as creative. The turning point in my life came when I wrote an essay in school and my English teacher spoke to me about it privately. He told me that I had a special way of expressing myself and that if I developed my creativity I would discover untapped powers and accomplish a lot. I argued, saying that I wasn't that creative; but he told me that if I had been able to write and express myself the way I did, that itself was creativity.

I had to agree with him. This exploded the blocks that had stifled my creativity until then and opened up an entire wellspring of originality that has made a major impact on my entire life.

I was an average yeshivah student. I was painfully aware of my many faults, and while I enjoyed learning, I didn't consider myself one of the most successful students in the yeshivah. When I heard people talk about inferiority feelings, I said to myself, "They're talking about me."

Then a friend of mine told me one day in passing that he admired me for having a heart of gold and a sensitive ear for the cares and concerns of others. He added that he had overheard the Rosh Yeshivah telling someone that he considered me one of the truly good students in the yeshivah, and that he appreciated my sincerity and felt that I was smart.

I hadn't realized that the Rosh Yeshivah thought this way about me. I didn't think he noticed me at all. I immediately felt a tremendous difference. My brain started working better than ever before. I felt terrific about myself, and besides the improvement in my studies, I davened better and was able to be more of a positive force in the lives of younger students.

I considered myself inferior my entire life. I wasn't very bright and I never had anything especially interesting to say. Nor did I have any special talents. Even though my children, other family members, and friends would tell me that they enjoyed being with me, that I was smarter than I gave myself credit for, that I was talented and admired, I still couldn't really appreciate myself.

But then one specific incident changed my view of myself.

I was visiting a friend in the hospital who was scheduled for heart surgery the next day. The nurse in charge suddenly looked at me and said, "I know you."

I told her that she didn't look familiar to me and that I had never been a patient in that hospital. She replied, "But I remember you. Some 20 years ago you worked in a hospital where a child of mine needed surgery. I was overwhelmed with worry and anxiety. You spoke to me with such care and sensitivity that your words encouraged me then and have stayed with me all these years."

This nurse didn't realize the powerful effect her remarks had on me. If someone could remember *words of encouragement that I said to them 20 years ago, I realized, then I must be a valuable person.*

From then on I felt so much better about myself. In one minute, this stranger had the dramatically positive influence on me that years of reassurance from others didn't.

Part C: Reframing: Solution to anger

1. What Is Reframing?

"A person who loses his temper easily might have difficulty understanding how someone else is able to remain calm in situations when he would become furious," says Rabbi Yeruchom Levovitz. "Conversely, someone who is able to remain calm might have difficulty understanding why another person becomes angry in a situation when he remains calm. A quick-tempered person should try to learn from someone who remains calm" (*Da'as Chochmah U'Mussar,* vol. 1, p. 141).

R' Yeruchom is telling us that not only do we have a choice of how to react to any given situation, but that it is our perception of the situation that will determine our reaction. A person who remains calm in a potentially anger-provoking situation is telling himself something different about it than the person who explodes when confronted with that same situation. This is a Torah insight that can transform the emotional quality of our lives. Mastering the right way of looking at things frees a person from needless frustration, anxiety, sadness, and anger.

This concept has gained contemporary popularity and is known as reframing.

We all have immediate and spontaneous reactions, based on past experience, to situations we encounter in life. Then, after our initial reaction, we think about what happened. What we tell ourselves about what happened — both the initial perception of the event and the mental summary — will be the key factor in our emotional response.

Our goal is to develop attitudes, perspectives, and ways of looking at events and situations through the lens of Torah, so that our initial reaction — and our later interpretation — will be consistent with the way our Father, our King, would want us to look at what happened. This in turn will affect our inner response and the outward expression of it. Until Torah attitudes become automatic, so that even our initial view of the experience is consonant with them (and this is a lifetime task), most of our efforts will go towards changing how we view what has already happened. Regardless of how we initially perceived an event, when we think about it later, even if this "later" is only a few minutes afterwards, we can change our attitude.

To reframe an experience means that we take our initial evaluation and label — "This is terrible"; "I just have to feel angry when someone says this," etc. — and remove the picture (the original experience in all its details) from the "frame" we originally put it in. The term was taken from the art world, where it is known that a picture's frame is an integral part of what we see when we look at the picture, so that a better frame gives us a better feeling about the picture on the whole. A poor-quality frame will not do justice to a beautiful painting; the painting should be taken to be reframed.

Our human perception of events is flawed; the Torah reality is the true picture. It is only because we do not live with the awareness that our lives are a manifestation of the love of our Father, our King; and that all people are created in His image; and that any given experience is part of our personal life-test to act according to Torah principles even when it is difficult — that we misinterpret and put the wrong "frame" around events. However, once we understand that the choice is ours, it will be easier for us to learn how to change these frames at will, improving our outlook on life and hopefully eventually reframing everything that happens to us according to Torah.

Be aware of your initial reactions to what happens. Be aware of both your thoughts and your feelings. Don't deny angry feelings by telling yourself that you shouldn't be angry since you should be viewing this event differently. Initially, just notice your angry feelings as they arise. Don't worry if at first you find it hard to get in touch with your feelings. Some people know exactly what they are thinking and feeling at any given moment, while others need time to reflect. Some people are aware of their thoughts but not their feelings, while others find the opposite to be true. Becoming more aware of both will broaden your self-knowledge and allow you to change.

Negative reactions to life come from the way we frame our experiences. Disappointment, irritation, frustration, feeling miserable, being upset or angry and many other painful and counterproductive emotions are all products of poor framing. Reframing the situation in a more positive way will change these inner reactions. By mastering the art of reframing, we can become masters of our emotions. Even though we certainly cannot control all external factors, we always have the ability to reframe — no matter how long ago the event occurred.

2. Poor reframes cause anger

Our evaluation of events can be the cause of anger, or its antidote. Internalizing Torah evaluations of situations will eliminate most anger.

Most angry feelings are preceded by hurt feelings. We feel hurt about an act of commission or omission. These hurt feelings have a powerful tendency to turn into anger, and the greater the hurt, the greater the anger. The reason we feel hurt is because of what we tell ourselves about what happened. For example, suppose someone you think should have called you or written to you failed to do so. You take this neutral act and tell yourself that the omission was meant as a slight, that the other person does not consider you worthy of his time and attention. Once you have framed the event this way, you feel hurt by this insult. You take it as a sign that you are unloved and unappreciated. Your hurt flares or festers (depending on your personality) into resentment and finally anger at the other person for his treatment of you. But the actual event — not receiving the call or letter — is not in and of itself cause for anger. It's the wrong frame that is to blame.

We have other choices.

Some people will frame the lack of receiving a call or letter as an opportunity to judge favorably. They will think of all the many reasons why they might not have heard from the other person: "Perhaps they called and my telephone was busy"; "Perhaps they are preoccupied with stressful life events and need my empathy, not my anger"; "Perhaps they don't realize how much a call or letter would mean to me." A person might decide to talk to the reluctant caller or letter-writer and tell him how much he looks forward to hearing from him. Or, he might use the disappointment as an opportunity to improve his ability to give unconditional love, not dependent on whether or not the other person does what he wants. Instead of choosing to feel hurt, he thinks, "If I can love this person even though he doesn't write or call, that makes my love for him more valuable and precious."

Many people feel that the way they automatically view an event or situation is the ONLY way to see it. But the truth is that on the completely objective level, events, occurrences, and situations are just that, nothing more. It is the viewer who evaluates them as either positive, negative, or neutral. It is he who attributes meaning to his experiences.

When you evaluate a situation as neutral, you won't be affected by it. Let's imagine, for instance, that you are walking down the street and notice a box lying on the sidewalk. It registers in your mind that the box is there, but it makes no difference to you one way or the other. You have framed the box as neutral.

But let's say you were to pass by that same box and recognize it as the box of used clothing you asked your spouse to take to the local charity. You might wonder why it is sitting on the sidewalk, or you might be furious that it is still sitting on the sidewalk.

Alternatively, how would you feel if you suspected a hidden bomb in that box? Your anxiety would not depend on how dangerous the box actually is, but on your own inner fears.

And if your neighbor, who is moving, was out looking for boxes, he might be overjoyed at seeing that same box.

Make it a high priority to master the skill of reframing. It is one of the most valuable skills a person can have, especially if he wants to reduce anger. All you need is one experience of exchanging a poor reframe for a more positive one to see that you have the ability to do so.

3. Reframe yourself out of frustration

Frustration, which is a form of anger, is a product of a poor initial frame. Frustration comes when we want something to be a certain way — faster, easier, more perfect — and it isn't. Picture, for example, the frustration of spending five minutes instead of the expected five seconds to open a jar, half an hour instead of the anticipated five minutes to print a letter, two hours instead of one to get through rush hour traffic. Frustration is linked to expectation.

While waiting in an airport for a delayed plane can evoke feelings of frustration, just 100 years ago people would have viewed the time it now takes to get from one continent to another, even with the long delay, as an unbelievable miracle. Computers, fax machines, microwaves, washing machines and dryers, and all the other benefits of modern technology save us time and effort. Yet it is highly possible that people living in the future will feel frustrated with the "slowness" of what we presently view as miraculous. The correct way of looking at life is to feel gratitude for what goes right while realizing that what goes wrong is the price we pay for the benefits of what goes right.

I knew a Torah scholar who never became frustrated or irritated by delays. I asked him how he does it. He told me that he has a special learning seder in which he reviews certain tractates over and over again.

"I am not the one who decides how long each review session will last. That I leave up to Hashem. The longer the delay, the longer He wants this particular session to last."

After hearing his reframe, I, too, began to utilize waiting time and no longer feel so frustrated.

My Rebbetzin never seems even a bit upset whenever her washing machine, telephone, or refrigerator breaks down. She told me that she tends to take them for granted. Therefore, she views their breaking down as a Heavenly reminder to appreciate them when they do work.

View every potentially frustrating situation as an opportunity to develop a greater amount of patience. It can also serve as an indicator of how much progress has already been made in conquering anger. Less frustration felt is an indicator of real progress.

Experiment with telling yourself that "The more frustration I begin to feel, the more I will switch tracks to think in ways that create joy"; or, "When I start to feel frustrated, I will move over into empowering states."

How did you reframe these suggestions? Some people will reframe them as ridiculous and certainly impossible for them personally. Other people will be curious as to how they might work in their own lives. Certain people will immediately envision how they will put this idea into practice, while others will realize that they already do it. How you personally reframe this idea is up to you. If you don't like your initial reaction, you don't have to be stuck with it.

Practice using your intellect to help you experience more and more joy every second of the day. When you become a master "reframer," situations that other people would consider highly frustrating will feel like only minor annoyances to you, or even turn into sources of humor and enjoyment.

4. Reframe insults to reduce their sting

Insults frequently cause distress and anger. But if we look at them with total objectivity (which can be very difficult to do when we are their target!), what is actually happening? Someone says a number of words that contain a certain verbal energy. These words and the energy with which they are said are different from the words and energy of what we would call praise. Our reaction is not caused just by the other person's words. It is our personal and subjective reframe, or evaluation, of those words that creates our reaction.

If we were to reframe those words as totally neutral, they wouldn't affect us one way or the other. Suppose the words were said in Chinese. Assuming we don't know the language, our feelings would be neutral, even if we were on the receiving end. Because the words have no meaning for us, we reframe them as neutral. Or, suppose we thought the person was practicing his lines in a play. We would also reframe his words as neutral.

A person who has mastered the ability to think that "whatever someone says is really a statement about themselves personally," would probably also be relatively unaffected.

If the words are viewed as "an awful attack" with the listener blaming the person who said them, he will feel angry. The more negative the initial frame, the more pain and anger experienced.

On the other hand, imagine that someone offered you a million dollars for any insult you were to endure during the next three days. If during that time someone were to insult you, you would view each insult as a money-making opportunity and feel deliriously happy.

You might choose to feel grateful that someone is sending only verbal energy your way and nothing more. Also, if you internalize the awareness that you can elevate yourself by being able to forgive others for the wrongs they do, you will feel spiritually elevated whenever you have that opportunity.

It is impossible not to react to an insult. The whole question is: Will you reframe it as negative or positive? It takes effort to learn to reframe insults positively. But it is worth this effort. The *Rambam* (on *Pirkei Avos* 4:4) notes that a righteous person was once asked to name the most joyous day of his life. He replied that it was the day he was on an ocean voyage and the people on the ship mocked and jeered at him, even throwing garbage at him. Why was this a day of great joy? Because the traveler was able to refrain from responding angrily, he defined the incident in terms of improved character development and self-control. He reframed this day as one of liberation from fear of other people's insults.

> I have always respected my Rabbi and now I respect him even more. Someone who is a bit high-strung, verbally attacked him in front of a number of people. The person's complaints were ridiculous. The Rabbi had mentioned that it would be of benefit to pray for the welfare of five people from a different city who were hospitalized following a car crash. This congregant felt that being asked to pray for someone he didn't know was an imposition. He screamed at the Rabbi, saying that he had a nerve to make such an unreasonable request, and that praying for strangers makes people less likely to pray for those in their own community.
>
> The Rabbi listened to him calmly with what I felt was exemplary patience. After 10 minutes of this tirade, the Rabbi politely and respectfully thanked the person for expressing his reaction and then told him that he would now be leaving to attend a meeting.
>
> "Rabbi," I asked him as we walked to the car, "why didn't you tell him that what he was saying was nonsense?"
>
> "This person has a need to feel important," he replied. "By showing him respect now, I have a better chance of getting him to listen to what I have to say on more important issues. He has been through a lot, and we should all treat him with compassion."

5. Reframe into joy and happiness

People who experience joy, happiness, and elation in their lives do so because of the way they reframe life events. People who enjoy being kind and compassionate are able to find pleasure in giving and helping because of the way they reframe their relationships with other people.

> I saw a prominent halachic authority patiently answer some questions that were ridiculously simple. He was asked why he never mentioned to the questioners that they should know the answers themselves.
>
> "I know that they are only asking the questions as an excuse to be able to tell others they spoke to me. Since this makes them feel good, I have pleasure that I can do this kindness for them."
>
> Instead of viewing this as a source of annoyance, he reframed this as a chesed opportunity.

Ask people who are usually joyous, serene, and kind how they would have seen and responded to various incidents that made you angry. Find out their underlying reframes. You will be surprised to see what you might have considered absolute reality reframed in a different, more positive light. Thinking about these other reframes will enable you to internalize them.

Practice reframing events that in the past have angered you. See them now as exciting challenges and adventures in personal growth and character refinement. You can even look at each situation that used to elicit an angry reaction as an opportunity to improve your skill at reframing!

There is no event so positive that creative negative reframers can't find something wrong with it. Cynical, pessimistic, bitter, gloomy, or self-pitying people constantly reframe events to evoke those emotions. Even if something is admittedly enjoyable and wonderful, a champion negative reframer will say, "It won't last."

On the other hand, a person with a creative sense of humor can find humor in things that frustrate others. Positive reframing is what anyone with a spiritual or poetic view of the world does constantly. Someone once asked jokingly, "How many reframers do you need to change a lightbulb?"

"None," I answered him, "because a reframer will find the benefits of darkness and enjoy it."

Is there a danger that a positive reframer might not be living in total reality? Might a positive reframer not take action when action is needed? Hopefully not. Unlike the person in the lightbulb joke, someone with clear thinking will know when it is best only to reframe and when it is best to take action. A person who thinks clearly will differentiate between a positive reframe based on reality as opposed to wishful thinking, self-delusion, and rationalization. But keep in mind that a negative reframer is not living in reality. He is creating a life of misery and anger, constantly reframing in ways that destroy his own life and at times the lives of others.

When you reframe an event in a way that is real to you, your feelings will be consistent with that new view. Consider, for example, your feelings when someone for whom you have done many favors refuses to do you a badly needed favor. If you view his refusal as "awful," you will resent his refusal. You will then have to find a way to dissolve this anger so as not to transgress various Torah prohibitions, such as holding a grudge, taking revenge, etc. Someone who is skilled at reframing, though, will be able to tell himself, "While I would have liked him to do me the favor, if he doesn't, it's not that terrible. After all, I would rather be the kind of person who does favors because it is a mitzvah, rather than for any expected personal gain."

I once saw someone refuse to lend a Torah scholar one of his books. When the person said, "I have a policy not to lend out my books," the scholar smiled widely. I later asked him why he reacted this way.

"I now have an opportunity to fulfill the mitzvah of not taking revenge. The next time this person asks me to lend him something, I will gladly do so and I will not even mention this incident so as not to violate the prohibition against bearing a grudge. What I gain from these mitzvos is greater than if he were to grant me this favor."

Some people are able to internalize reframes very quickly. As soon as they hear a new and better way to view a situation, they immediately integrate this information. Their emotions follow suit and become positive, too. Other people need time to reconsider their original view. We are always reframing, whether we are conscious of it at the time or not. Realizing the subjectivity of our reframes will make us more flexible about reframing negative ones.

The benefits of learning to reframe are so great that it is worth devoting much time and effort to becoming an expert at this skill.

6. Nine Torah reframes to decrease anger

The following Torah reframes can elevate us, bringing us closer to the Torah view of reality, thereby diminishing anger and increasing happiness. Just thinking of a reframe will not necessarily change the emotional reaction. It must be experienced as reality. Asking the companion REFRAME QUESTIONS throughout each day will make the Torah reframe just as emotionally real as the original perception. Practice asking yourself these reframe questions until they become automatic.

Torah Reframe One: "All that the A–mighty causes to happen is for the good." *Rom 8:28*

Rabbi Akiva was once traveling from one place to another. Towards evening he reached a certain city which he decided would be a good place to spend the night. The residents of this town, however, refused to let him stay. Rabbi Akiva's only comment was, "All that the A–mighty causes to happen is for the good."

Rabbi Akiva went to a nearby field to stay overnight. He had with him a rooster (to wake him up, according to Rashi); a donkey (for transportation); and a torch (for light). Suddenly, the wind blew out his light. Then a cat came and ate his rooster. Finally, a lion came and ate his donkey. After each occurrence, Rabbi Akiva's sole reaction was, "All that the A–mighty causes to happen is for the good."

In the middle of the night an enemy army came and captured the city that had refused lodging to Rabbi Akiva. The sage commented, "See how everything that the A–mighty causes to happen is for the good." Rashi explains that Rabbi Akiva realized that if his torch had still been lit, the enemies would have seen him, and if the donkey or rooster had been alive, their noise would have attracted attention and led to his capture (*Berachos* 60b).

The *Shulchan Aruch* tells us that it is good to get into the habit of repeating, "All that the A–mighty causes to happen is for the good" (*Orach Chaim* 230:5), as did Rabbi Akiva. It is noteworthy that Rabbi Akiva's teacher was Nachum, Ish Gam Zu, who used to say, "This too is for the good" (*Taanis* 21a).

We only become angry when we feel that someone wronged us or caused us a loss. When we realize that whatever happens is for the good, we will be free from anger. Even if the person did not intend it for our benefit, our Father, our King, did. The more we habituate ourselves in this belief, the happier our lives will be.

Each situation that is not exactly the way we would want it to be is an opportunity to accept the will of our Father, our King, with love, and to realize that He has planned every situation for our benefit.

• If someone or something delayed you and you missed your plane, it is because it is better for you to have missed that plane.

• If you weren't invited when you expected to be, it is because it is better for you to be somewhere else at that time.

• If you weren't hired for the job you wanted, it is because there is something better in store for you.

• If someone didn't give you a message, it is because you weren't meant to hear that message right then.

A person who masters the ability to experience all that happens to him as being for the good lives a wonderful life. The same experiences that cause others distress, anguish, and disappointment will be for him a source of joy. Every difficulty in accepting the Creator's will is a test. When we overcome the reluctance to part with our own agenda, we become greater people and experience a joy in living that is impossible to feel otherwise.

It is often impossible to see the positive, beneficial aspect of any given situation immediately — it can take hours, days, weeks, and sometimes even a lifetime. Rabbi Akiva had to wait until the following morning to actually see how the events of the previous evening were for his benefit. Yet this did not prevent him from reacting positively at the time. Even before he saw how events would turn out to be for the good, he knew intellectually and emotionally that what had occurred was beneficial for him. Instead of reacting with distress, each occurrence was a source of joy, yet another manifestation of the A–mighty's kindness.

We can compare each moment of our day to a present given by a wealthy relative who loves us. Until we open the gift wrap, we don't know what is in the box. Still, we are positive that whatever is inside will be something valuable and something we'll like.

Let's imagine how a negative reframer would have reacted in Rabbi Akiva's place. Our negative reframer is exhausted from traveling and relieved to ride into a city where he hopes to rent a room for the night. He stops at the first house he sees and knocks on the door. When the door opens a crack, he voices his request, only to get the gruff reply, "We don't take in strangers." With that, the door slams in his face. Our traveler feels disappointed and angry. His resentment and anger towards the town and its residents increase with each person who refuses to give him a room. The negative reframer bitterly complains about how he now has to sleep in a deserted field. "At least I have a torch for light," he consoles himself, "plus a rooster for an alarm clock and a donkey for transportation." But suddenly there is a strong wind and he is left in the dark. Imagine the distress and increased bitterness towards those cruel and callous people who wouldn't let him stay in their town. When the rooster and donkey are killed, he feels even worse. What is happening to him, he decides, is not only terrible, but unfair. He blames the residents of the city for his plight. "How am I supposed to get a decent night's sleep?" he fumes. (And with his angry thoughts and feelings, he probably won't.)

The next morning, when he discovers that everyone in the city was captured while he was saved, he will probably feel even worse. He will then blame himself for wrongly interpreting the previous night's events.

If our negative reframer had been a traveling companion of someone with Rabbi Akiva's view of life, he might very well have complained about the fellow being "naive" and "out of touch with reality." His distress at the unexpected turn of events would have been compounded by having to be in the company of what he might call a fool.

Most of us want life to go smoothly — whatever that means. We would rather be given a room for the night than have to sleep out in an open field. Emulating Rabbi Akiva's positive approach in the right way does not mean that if we had been asked our opinion beforehand we would have voted in favor of what actually happened. It does mean that once something has already happened, we remind ourselves that it can only be for our benefit.

Try to look for the good in every experience. If you can't think of any benefit right away, try saying to yourself, "I will hold off my judgment. Eventually I may see how this was actually for my benefit."

Realizing that all that happens is for the good will transform potentially anger-provoking situations into opportunities to increase *emunah* and *bitachon*. Pray to our Father, our King, for the ability to see the good in all that He causes to happen in your life. Ask Him in your own words to let you see His love and compassion in all of your experiences. People pray for health, wealth, good fortune, and many other things. The ability to experience all that happens to us as being for the good is the most precious ability we can have.

• Reframe Question One: "What is good about what is happening?"

Torah Reframe Two: "The reward is according to the pain involved" (*Pirkei Avos*, ch. 5, last *Mishnah*). Ex 2|. 25- 27

"For people whose love for the A–mighty is so strong ... the greater the obstacles in their path and the more effort it takes for them to overcome them, the greater will be their joy in being given the opportunity to demonstrate their *emunah* — just as a powerful general will prefer difficult military assignments because victory in such a challenging situation will reveal his strengths and abilities to the utmost. Similarly, anyone who feels a strong love for someone else will experience joy when he finds opportunities to express the extent of his love for that person" (*Mesillas Yesharim*, ch. 19).

The more difficult it is for you to control your temper, the greater the reward for doing so.

It might be difficult for you to control your temper because ...

... of your basic nature

... you had angry role models

... you are in a difficult situation

... you have to interact regularly with someone who consistently provokes you.

In these cases and all others, controlling your temper and what you say when you are angry will increase your reward for doing so.

It makes sense. A more difficult job pays more than an easier one. Everyone finds it easier to accomplish a difficult task when offered a larger payment than a smaller one, say a $1,000 versus $50. It's even easier to do something difficult for a million dollars. And what wouldn't be easy to do for $25,000,000! Yet all the wealth on our planet is insignificant compared to the value of eternal reward for fulfilling the will of our Creator. This Torah reframe is very powerful.

When you are angry at someone and still do not do or say things that violate Torah regulations for interpersonal relationships, your reward is greater than when you do not feel provoked. In any situation, if you act with kindness, compassion, love, and respect towards another person when — for whatever reason — you find it difficult, your reward will be greater than if you were to find it easy. In other words, increased difficulty in mitzvah performance is like a value added tax. The worth of your mitzvah automatically increases, on the spot. When obstacles stand in your way, appreciate them for the bonus they represent. Remembering that Hashem sends every difficult situation for our eternal benefit is a powerful anger-reducing Torah reframe.

• Reframe Question Two: "How am I gaining merit from this?"

Torah Reframe Three: "This is an opportunity to improve my *middos,* character traits."

We are expected to emulate our Creator, as much as is humanly possible (*Devarim* 28:9; *Rambam, Hilchos De'os,* ch. 1). Every difficult situation we handle well helps us come closer to refining our character traits, which should be one of our major goals in life.

Think about the *middos* you feel a need to develop further. Potentially frustrating situations will help you measure where you stand now and will highlight areas that need improvement. Anticipate and look forward to situations that will enable you to grow in self-control, emotional maturity, patience, humility, unconditional love, compassion and empathy, respect for other people, and judging favorably. Without these challenges in life, we would stagnate spiritually.

View every difficult person you encounter as your partner. This is an important way of reframing the way you view stressful encounters. The specific individual or the type of person you might once have viewed as your nemesis will now become transformed into your study partner. His role is to pose the difficult question; your role is to answer it correctly. With an attitude like this, it becomes almost effortless to reframe every potentially explosive situation into a lesson in *middos* improvement.

Looking at people you find it difficult to deal with as "adversaries" creates problems. Seeing them as selfish, stubborn, power-hungry, manipulative, or "off-the-wall," etc., breeds anger. Reframing such people as "my partner in character development" creates solutions. Interacting with this "difficult person" now becomes your chance for greatness.

> *I used to hate repeating myself. I viewed it as a total waste of my time. I felt that if a person didn't listen carefully enough the first time I said something, that was his problem. If he is too slow to follow, let him find someone else, someone who doesn't value his time as much as I do.*
>
> *But then I heard how Rabbi Chaim Shmulevitz said that when Rabbi Preida repeated each lesson to his student 400 times, he himself was developing his OWN patience. I understand now that being patient with another person isn't a waste of my time. Just the opposite. I am actually using that time to develop my character. I now feel ready to respond even to someone who needs 400 repetitions.*

When you anticipate meeting someone with whom you have found it irritating to deal in the past, mentally prepare yourself in advance. Think about the specific traits you will be developing during your encounter.

Reframe all interactions with "difficult people" as part of your world-championship development program. If you were to have an international audience of millions of viewers watching you, it would motivate you to do your best. Let the knowledge that your Father, your King, is watching, be an even greater incentive.

An added benefit is that the more love, compassion, and empathy you feel for someone, the greater the possibility that he will eventually act in ways towards you that will no longer classify him in your mind as difficult.

• Reframe Question Three: "What traits or qualities can I improve thanks to this experience? What can I learn from this experience?"

When you see how someone else's behavior distresses you, observe yourself to see if you do anything similar that distresses others.

Someone else's behavior might initially be bothersome to you, but you might find that you can learn a lot from what that person has said or done. For example, if someone is assertive and speaks up in ways that you don't, perhaps you will find positive ways to be more assertive than you presently are. This person will serve as a partial role model. Similarly, the person might express himself with total confidence. You might fail to do so even when it would be appropriate. Now you can learn to express yourself with more confidence.

Torah Reframe Four: "This is just a test."

All anger-provoking situations are tests. They test our love for our Creator and our readiness to do His will. Telling ourselves, "I will do all I can to show my Father, my King, that I will pass His test," is a powerful reframe.

Money issues are often at the root of anger. Both a person with a large amount of money and a person with hardly any money at all are tested by the way they handle money (*Mesillas Yesharim,* ch. 1). If you ever feel that you are about to get mad at someone over money, realize that this money is testing you. Whether the issue is minor or major — even if it gets to *beis din* — you are being tested to see if you talk and act in ways consistent with what the Torah expects of you.

> *I used to view money as a precious commodity deserving my maximum efforts at acquiring as much of it as possible. The common expression, "How much is he worth?" gave me the feeling that the more money you have, the more value you have as a person. I looked at any financial loss as a loss of my own self-worth.*
>
> *Now that I am aware of the concept of reframing, I see how my perception of money and its importance led to a lot of anger. I used to take people to task over even small losses and really blow up over expenses I felt certain could have been avoided. Now I look at situations involving money as my opportunity to demonstrate that I value human dignity and respect more than money. I look at my money as a means of elevating myself spiritually.*
>
> *I have been amazed at how this reframe has almost eliminated my anger over money issues.*

> *When I started thinking about finding work after graduation, I decided it would be a good idea to learn touch typing. I bought a computer program and practiced hard to improve my speed and accuracy. The program has various levels, from beginner to*

advanced. At the end of each lesson, there is a timed test, which is graded automatically by the computer. I was never a good test-taker in school and used to dread every exam, yet I found that I enjoyed taking these tests. It gave me a sense of satisfaction to see my speed and accuracy improving.

This experience gave me a whole new understanding of the concept of, "It's all a test." I can't say that I try to look for situations that will test my character, but whenever I am tested I think of the computer test and how much fun it is to measure my progress. I immediately feel better about the test at hand.

• Reframe Question Four: "What would an expert reframer be able to say about this?"

An expert reframer will always be able to find something positive. Even if you say a reframe in jest, it still takes away some of the heaviness of the situation. Just becoming more in touch with various possibilities of how to view this situation will decrease the power of your negative reframing.

How about:

• "Once I get through this, I'll be able to tackle anything!"
• "It's a difficult situation, but I'm going to feel great about myself if I handle it well."
• "This is one way to get me to increase my sensitivity to others."
• "These insults are giving me a good practice session on how not to be so affected by what other people say."
• "This person's refusal is just par for the course for anyone who wants to get things done. I'm not going to give up. I'm going to take that 'no' as the first step in our negotiations and go on from there. I don't have to be afraid of rejection or failure — I only need to try my best."

Torah Reframe Five: "This is a *kapparah*, an atonement."

Every time we suffer, it is an atonement for the wrongs we have done (*Midrash Rabbah, Bereishis* 65:4; *Chochmah U'Mussar*, vol. 1, p. 347; *Da'as Chochmah U'Mussar*, vol. 1, p. 365).

Feeling appreciation for this atonement will save us from much anger. Instead of becoming angry over many of life's inconveniences, we will realize how much we have to gain. Even minor inconveniences such as expecting hot water and getting cold, or reaching into a pocket for three coins and pulling out only two, are a form of suffering, and as such, serve as atonement (*Arachin* 16b).

Anyone who has flown on an airplane has probably witnessed the following scene: The airport lounge is filled with passengers waiting to begin boarding. Suddenly, the airline announces that it has overbooked the flight and is offering either a seating upgrade, a free ticket, or a cash refund to any passenger willing to give up his seat. It is almost a certainty that there will be not one, but several volunteers. In fact, the airlines can deliberately overbook because they count on people willing to inconvenience themselves for physical or financial reward. In the same way, if we would only realize the benefits we accrue — the cleansing and healing of our *neshamah* (soul) — through accepting inconvenience and unpleasantness, we would feel joy and not anger.

> My grandmother always used to say about whatever went wrong, "It's a kapparah." I took it for granted that this was the proper response. I didn't notice it when I was younger, but now I realize that she hardly ever became angry over anything. Her kapparah reframe transformed every potentially anger-provoking incident into one of spiritual purification. I hadn't realized

the power of her response until I was old enough to visit other people's homes. Then I saw others react with frustration and irritation in situations where my grandmother remained calm.

• Reframe Question Five: "How would I feel now if I realize this is a *kapparah*?"

Torah Reframe Six: "Love your neighbor as yourself" (*Vayikra* 19:18).

How easily we forgive ourselves for behavior that might irritate or infuriate us if done by someone else. When we are angry at another person it is all too easy to forget that he is still deserving of our love and respect. A good technique to prevent this mistake is to remember the other positive feelings you have for that person. If it is a child, think about the love you felt for him when he was a baby — or when he's sound asleep! If it is a parent, spouse, friend, relative, employer, or employee, think about all the wonderful aspects of this person that you enjoy and feel grateful for.

Remember too that the object of your anger is also a child of your Father, your King, Creator and Sustainer of the universe. That makes him a relative, giving you something in common. This will make it easier to feel close to him, and the closer we are, the less angry we feel.

A neighbor owed me money for a long time and it did not seem like he was going to pay me back in the near future. I was angry and told him that I felt he had betrayed my trust.

After my tirade, I noticed that he avoided me.

Weeks later, when we read Parashas Kedoshim, the

Torah portion that mentions the mitzvah to love others as we love ourselves, I decided to change my attitude and approach that person with unconditional love in my heart. I realized that I personally violated a Torah law by pressuring him about paying a loan. My anger caused me to react without thinking.

He looked embarrassed when I came over to him. "I'm really sorry that I spoke so strongly to you," I said with heartfelt sincerity. "I have been thinking about how I would want someone to treat me if I were having a hard time paying back a loan. What I did was wrong and I ask your forgiveness. Don't worry about it — I can manage, even if I have to wait a long time. I wish you tremendous financial success, and hope that things go so well for you that paying back this loan will be easy."

I didn't expect to get my money back too soon, but to my great surprise the person came over to me with the money only a few days later. He said that he was sorry he had made me wait so long and told me that he very much appreciated the positive way I had approached him. He felt so good about it that he had sold something he didn't use very often in order to pay me back right away.

I am very sensitive to noise and often become angry at my neighbors for making too much noise. They can't relate to the distress I feel, so I have to keep reminding them. I get so angry when they are noisy that when I tell them to be quieter my tone is very aggressive. I always felt that if I changed my tone of voice without changing my inner feelings, my insincerity would be all too obvious.

One day I sat down and made a mental list of all the good qualities these neighbors have: They are good-hearted and cheerful people; they always have a lot of guests and are happy to do favors for everyone; and on and on. Remembering why I liked them made it easier for me to overlook this one irritant. The next time I spoke to them about the noise, my voice reflected my inner feelings of respect for them. They said that they would try to be much more careful in the future. They also asked me to feel free to point out to them whenever they were disturbing me.

I found the difference in their response this time amazing. I guess they felt the same difference between how I used to speak to them and how I spoke to them this time.

• Reframe Question Six: "What positive qualities does this person have that I can appreciate?" or, "In what ways am I grateful to this person for what he has done for me in the past?"

If someone has done positive things for you before even though right now he refuses to do something for you, your sense of gratitude for the past will decrease your anger in the present.

Torah Reframe Seven: "Judge other people favorably" (*Vayikra* 19:15).

Anger comes from blaming. Even if you don't like what happened, if you don't blame anyone for it, you will not have as strong a response as when you do blame. Even if your judging favorably doesn't totally exonerate someone, if it lessens the degree of blaming, the anger will be decreased. For example, if someone were to step on your toe, you might blame the person for not being more careful when he is walking. If you were to see that the person was blind, you would certainly blame him less. If the person were running to do you a favor, you would blame him even less. And if he were running to save your child from being run over by a car, you would be grateful.

It is impossible to know all the factors motivating a person's behavior. Before blaming someone, ask yourself, "How can I be sure that this person is really to blame for what I am about to blame him for?"

The answer is, you can't.

> *Judging favorably has always been a bit hard for me. I am a realist and feel that it's a high priority to live in reality. I grew up with people who felt that assuming the negative was more intelligent than trying to think up some imaginary excuse that might not even be true.*
>
> *But then I was accused of something when I was totally innocent. A student of mine told me something in confidence and asked me not to repeat it to a soul. I pledged my word of honor.*
>
> *A week later, he came over to me in a rage. "I told you not to repeat this," he shouted.*
>
> *"I didn't," was my honest reply.*
>
> *"I was asked to leave the school," he said. "The principal of the school heard from someone what I had told you in confidence. You are the only staff member to whom I told this. You are definitely guilty and now you are lying."*
>
> *I knew I was innocent. But at the time of this encounter, I had no way of knowing how that information became known to the principal. I inquired into the matter and found out that this student had related the same information to a friend of his. A third person*

in another room had overhead their conversation and reported it to the principal.

Ever since then I find it much easier to tell myself that since I don't know the whole picture, I will just have to assume there are facts of which I am unaware. I now have a wonderful feeling every time I judge someone favorably.

• Reframe Question Seven: "How can I judge this person favorably and look at his behavior in a way that will free me from blaming him?"

When you judge another person favorably, you fulfill a Torah commandment. Keeping your focus on the joy of fulfilling this mitzvah will free you from much anger.

In *The Other Side of the Story* by Mrs. Yehudis Samet you will find many wonderful ideas and stories about judging people favorably. Even one reading of the book will make it much easier for you to find favorable ways to judge others.

Even when you won't consider the other person as having been totally not at fault, understanding why someone did what he did will decrease your anger. This is especially important for people who tend to think that others spitefully do things against them.

For example, you might be annoyed with someone for frequently being late. Understanding how his attitude towards time is different from yours will enable you to be more tolerant of his tendency to be late. Even though he should still be on time, your decreased blaming decreases anger.

You might be angry at someone for what appears to you as overreacting. But from his perspective his reaction might have been quite normal. Also, if you were to know his unique temperament and life history, you would be much more tolerant of him. It could be that he suffered greatly in the past and that is why he reacts the way he does now.

You might be angry at someone for being emotionally cold. Understanding how this person's emotional nature is different from yours will free you from anger. You might even find that you gain greatly from him because of his practicality, his clear reasoning, or his intellectual creativity.

Torah Reframe Eight: "This is an opportunity to emulate the A–mighty."

Rabbi Yechezkel Levenstein wrote: "While we have an obligation to be extremely careful not to insult another person, if someone insults us, we should still strive to be kind to him. This, as *Tomer Devorah* explains, is part of the commandment to emulate the A–mighty, Who continues to bestow us with life even when we do things that are against His will. This is not an easy level to reach. It takes a great deal of hard work and effort to train ourselves to ignore the insults of others. It first requires an awareness that other people's insults cause us no real harm.

"Part of the difficulty of mastering the proper attitude is that we need to have a double standard when it comes to insults. As regards the insults of others towards you, learn to tolerate whatever they might say. At the same time, be extremely sensitive not to do or say anything that will constitute even a minor slight to the honor and respect due another person.

"If a person identifies himself as a body, it is truly difficult to develop these antithetical positions. By realizing that you are a soul, however, you will be aware of having been created in the image of the A–mighty, and you will therefore find it possible to emulate His attributes" (*Ohr Yechezkel,* vol. 4, *Middos,* pp. 90-2).

> *I bought a new ironing-board cover for my wife in a store that is just around the corner from our home. The first time she used it, it shed tiny metallic flakes*

all over the pants she was ironing. Not only that, but it deposited a sticky layer on our new iron.

Since we are frequent customers in this store, I was unprepared for their refusal to give me credit for the ironing-board cover when I returned it the next day. The money involved wasn't that much, but it was the principle of the thing that bothered me. I asked to speak to the manager, and he too refused to give me a refund. I was furious. I controlled myself from doing what I would have liked to do, but the anger in my voice let him know loud and clear that he had lost a customer.

I was burning up over the injustice. I had paid them good money and deserved value in return.

Then it hit me. Wasn't that exactly what Hashem was doing with me? Wasn't he giving me everything? And what was I giving him in return? Have I been giving Him full value?

The instant that thought crossed my mind, my anger vanished. The situation still existed, but it no longer bothered me. My blood pressure went back to normal. I guess you would say I reframed the incident.

The funny thing is, the next morning the store owner called me up at home to say that my refund was waiting for me at the store.

• Reframe Question Eight: "How would I like Hashem to treat me in such a case?"

Torah Reframe Nine: "This too shall pass."

Tradition has it that King Solomon, the wisest of all men, had a ring engraved with the saying, "This too shall pass." We, too, would do well to remember that any unpleasantness we experience is only temporary. This reframe will shrink it to manageable size — and make us less angry at whomever we'd like to pin the blame on.

> *My mother-in-law was with us for a month-long visit. Although she is a wonderful woman, it was still a strain for me to have another person in the house. I wanted the children to behave perfectly at all times so that she would be proud of them (and us), I tried to make the meals special, the house always clean — in short, I was under a lot of tension. A close friend told me that I should relax and just be myself, that it was unfair to put such a strain on the family, and that we would all enjoy my mother-in-law's stay a lot more if I didn't try to live up to the imaginary picture-perfect standard I had set as my goal.*
>
> *But her advice had no effect, because relaxing was easier said than done. One casual comment, though, did sink in. She said, "Well, just remember: this too will pass."*
>
> *I realized she was right, and I started imagining the house after the four weeks were over, with all of us back into normal life. I felt my resentment vanish. Since all this tension was eventually going to pass, I told myself that I might as well let it pass right now and save myself unnecessary anguish.*

• Reframe Question Nine: "Why is this not so important?" and "What is funny about this?"

When you view what happened as important, you give it more power over you. When you realize that your loss or damage is minor, it will frequently not be worth getting angry over. An alternative question is: "Why is this a triviality?"

Think about how long you will remember what happened. How will you feel about this a year from now?

In the entire context of your mission on earth, what is the size of what happened?

When you find humor in something that happened you will laugh instead of getting angry. It is impossible to remain angry when you laugh. The physiological responses of anger and laughter are incompatible. Since it's both healthier and more fun to laugh than to get angry, develop the habit of laughing in those situations that previously got you angry.

An alternative question: "What would the funniest person I've ever met say about this?"

People often say about challenging situations, "I'm certain that in the future I'll look back and laugh." Why wait? You can look back and laugh right away.

7. Reframe past events

Practice reframing past angers to release the anger associated with them. These successes also strengthen our belief in our ability to reframe effectively.

Remember a time when you felt very angry. You may still feel some of that anger. Now ask these following reframing questions about what happened:

- "What were the positive benefits of this situation that I can see now but couldn't see then?"
- "What did I learn from what happened? What can I still learn?"
- "What did I learn about myself? How was this incident 'Rebbe gelt'?"
- "What will make me feel grateful for what happened?"
- "Now that I look back, can I find a way to judge the person (people) involved favorably? Could I have done it then?"
- "How can I now understand their behavior in a way that will free me from blaming them?"

- "Now, from the perspective of time, how important actually was this event?"
- "In terms of Jewish history, how important was this event?"
- "Was there anything humorous about what happened?"
- "What might an expert reframer have to say about it?"

The more you repeat these questions, the more they will become habitual. The goal is for them to pop up in your mind as soon as you become angry. Try a few "trial runs." Take some past incidents and reframe them using these questions as a guide.

> *A great Torah scholar used to relate that when he was a young student, he felt like leaving yeshivah and going for a menial job. He saw a sign outside a store saying, "Boy Wanted." When he asked the manager for the job, he was told that someone had just been hired. He decided to continue his yeshiva studies and eventually became an outstanding scholar.*
>
> *His entire life he looked back on that incident as the turning point of his life. At the time, he felt crestfallen. But for many years to come, he would look at that incident as one of the greatest things that ever happened to him.*

I thought reframing questions were great in theory, but doubted whether I'd be able to remember them on the spot — when I most needed them. I asked an expert reframer and he advised me to repeat a list of reframe questions 10 times a day for an entire month. I must

admit, I was skeptical. It seemed silly and meaningless. But after losing my temper a few more times, I decided I didn't have much choice.

I was pleasantly surprised to find the questions popping into my mind whenever I started getting angry. They made me pause and look at the situation from a different angle. Once I got the hang of it, reframing changed my life.

8. Get your priorities straight

What are your real priorities in life? Where on your personal priority list are the following:
- Loving G-d and serving Him
- Living by the Torah
- Improving your character
- Not causing other people pain

And where on that same list are:
- Having things your way
- Getting maximum comfort and pleasure
- Winning approval
- Seeking honor

What we become angry about and what we don't, as well as what we say and do when we feel angry, is an expression of our real priorities.

It's wonderful to have a neat house and for everyone to do things on schedule. But it's even more wonderful for children to grow up in a happy home.

It's wonderful to have employees who implement your instructions the minute they hear them and are consistently efficient. But it's even more wonderful to have employees who love working for you because of the courteous and considerate way you interact with them.

It's wonderful to be on time. But it's even more wonderful to enjoy the journey and arrive calm and relaxed.

It might seem that it would be wonderful if everything in life would go the way you want it to. But it's much more practical and realistic to expect that it won't. And the way to have a wonderful life is to master the ability to feel positive no matter what. A master Torah reframer is ensured such a life. Having a spiritual outlook on life, you realize that things are exactly the way they should be.

A person with confused priorities will make minor and trivial matters a high priority and therefore will get angry when some of these trivialities are not the way he would wish. When you make it a high priority to live a life of joy and inner peace, you won't allow yourself to ruin this with anger. As Hillel said, "Better that someone should lose 400 gold coins than that Hillel should get angry." The vast majority of things that people get angry about are just not worth the cost in emotional wear and tear, and the pain and distress caused to others.

I recently interviewed a person who rarely gets angry, and asked him what attitudes enabled him to stay in positive states and not become angry. He replied, "Life is too short to waste it on anger." Viewing anger as a waste of life will be helpful to you just as it was to him.

Making it your highest priority to increase love for the Creator will enable you to live an elevated spiritual life. This priority will give you many opportunities for joy and decrease the amount of situations that elicit your anger. Knowing that He is in charge will help you live a calmer and more serene life.

9. Metaphors are reframes

The metaphors you use are a factor in whether a situation will elicit your anger or not. Once you say a metaphor, you look at the situation as if your metaphor is the reality. In truth, a metaphor is nothing more than a subjective reframe.

What does this mean in practical terms? Suppose you ask someone to do you a small favor and they don't. If you tell yourself, "I felt like I was drowning; I asked this person to throw me a life preserver and he refused to do it," you will now look at this person's not buying a relatively minor item for you when he went shopping as if he caused you to drown. You can defend this metaphor, "But I felt like I was drowning in work." That's exactly the problem. Fortunately, you weren't actually drowning. It would be preferable to say, "I'm disappointed that you didn't buy what I asked for." This reframe is a lot lighter than the drowning reframe.

Some anger-provoking metaphors are:
- "What he said killed me."
- "He threw me to the wolves."
- "Talking to her is like arguing with a Mack truck."

Whenever you are about to use a metaphor of what a situation is like, ask yourself, "Is this metaphor helpful?" A metaphor is beneficial and useful when you are trying to give someone a picture of what you are feeling so he will be more motivated to do or refrain from doing something. A metaphor is counterproductive if it just increases your fury so it becomes like a raging fire burning entire forests, and you become like a raving maniac who should be locked up. Notice the effect of the last sentence. Metaphors add power. Use them carefully and wisely.

There is another issue with metaphors. Your metaphor for anger will affect how you view it. For example, "Anger is like a time bomb that can blow up at any moment without warning," or "Anger is like you have a volcano inside of you. Even when it is quiet it can explode at any moment." Compare how you feel about anger: Do you view it as a bomb or volcano; or do you consider anger as your inner teacher that gives you insights into yourself, your priorities, your character, and your self-mastery; or as a precious biofeedback mechanism that supplies you with feedback that there is something about the present situation that calls for a constructive change.

10. Reframe choices

The situations presented here recur again and again in life. They tend to evoke a range of negative emotions, ranging from frustration to hopping mad. Evaluations that typically provoke anger are presented first, followed by anger-reducing reframes that can be easily substituted. It is easy to see how the anger-producing judgments are arbitrary and subjective, and certainly not the only "reality."

❑ Example 1: When someone is late:
Anger-causing evaluations:
• "He doesn't respect me — otherwise he'd make sure to be on time."
• "If he can waste my time like this it shows the level he's on."
• "He knows I can't stand it when he's late. He is just doing this to aggravate me."
Anger-reducing reframes:
• "He may have valid reasons beyond his control for being late."
• "He probably doesn't realize how important it is for me that he be on time."
• "Now that I know how it feels to be kept waiting like this, I'll try to make more of a point of being on time."

- "This is a good opportunity for me to practice reacting positively. Instead of berating him when he finally does come, I will say, 'It's so good to see you.' "
- "He seems to have a problem with time management. Maybe I can find a way to help him with this."
- "I can use this time to say *Tehillim* or review the *daf yomi*."
- [Add your own reframe.]

❏ Example 2: When someone blames you for their mistakes:

Anger-causing evaluations:
- "What a chutzpah! It's his mistake — why is he trying to pin the blame on me?"
- "Does he think I'm stupid enough to take the blame for what he did wrong?"
- "I refuse to be his scapegoat. I'll show him that he can't do that to me."

Anger-reducing reframes:
- "Maybe some of what happened is my fault."
- "Let this be a *kapparah*."
- "I wonder if I ever blame other people for my own mistakes?"
- "This is another chance for me to practice making my own emotional state independent of what anyone else says or does."
- [Add your own reframe.]

❏ Example 3: When someone doesn't follow your advice:

Anger-causing evaluations:
- "Boy, did he waste my time."
- "He must think I'm stupid and not worth listening to."
- "He's probably going to wind up blaming me for not making sure he followed the advice I gave him."

Anger-reducing reframes:
- "You can lead a horse to water but you can't make him drink."
- "Maybe it's a good thing he didn't listen to me. Who knows how things will eventually turn out?"
- "He's probably asking a few people for advice, just like most of us do."
- "Any time or energy I spent trying to help him is all to my credit, whether or not he takes my advice.
- [Add your own reframe.]

❑ Example 4: Someone criticizes you:

Anger-causing evaluations:
- "He's worse than I am so how does he have the nerve to criticize me?"
- "Just who does he think he is?"
- "He's always criticizing me. He's so negative. I wish he would leave me alone."

Anger-reducing reframes:
- "He is paying attention to me. This shows that he cares."
- "I can certainly learn from this how to be more tactful when I criticize others."
- "This is a good way to learn humility!"
- "Isn't it funny how easy it is for all of us to see our own faults in others. I must do it too."
- [Add your own reframe.]

❑ Example 5: When someone keeps misplacing your things:

Anger-causing evaluations:
- "Can't he put anything away?"
- "What am I, a nothing to him?"
- "He can't keep track of a thing. Who knows what losses

this will cause us in the future?"

Anger-reducing reframes:
- "I guess I'm not meant to find this right now."
- "This will give someone an opportunity to fulfill the mitzvah of returning a lost object."
- "On a scale of zero to ten in importance, this is about a minus two."
- "At least I have things that can be misplaced."
- [Add your own reframe.]

❑ Example 6: When you are driving and someone tells you to be more careful:

Anger-causing evaluations:
- "Who needs a backseat driver? Doesn't he know that I'm a good driver?"
- "If he doesn't keep quiet, I'm going to get so mad that we might have a real accident."
- "What kind of a driver is he that he thinks he can tell me how to drive?!"

Anger-reducing reframes:
- "She cares about the welfare of your children."
- "We're almost there. It won't hurt me to let him talk until we get there."
- "He is nervous. Anything I can do to put him at ease is a kindness."
- [Add your own reframe.]

❑ Example 7: When someone brings out the worst in you:

Anger-causing evaluations:
- "I hate him for bringing out the worst in me."

- "If he treated me better, I'd treat him better."
- "I don't act this way with most people. It's all his fault."

Anger-reducing reframes:
- "He can only evoke that reaction in me because I have not yet mastered self-control. This teaches me what I need to work on in myself. I'll do all I can to improve."
- "In my next encounter I'll be able to check to see if I am making progress. This person is like a biofeedback machine for me to notice my growth."
- "I certainly have a better appreciation for those who bring out the best in me."
- "What can I do to bring out the best in others?"
- [Add your own reframe.]

❑ Example 8: When someone is unfair:

Anger-causing evaluations:
- "He should be strongly condemned for his unfairness."
- "If this is how he acts now, who knows what he'll do in the future?"
- "People are always unfair to me. I must be a weakling for them to treat me this way."

Anger-reducing reframes:
- "Everything Hashem does is for the good."
- "Maybe in this person's eyes he is being fair. Let me try to see things from his point of view before I discuss the issue with him."
- "I am grateful for this atonement for other wrongs I may have done, either in this lifetime or a previous one."
- "Even if this is unfair, it is only a trivial issue in the entire context of my life."
- [Add your own reframe.]

❏ Example 9: When someone laughs at you:

Anger-causing evaluations:
• "He is embarrassing me, which is a very serious Torah transgression."
• "People have always laughed at me. It has always been painful and difficult to cope with."
• "This person is what they call abusive."

Anger-reducing reframes:
• "Any mitzvah I do despite someone making fun of me greatly increases its worth."
• "Being embarrassed in public wipes away all transgressions."
• "Now that I know how terrible it feels, I will make sure never to make fun of anyone else."
• "Actually, nothing bad really happened to me. I didn't melt or disappear. The amount of distress I choose to feel is up to me. I am going to use this experience to increase my ability to view similar situations objectively. This will eventually free me from feeling pain in the face of anyone's disapproval."
• [Add your own reframe.]

11. Prepare yourself in advance

What is a surefire way to push your buttons? What is guaranteed to burn you up? Are there any situations that repetitively elicit angry reactions in you? If so, you will now be able to practice reframing them. You don't have to wait until you are in the midst of those situations. When you are calmly, or at least relatively calmly, reading a book, you will be able to think more clearly and more creatively.

What anger-producing situations tend to repeat themselves in your life? It might be the type of situation you will have to deal with today or tomorrow, or only on Friday or Shabbos, or when you encounter specific people.

What reframes or inner thoughts are at the root of your anger? What reframes would enable you to remain more centered and balanced or even calm and relaxed in those situations?

It will be helpful to write down a list of those situations. Write down your anger-producing thoughts. Then write positive and beneficial reframes. As you think about those situations in the next few days, keep adding new reframes or repeat the ones that seem the most effective to you.

How can you test if a reframe will work? It is really quite simple. If the next time you are in the same situation you don't become angry at all or at least not as angry as usual, it shows that the reframe is working. There is always the possibility that any given reframe will work for you in one specific situation and not in another, but if it works even once you will at least be certain that you are moving in the right direction.

You can even test a reframe before you find yourself in an actual anger-producing situation. When you think about situations that elicited your anger in the past, you will presently experience some level of an angry reaction. The more relaxed your muscles are, the easier it will be for you to be aware of even slight angry reactions. Think about various reframes for those situations. Now think about those situations again. When you presently decrease or eliminate an angry reaction as you imagine those scenes, it shows that you are making progress.

12. You are always a role model for others

Whether you want to be or not, the way you personally reframe situations and events serves as a role model for others. One of the greatest things you can do for your children is to model positive reframing for them. They will pass it on to your grandchildren and great-grandchildren. All parents teach their children how to reframe events. If a parent becomes angry at his children, or angry about other things in front of his children, he is automatically teaching them how to handle such situations in their own lives. Even before those children become parents they will have learned patterns. It is up to us as parents to teach them positive ones.

It is impossible not to have our own reframes influence others because every comment we make puts a certain frame on the experience. Teachers automatically teach their students how to reframe, as do friends. For example, if it's raining, we can say, "What a shame the weather is so terrible today," or you can say, "Look at that rain! What a blessing." When someone is late, the choice is ours, either to see the lateness as very negative, both in terms of the person who is late as well as the inconvenience to ourselves, or to see a broader picture and use one of the Torah reframes to feel positively at that moment, perhaps commenting, "He probably has a good reason for being late."

Even when we don't consciously intend to influence others, we do. People see our reactions and they immediately become part of their mental library. By being a positive reframer, we not only have more joyous lives ourselves, but we create more joy for many other people. You can never know who has witnessed your positive reaction and will adopt it in their own life.

I was visiting a friend of mine who had been married a number of years. When I spoke to him, he was in the kitchen washing the dishes. I noticed how he seemed to be enjoying himself. He was a diligent scholar and didn't waste time from his studies. I told him how I admired the positive attitude he had towards doing the dishes. He told me that since his wife wasn't feeling well, he had an obligation to wash the dishes now, and whatever we are obligated to do we should do joyously. This reframe came to my mind whenever I did the dishes myself.

I was standing in line at the bank the other day for quite some time. I was starting to feel impatient as were most of the others. I noticed one man, though, who looked pretty calm. Then I overheard him say casually to the person standing next to him, "I love waiting in lines. It gives me a lot of time to think."

Ever since then I began to see waiting in line as a golden opportunity to spend time in productive thought and planning.

13. Mastering reframing takes time

People differ greatly as to how long it takes for them to change their initial reactions. Some are immediately able to change their feelings as soon as they hear a reframe. Most people, however, need more time. Learning to master the art of reframing is a lifetime process. It can't be mastered overnight. Focus on your progress and appreciate even small improvements.

A question that is frequently asked is, "How can I reframe when I am boiling mad and can't think of anything except my overwhelming feelings?" The question is valid. When anger is too strong, we can't think clearly.

When you are too angry to think about alternative reframes, breathe slowly and deeply. As you exhale, tell yourself that you are releasing stress and tension. As you inhale, tell yourself that you are taking in positive energy. If it is hard to do this when you are in the midst of a rage, just count your breaths. The process of slow, deep breathing automatically has a calming effect on your nervous system. The more you practice, the quicker you will be able to calm yourself in the future.

The more you practice reframing when you are relatively calm, the better you will be able to reframe even when you are angry. After a while, your brain will automatically come up with the word "reframe" whenever you come across a challenging event.

14. Reframing for others is an act of kindness that takes skill

Calming a person who is angry is a great act of kindness. Yet care must be taken to do it in the right way, and not in a way that elicits even more anger. When someone is angry and you feel you can help him reframe whatever is bothering him, hold off doing so unless you feel confident enough about your skills. While it may seem easy to just repeat any of the reframes mentioned here, just telling someone a reframe does not mean that he will automatically change the way he views what happened.

Timing is of foremost importance. The Sages tell us not to try to calm an angry person when he is in the midst of his rage (*Pirkei Avos* 4:17). It is much better to wait until he calms down sufficiently to be able to listen to what you want to say, no matter how long this takes. After time has passed, he will automatically have a different perspective. What originally encompassed his entire consciousness will now be only a memory, and often a small one at that.

It is also vital to look at the anger-provoking incident from the person's point of view. In many situations, empathy and compassion are prerequisites. Before a person will be ready to listen to the reframes you suggest, he needs to know that you understand how he feels. Even if the specific situation that bothers him would not get you angry, try to see what this means to him.

Never suggest a reframe as a form of criticism, saying, for instance, "This shouldn't bother you — everything that happens is for the good"; or, "Don't be angry, judge favorably. I'm surprised you haven't judged that person favorably on your own already." Being on the receiving end of those types of comments is painful, not pain relieving.

Try to choose reframes that are real to the person you are trying to help. Often it will be better not to even mention the word "reframing." Just suggest a new way of looking at the situation and see how the person responds.

Don't use reframing as a weapon and be careful not to make people hate the word "reframe." If you yourself provoke someone and then when they respond angrily you tell them, "Just reframe it," they will most likely be irritated.

Those of us who are less emotional by nature usually find it easier to reframe faster than do people with highly emotional natures. Take this into consideration when suggesting an alternative way of looking at things.

Asking questions, rather than making blanket statements, is a more helpful approach. For instance, "Is there any way you think you might gain from this?" is better than, "You have a lot to gain from this." Or, "If you could look at this in a positive light, what would you say about it?" rather than, "Try to look at things more positively."

Even if a person is not open to reframing an anger-provoking event or situation right away, as time passes he will be more receptive to the idea. If you tried to help someone gain a different perspective on what happened, but to no avail, try again at a later time. Both you and the other person will have acquired more life experience by then. Your expertise will have grown. And remember, too, that although at the time the other person did not accept your suggested reframe, your words did make some impression. He will now be more aware of the fact that it is possible to see a situation from a different angle, and just knowing this will make him more flexible.

Helping others master the art of reframing is a *chesed* that will benefit them not only in the present, but throughout their entire lifetime. As you talk to others about reframing, you gain greater mastery yourself, which will in turn greatly enhance all aspects of your life.

Step 4

Communicating Without Anger

Step 4

Communicating Without Anger

Even if we sincerely aspire to conquer anger, until we reach our ideal we will become angry from time to time. Therefore, it is highly important to be in control of what we say and how we say it even when we do feel angry.

The secret of effective communication can be summed up in three words: Know your goal. Once you have your goal clearly in mind, decide to follow this three-point plan for successful communication at all times:

A. Know what to say.
B. Know how to say it.
C. Know what not to say.

A. Know what to say

1. Know your goal when you speak

It is always a good idea to think before speaking, but when we are displeased with what someone said or did, having a specific goal in mind for the conversation becomes an even higher priority. As our Sages tell us, "The wise person focuses on the outcome" (Tamid 32a).

Why do we communicate with others? Because we want to give them a message. The question to keep in mind is: "What message do I want to give this person right now?" Once our purpose is clear, we can then ask ourselves, "How can I word my message for maximum effectiveness?"

An angry message conveys lack of control. Instead of the other people hearing that the matter being discussed is important, they will be saying to themselves: "He sounds like a raving maniac!" or, "She sounds totally hysterical." Yelling, whining, shouting, screaming, scolding, or insulting are all painful to the ear. The distress causes the person on the receiving end to "turn down the volume" on the broadcast. He probably won't even hear, let alone pay attention, to the content of the real message. All he will hear is the anger coming through loud and strong. The person doing the shouting might protest, "But I want him to know that I'm angry. That's the whole point." But is that really the point? Isn't the real message the issue that provoked the anger in the first place? Why not just say it? But say it in a way that the message can be heard.

Let your anger subside before you begin to talk. By allowing the anger to ebb, your tone of voice and the content of what you say will convey your essential message in a way that will make it easier to be heard accurately. Even if you are boiling inside, it is possible to control what comes out of your mouth. An added benefit is that when you express yourself in a dignified manner with respect for the other person as well as yourself, the reply you get will often be one that alleviates your anger.

"There are those who speak like a sword that stabs; and the words of the wise heal" (*Mishlei* 12:18). The Vilna Gaon comments on this:

> There are two basic approaches that are possible to take when you see someone doing something wrong. One is to speak harshly to the person and tell him that what he is doing is wrong. But this approach does not tell people how they should behave and how they can correct what they did wrong. This is like stabbing someone with a sword; it is not a healing approach.
>
> The approach of the wise is to show people how they can correct what they did wrong. This is a healing approach and the only words that are said are those conducive to healing.

Be wise. Learn to speak in a healing manner. The good that your words can do is immense. Whenever someone does or says something that irritates, annoys, or disturbs you, you have an opportunity to speak to that person in a healing manner.

The way you speak to someone when you are angry at him is a key factor in whether you will improve a situation or make it worse. Speaking the right way, you can find solutions to difficulties, you can calm down other people, and you can even transform an adversary into a friend.

Words spoken in anger, on the other hand, can easily cause an escalation of the argument. The other person will match your angry words with more of his own. Verbal punching matches can be every bit as painful as physical ones. Instead of working out the original issue that was bothering you, you will now have to put out the fire caused by your angry remarks. Everyone loses and there are no winners.

It is definitely not worth it.

Before speaking in anger, get in the habit of asking yourself, "What is the best way to express myself to reach my goals?"

Many times, this question alone will guide you to thinking of a better way to express yourself than if you just impulsively said the first thing that came to mind.

Speaking with calm confidence is much more powerful than an angry outburst. When you express yourself with restraint, you impress upon others that you have a strong belief in the validity of your position. Casting aspersions on the character of another person, however, does not in any way prove that you are right about the issue at hand. When you speak in a dignified manner, even though you have reason to be angry with someone, it is a sign of self-discipline that will ultimately gain you the respect of others — and it will certainly increase your own self-respect.

> *Once I started thinking about the subject of anger and communication, I realized that when other people spoke angrily, I didn't take them seriously. I couldn't hear the words that they were saying because the only thing that registered in my mind was that they sounded awful. Finally it hit me that I must sound the same way when I blow up at others. As soon as I realized this I felt embarrassed. From then on I was resolved never to sound like that again. Every once in a while, I slip up a bit. But as soon as I do, I immediately listen to how I sound. That's all it*

takes for me to renew my resolve to be careful about how I speak.

If you find that you have great difficulty controlling what you say when you are angry, walk away from the scene for a few minutes. It is important that you define your leaving the room as taking time to calm yourself down, rather than as an aggressive act. You might tell the other person, "Excuse me, I have to leave the room for a while to gather my thoughts"; or, "I will be right back after I take care of something" (your anger), and go to a different room until you calm down.

A major reason why people insult others when they are angry is because they haven't worked at developing effective communication skills. If someone wrongs or annoys us, it is easy to make disparaging remarks. But if you think the matter over, what is your real goal? Isn't it to influence the person to do something or to stop doing something? When you have mastered positive approaches, you will accomplish much more than if you were to verbally attack the person you want to motivate.

Skilled leaders know that other people are more open to complying with requests when they respect and admire the person making them. The opposite holds true as well. Insults that breed hurt feelings and resentment make for disgruntlement and lack of willingness to comply. Even if fear seems to get immediate results, in the long run it loses out to resentment.

Let's say that Shimon is trying to read and feels irritated by the noise someone nearby is making. At first he tries to ignore the disturbance, hoping it will stop. But it doesn't and his annoyance grows. Finally, feeling himself at the end of his rope, he shouts, "Can't you keep quiet over there?! How selfish can a person be! Have some consideration for the other fellow. Can't you think of anyone else besides yourself?! If you don't keep quiet, I'll make sure that you are sorry you didn't!"

Now imagine that you were the person making the noise. You might not even have realized that you were disturbing anyone. Suddenly, Shimon shouts at you this way. How would it feel to be on the receiving end of this form of "communication"? How willing to comply with his request would you be? If you were making noise that someone else found disturbing, wouldn't you prefer hearing, "I'm sorry to interrupt you, but I find that noise a bit too loud for me. Could I please ask you to be quieter?"

Seeing these two possibilities side by side makes us wonder, "Why would anyone use the first approach when the second is so easy? It will probably work, too, so why create needless ill will?" Unfortunately, variations of the first approach are unthinkingly used by people who are usually kind and pleasant.

There is an important principle of communication: The meaning of your communication is the results that you get. That is, you might say something hoping to elicit a positive response. Instead, the person reacted negatively to what you said. The meaning of what you say is not only dependent on what you as the speaker meant to say; the listener is an integral part of the interaction. In the total picture, it's the listener's reaction that counts. If what you say distresses someone, take responsibility for having caused that person pain and stop immediately.

Resolve to use only respectful and tactful approaches. Appeal to the other person's sense of values and ideals. The incident portrayed above might best be handled by saying, "I know you wouldn't intentionally want to cause others suffering. You are probably not aware that I'm finding the noise very irritating."

Don't expect instant results. You may not get what you want, even if you ask nicely. But you will have avoided an

angry confrontation, thus leaving open the lines of communication.

Authority figures

If you are in a position of authority, your very position
gives you power. The people who view you as an authority
figure know that they have to listen to what you have to say.
You don't need to insult or shout at subordinates. Actually,
the kinder and more considerate you sound, the more coop-
eration you will get.

It is amazing that it is often the people with strong personalities, who would be listened to even if they whispered,
who feel a need to intimidate others by raising their voices
and threatening. People always return respect with respect.
The greater your authority, the better people feel when you
treat them with respect, and the more they will want to follow your leadership.

---

2. Attack the problem, not the person

Whenever you are dissatisfied with what another person
says or does, a general rule to follow is: Attack the problem,
not the person.

Use descriptive language, rather than blaming language.
With descriptive language you describe in neutral words
how you would like to see the situation changed. Blaming
language attacks the person.

When you begin a sentence of complaint with the words,
"You are ..." the person you are talking to is going to feel
under attack. Focus on finding solutions to the problem at
hand instead of making a verbal attack on the person you
wish to influence. People differ greatly as to what they

would consider a personal attack. We may think someone is being "overly" sensitive if he reacts defensively to remarks we think are neutral. But it is the recipient who defines what is hurtful or not, and this is very individual. Our obligation is to be careful with other people's feelings and avoid hurting them. To be on the safe side, it is best to begin statements with words that clearly show an interest in finding solutions rather than attacking the person. For example, "Some difficulties have come up. I think we might be able to solve them in the following manner"; or, "I see that we differ about this. Let's work on negotiating a solution we can both agree upon." Even if you differ greatly and you think that the other person is totally wrong, this latter statement is a good way to begin.

What would happen if someone were to start off by saying, "I think you are totally wrong about this. I don't know how you can be so stupid and irrational as to think the way you do!" There is hardly a chance in the world that the recipient will respond calmly and say, "You have a good point there. I am grateful that you are here to show me the right way. Yes, I am stupid. Fortunately you are here and you can teach me the rational way to think."

Strong verbal attacks lead to angry responses and resentment. At times the victim might not feel confident enough to express this inner resentment, but it will surface in some way in the future. Shouting matches are never conducive to reaching an agreement. When you hurl insults at someone, battles begin. A display of histrionics by one person leads to emotional outbursts in response by the other person. If what you say calmly is not effective right away, don't give up. Repeat your request a number of times. If that does not work, search for creative ways to motivate the other person.

There are many instances when we become angry at another person over something that was not really his fault.

By attacking the problem and not the person, you will quickly realize that the issue is a minor one and the person did not do anything to maliciously harm you.

For example, if someone bumps into you, it is easy to feel like bumping him back — with words. In maximum security prisons, bumping into someone even accidentally is a highly dangerous thing to do. But that's exactly why those people are there. We have more control over our actions and should extend this to control over our verbal reactions as well. In a normal situation, when someone bumps into us what did he actually do wrong? He was probably in a rush or thinking about something else and careless about how he was walking. He certainly didn't do it on purpose, so why get angry? Some people argue, "But I might have been carrying something fragile. If this person doesn't learn now, he'll never be careful. Better for me to get angry at him now than have him cause real damage some day." This line of reasoning is flawed. Even though there was no damage right now, anticipation of future loss is used to justify anger in the present. Yet what is the actual goal? To get the other person to be more careful when he walks. First of all, the damage you are concerned about might never even happen. Secondly, feeling and expressing care for him as a person will be more helpful in encouraging him to correct a fault than will attacking him.

Global attacks

Be especially careful not to make global attacks when you are angry. They can have a devastating effect on the person receiving them. For example:

• "You ruin everything you touch." (No one ruins "everything they touch.")

• "You never do anything right." (That's impossible. He must do many things right many times.)

- "You're no good." (Will this make a person want to be better?)

In a global attack, you are attacking the very being of the victim. Motivate people to improve by offering encouragement and practical suggestions. The better someone feels about himself, the greater will be his effort to live up to his positive self-image.

3. Speak up right away to prevent anger

If you feel annoyed, don't let your irritation simmer. If you wait until you are very annoyed, you are more likely to explode, or at least say something in anger that you would not have said had you spoken up earlier. By speaking up when you first feel annoyed, you will be able to speak much more politely and respectfully.

For example, a co-worker has closed a window without asking you. You feel irritated. "Can't we have a little air in this place?" you wonder, as your resentment escalates at what you feel is lack of consideration. "Does he think he owns the office?" But it's much simpler and better to nip your anger in the bud by saying, "Excuse me, but it bothers me to have the window closed. Would it be okay with you if we left it open?"

If you find it difficult to speak up when you are annoyed, analyze your fear. What exactly are you afraid of? You'll find that fear of speaking up is based on an illusion that something terrible will happen if you do. Once you try it a few times and realize that not only is it safe but that it also works, you will find it progressively easier to do.

To make it easier to speak up when you feel a need to do so, practice visualizing yourself speaking up. Mentally practicing what you will say will make it easier in real life.

Role play. Practice speaking up when no one is in the room. Then practice with a friend. After a number of practices you will find it easier to be assertive in actual situations.

Right this moment, think of an irritating situation involving another person that you have put off discussing. Try to pinpoint what it is that you find hard to say. Now practice saying this out loud. Once you can say something with no one present, you will eventually be able to say it to the person you currently find it difficult to confront. By dealing with the problem at an early stage, you preempt wild, emotional outbursts and save yourself from angry encounters.

B. Know how to say it

1. Tone of voice makes a major difference

After knowing what to say, the next thing to master is the ability to say it in a calm tone of voice. A loud, angry tone of voice adds fuel to the fire of anger in two ways. For one, it makes you yourself angrier. As the *Ramban* points out, "Accustom yourself to speak whatever you say in a pleasant tone of voice to each and every person at all times, and this will prevent you from getting angry" (*Iggeres HaRamban*). Secondly, an angry tone of voice will inflame the anger of the person you are speaking to, or stated positively, "A soft reply turns away anger" (*Mishlei* 15:1). Even when someone else is already angry at you, if you speak to him in a soft tone of voice and say the right things, he will calm down.

Tone of voice is a form of energy. The energy sent someone's way affects both speaker and listener. Think for a moment of the energy sent your way when someone speaks to you in a kind and caring tone of voice when you are exhausted or ill. The energy itself is healing.

Now think of what it feels like to be on the receiving end of someone's angry outbursts. Besides any content, the energy alone is painful. It creates within you negative energy that must be discharged. This is one reason why people who have been screamed at feel like screaming — yelling back releases some of the negative energy. There are certainly much healthier ways to release the energy (slow, deep breathing or vigorous physical exercise, for example) but the principle remains the same: After absorbing a blast of negative energy, we feel a strong need to release it.

Rabbi Yechezkel Sarne *zt"l*, Rosh Yeshivah of Hebron Yeshivah in Yerushalayim, compared speech with song. When singing, every note has to be exactly right to have the proper effect. So, too, when speaking to someone, even when you need to correct him, your tone of voice has to be pleasant in order for it to be accepted. Just as a wrong note will have a negative effect on the quality of the song, the wrong tone of voice will prevent your message from being heard (*Daliyos Yechezkel*, vol. 2, p. 305).

> *I used to feel that tone of voice didn't make too much of a difference. I didn't think that someone else's tone was important when they were speaking to me. It's what you say that counts, I used to think. And if what I said wasn't mean or attacking, why should anyone care how I say it?*
>
> *What woke me up to the importance of the tone happened when I was a Shabbos guest at the home of a family of great singers. The entire meal was fantastic. They all sang the most beautiful songs. I felt my spirit soar. I noticed that whenever one of the children sang off key, the father gently motioned with his finger that a slight change was needed. I can't sing very well, nor do I have more than a layman's ear for*

music. It puzzled me that it made such a difference to the father if someone was slightly off key, and I decided to ask him about it after the meal.

My host explained that each song has a special melody that elicits a certain feeling. When a song is sung perfectly, it brings out the full richness of that song in the way that was originally intended. If someone sings off key, the listeners will not have the experience they could have had.

Upon hearing this, I realized that this is a powerful metaphor for our tone of voice when speaking. Not everyone can sing well. But every person who speaks has a tone of voice which affects the listeners. A professional singer does all he can to sing each song in the best possible way. We are all professional speakers when we speak to another human being. Our tone of voice will make a difference.

Your tone of voice affects the tone of voice of the person at whom you are angry. By speaking in a lower tone of voice and sustaining this regardless of what the other person says, you will eventually have an effect on his tone of voice and it will become lower. If you ever find yourself in a screaming match with someone, try saying, "Let's both speak in a lower tone of voice so we can hear each other better." Even if you feel that only the other person is speaking angrily, using the plural, "let's both," is helpful. This way he will not feel that you are blaming him.

There are many ways to express the same message. Even the exact same words will sound differently based on the tone of voice that is used. This difference can be awesome. Listening carefully to the messages behind the words someone uses is important when you are trying to understand someone in order to help them cope with difficult situations.

I once collected 800 adverbs for the word "said." Here is a small sampling. Imagine being on the receiving end of statements that are expressed in an —

abrasive, abusive, accusing, acrimonious, aggressive, agitated, angry, argumentative, arrogant, attacking, barking, bellowing, biting, bitter, blaming, blunt, brazen, brutal, bulldozing, carping, catty, coercing, cold, contemptuous, critical, cross, cruel, defiant, demanding, denouncing, destructive, devastating, dictatorial, edgy, enraged, fierce, foolish, frosty, furious, gloating, gruff, haranguing, harping, icy, impatient, impulsive, inconsiderate, indignant, insulting, irritated, *kvetchy*, livid, mad, malicious, malignant, mean, menacing, militant, mocking, negative, pejorative, petulant, power-holic, pugnacious, resentful, rough, rude, sharp, spiteful, tough, or vicious — tone of voice.

And don't we all feel much better when someone speaks to us in an —

affectionate, appreciative, balanced, benevolent, brotherly, buoyant, calm, careful, caring, cheerful, compassionate, considerate, courteous, delicate, delighted, diplomatic, discreet, effervescent, elegant, elevated, empathetic, encouraging, enthusiastic, fatherly, flowing, gallant, generous, gentlemanly, genuine, good-humored, graceful, happy, harmonious, healing, hearty, heavenly, helpful, joyful, kind, live, loving, motherly, noble, peaceful, pleasant, polite, reasonable, serene, smiling, soft, soothing, sympathetic, tactful, tasteful, understanding, validating, vibrant, warm, wise, zestful — tone of voice?

Your tone of voice is something that you can practice even when you are not in an anger-provoking situation. Every once in a while, practice speaking in a centered and balanced tone of voice. Imagine speaking this way even when you are angry at someone. The more you practice this, the more automatic it will be if you become angry. You'll be amazed at the tremendous difference a change in tone of voice will make in your life and in the lives of everyone with whom you interact.

> *I used to think that people would take me seriously only if I spoke in a highly aggressive manner. One of my greatest fears was that people would consider me wimpy. Then I witnessed an interaction that totally changed my mind.*
>
> *A few gang members tried to start up with a small group of yeshivah students. One of the gang members claimed that someone from the yeshivah almost hit him with his car. He claimed he wanted justice, which was really a euphemism for revenge, and in fact there was a possibility that the entire claim was just a fabrication that served as an excuse for making trouble.*
>
> *The oldest student in the group under attack was a brilliant Talmudic scholar. In contrast to the aggressive tone of the low-life who was looking for a fight, this tzaddik engaged in a dialogue that was one of the most amazing I have ever heard. In a gentle, mild tone of voice, he placated the fellow. With tact and wisdom, he spoke in such a way that he won the respect of this belligerent troublemaker, who even ended up shaking his hand and apologizing!*

> *When I first got married, I frequently became irritated with my husband. I appreciated his lofty values and kind nature but I resented his absentmind-*

edness. If he washed the meat dishes, he would sometimes carelessly leave parve pots in the sink. I had told him a number of times to do the parve pots first, but he would always forget. This was just one example of similar issues that came up frequently.

I didn't realize it, but when I would point out his mistake my tone of voice did nothing to hide my extreme irritation. My husband has a very pleasant disposition and never reacted angrily to my comment. Once, though, my older sister was visiting when I pointed out yet another mistake to my husband in the unpleasant tone of voice I reserved for such situations.

My sister wisely said to me, "Your husband will listen to you even if you talk in a pleasant tone of voice. What you are doing to him is just as wrong as what you complain about."

I worked on speaking in a cheerful tone of voice even when I wanted to point something out to him. After a few days, my husband said to me gratefully, "Thank you for speaking so pleasantly. I never wanted to start a fight, so I would let it go, but your tone of voice in those situations always annoyed me. I had to work on myself not to scream at you. You might not remember, but right at the beginning of our marriage I asked you a number of times to speak more pleasantly. You didn't, so I gave up. I am grateful for the change."

It shocked me that my tone of voice caused so much distress without my realizing it. From then on, I was totally resolved to be careful to speak with a consistently pleasant tone of voice.

2. Watch your audience's reactions

What you say and how you say it has an effect on the person you talk to. When you speak to someone, there are ways to put that person into a joyous or happy state; ways to put him into a sad or depressed state; ways to put him into a calm and relaxed state; and ways to put him into an irritated or angry state.

Try the following brief exercise to see how this works:
• "What are your three favorite memories? When have you felt tremendous joy? When have you felt calm and relaxed? When have you done something that made you feel good about yourself? What are some of your biggest victories?"

Imagine that someone has just asked you these questions. As you think of your answers, you find yourself feeling happier and lighter than you felt before.

Now imagine being asked these questions:
• "When have you become irritated and angry in the past? When have you felt overwhelmed and awful? When have you made a major mistake or error? When have you felt really bad about yourself? When did you not like something that was said to you?"

Notice the difference in how you feel answering these questions when compared with how you felt before. What happened? Words elicit emotional states. Some words make us feel better and some make us feel worse.

Every time you speak to someone you have a choice. You choose whether you will speak to them in ways that elicit a better emotional state or a worse one. You will either remind that person of his successes, or his failures. You will either remind him of his enjoyable moments, or the moments he would prefer to forget. Normal conversation does not usually evoke as strong a state of mind as the above questions would if they were asked in person. Yet by choosing and using the right words it is possible to help lift another person's spirits and encourage him. The wrong words, or words spoken angrily, can just as readily send another person into distress and discouragement.

The prohibition against *ona'as devarim* is a prohibition against needlessly putting people into painful states. The mitzvah of doing *chesed* is the mitzvah of putting someone into a positive state. Blessing someone, especially a poor person, puts him in a better state. Saying encouraging words to someone who is ill or discouraged puts him in a better state. Eliyahu, the prophet, said that two people who always made others laugh merited a distinguished place in the afterlife (*Taanis* 22a). Why? Because they helped people who were in a sad state access a humorous state. This is such a major act of *chesed* that the benefits are eternal.

When you are angry, it is easy to speak to someone else in a way that will put him in a distressful state. Be aware of the state your remarks will elicit.

Notice nonverbal reactions

When you speak to someone, notice his nonverbal reactions to what you say. Watch his body language. Notice the muscle tension in his face, jaws, and shoulders. Notice how his tone of voice changes in response to something you say. This nonverbal feedback is very important for communicating according to Torah. It shows you whether or not you are causing pain (*ona'as devarim*) and whether or not you are doing *chesed*. Some people do this instinctively. Such people are usually naturally good communicators. Those who don't do this instinctively need to learn this very important skill. Mastery of this skill will enable you to do much good with your power of speech and avoid pitfalls and problems.

3. Disagree with respect

Since no two people think exactly alike, differences of opinion are inevitable. Some people get angry at others for not agreeing with them, not only on major issues, but even on small points. They are enraged that someone has the audacity to disagree with their position. But getting angry is not an effective way to influence another person to change his mind. Try to prove your points by citing facts and proof. The validity of an opinion is not increased just because the decibel level is raised. When you feel a need to resort to name-calling, mockery, or sarcasm, it shows that you are unable to prove your point with valid arguments. Between the First World War and the Second, some anti-Semites wrote a book titled, *100 Authors Against Einstein.* Professor Einstein phlegmatically commented, "If I were truly wrong, one would have been sufficient."

State your side of the argument calmly in a straightforward manner. When you speak in a condescending manner or with contempt and scorn, you will usually just strengthen the other person's resistance. There is a greater chance of influencing someone to agree with you when you show him respect than when you fail to do so. Speak with respect even though you differ.

4. Respond to questions with patience

It is all too easy to react angrily when we ...
... feel the person should know the answer himself

... are tired of answering the same question over and over again

... feel unsure of the answer

... are pressured for time

... sense an attack in the making

... resent being openly challenged

... feel the question is patronizing

... don't want our privacy invaded

... think the other person is just showing off

... can't stand the sarcastic tone of voice being used.

Be prepared to answer questions in a calm and respectful tone of voice — no matter what! When someone asks a question because he really needs to know information, be patient. Rabbi Chaim Shmulevitz used to compare this with the obligation to put ourselves in the shoes of the person asking us for a loan. Answer people the way you would want to be answered (*Shemos* 22:24, *Rashi; Love Your Neighbor*, pp. 185-6). Think about a time when you needed information about something that was important to you. How did you feel about asking someone for this information? How did they respond? How would you have liked them to respond? Keep this in mind when you are asked questions.

If someone is trying to challenge you or trap you, a calm, clearly thought-out reply will earn respect. When you are able to maintain a calm and balanced state, you will think clearer about the wisest thing to say. Mentally prepare yourself in advance to sustain a calm state regardless of what anyone asks you. If someone asks you something that throws you off balance, mentally prepare yourself to remain calmer the next time.

Hillel serves as our model for the ultimate in patience:

Two men made a wager that whoever made Hillel angry would win 400 gold coins.

One of them, anxious to win the bet, set off immediately for Hillel's home. It was a Friday afternoon and Hillel was washing his hair in preparation for Shabbos when the challenger stood outside Hillel's house and called out, "Where is Hillel? Where is Hillel?"

Hillel wrapped himself and went out to speak to the man.

"My son, what do you want?" asked Hillel.

"I have a question to ask," the man replied.

"Ask, my son, ask," Hillel said to him.

"Why are the heads of the Babylonians shaped the way they are?"

"My son, you have asked a great question," Hillel said to him, and gave him an answer.

The man waited a while until Hillel continued his bath, and once again called out, "Where is Hillel? Where is Hillel?"

Hillel again wrapped himself and went to speak to the man.

"My son, what do you want?" asked Hillel, as he had before.

"I have a question to ask," the man again replied.

"Ask, my son, ask," Hillel patiently said.

"Why are the eyes of the people from Tarmood shaped the way they are?"

"My son, you have asked a great question," Hillel said to him, and gave him an answer.

Again the man waited a while until Hillel continued his bath, and yet another time called out, "Where is Hillel? Where is Hillel?"

Hillel again wrapped himself and went out to speak to the man.

"My son, what do you want?" asked Hillel as he

had twice before.

"I have a question to ask," the man replied.

"Ask, my son, ask," Hillel said patiently.

"Why do the people from Africa have wide feet?" asked the man.

"My son, you have asked a great question," Hillel said to him, and gave him an answer.

The man then said to Hillel, "I have many questions to ask you, but I am afraid that you might become angry at me for asking them."

"Ask as many questions as you want," Hillel said with the utmost patience.

The man then explained how he had lost his wager, for he saw with his own eyes that nothing he could do or say would make Hillel lose his patience (*Shabbos 31a*).

For generations the role model of Hillel's patience has served as our ideal to strive for. Even when you are very busy and someone is asking ridiculous questions, be patient. It's all a test. Each test gives you another opportunity to elevate yourself.

5. Never insult someone for making a mistake

When we are in a position where we must point out mistakes to another person, whether as parent, teacher, boss, or customer, we will get better results if we are sensitive to the other person's feelings and use neutral language. There's no need to add salt to the wound, especially since most people feel bad enough already about their mistakes. In most instances it is sufficient to just point out the mistake. Don't attack the person's intelligence; don't speak sarcastically or condescendingly; and never name-call.

6. Material loss is no justification for anger

Some people become very angry if someone breaks something that belongs to them or spills something. But most probably it was a total accident and not a bit intentional. Some people are less graceful than others. Many feel guilty on their own over any loss they cause. Whatever the situation, telling someone or shouting at him to be careful is usually counterproductive. It will only make him more nervous and more likely to break or spill something. Also, insulting someone for being clumsy or careless is often a much worse offense than what the other person did. True, most people feel upset or angry when someone causes them a loss of money or gives them extra work. But don't take out those frustrations on a person who did not mean to do anything wrong.

Rabbi Chaim Shmulevitz, the Mirrer Rosh Yeshivah, used to present the following scenario to his students to drive home this point: A person is sitting at his dining room table when a family member accidentally drops a valuable crystal vase. At the exact moment the glass shatters, someone comes running into the room and announces that the lottery ticket purchased by the master of the house has won the grand prize in the national lottery. The joy in winning the fortune will be so intense that the person will not feel the slightest bit upset over the loss of the glass. This, said R' Chaim, should be our constant sense of joy for being alive. We should experience such intense bliss and ecstasy for being alive that any distress over trivial matters will be irrelevant. And what in this context is considered trivial? Almost everything.

Put your major efforts into mastering the ability to appreciate being alive. Life appreciation is such an important quality that we should work on it every day. And in fact, we do. The first thing we say every morning when we wake up is "*Modeh ani* — I give thanks." This is our statement that we are grateful to be alive. By experiencing the joy of life itself, we will free ourselves from much of the frustration that breeds anger.

Whenever anyone breaks or spills something, let it remind you that you are alive.

Loss of money

Some people become very angry at family members or associates for wasting money. It might be their keeping electrical appliances on when they are not needed, throwing out food that could still be eaten, or wasting paper or other items. When the loss is minimal, badgering someone about inconsequential matters only creates resentment and animosity. The loss of peace of mind and positive feelings is much greater than the loss of money. The wealthy person is the one who feels joy with what he has (*Pirkei Avos* 4:1). Keep this well-known *Mishnah* in mind whenever money issues arise. Joy with what you have is the key element that makes money worthwhile. Being miserable and angry over minor losses of money causes you a much greater loss than the loss of money. Causing pain to your children, spouse, employees, and roommates is going to be much more expensive than the loss that they caused you.

If larger sums of money are involved, or if the small losses are continual, speak to the other person in a manner that will motivate him to be more careful. Avoid any belittling remarks or insults. Make doing the will of your Father, your King, a higher priority than money. After all, you already spend money on mitzvos. Shabbos costs money, Pesach and

Succos cost money, Torah study costs money, charity and *chesed* cost money. Refraining from anger is also part of Torah observance, and the money you spend to do the will of the Creator is an investment with eternal payments in return. The size of your return is dependent on the size of your investment. The larger your loss, the greater your reward for speaking gently to the person who was the agent through which it was caused.

A Torah-consistent approach would be to say something like:

"I realize that it's just a small amount, but let's all try to be careful not to needlessly raise our expenses."

"We can't afford these big phone bills. I want us to keep the long-distance calls to a minimum."

"The more we save, the more we'll have to spend on the things we need and want."

---

7. How to talk to someone who is angry

Angry energy is contagious. When someone is angry at you, the anger he sends your way enters your nervous system and makes it easier for you to respond to him with anger. This will set off a chain reaction, with both of you becoming angrier and angrier.

When someone is angry, he is more likely to take offense at what you say. There are many things that you might be able to say to him when he is in a receptive state of mind that you should avoid saying when he is angry. Observing nonverbal reactions becomes even more important when you are speaking to someone who is angry. Observe the person's face, muscle tension, and tone of voice for feedback. Ask yourself, "Am I increasing or decreasing this person's anger right now?"

When speaking to someone who is in a rage, it is highly unlikely that you will be able to calm him down by saying, "Anger is wrong," or, "Don't be angry." If you don't know what to say, don't say anything. The person might be angry at you for not replying, but saying the wrong thing will make him even angrier. If what you would like to say will not be beneficial right now, you will just be causing the person added frustration. Remain silent until the person's anger subsides. Even if you feel that the person is making mistakes in what he is saying, and angry people will usually be making mistakes, when he is in the middle of his angry rage he is not likely to give you a fair hearing. After he calms down there is a better chance that he might. View your silence in such moments as an opportunity to gain greater self-mastery.

While you are waiting for someone to let off steam, view him as you would a distant mountain. Observe him objectively. Notice the muscle tension in his face, jaws, neck. Look at his mouth as he speaks. Compare this with its appearance when he smiles. Observe the color in his face and notice how this is different than when he is in a calmer state. Listen to the music in his voice. What does it remind you of? Compare this with the music of his voice when he is in a much better state.

It is an art to calm someone who is angry, and tone of voice is the key factor. A soothing tone of voice has a calming effect on the listener's emotional state.

Try to find a way to interrupt the anger pattern. The more irrelevant the statement you make the more power it has to interrupt the person's pattern. Someone might be angry because he was cheated out of a few dollars, and you might say, "I don't know why but this reminds me of that great vacation we once had." I once saw a Torah scholar observe two people who were furious at each other. He approached one of them and gently said that he would like to ask him a favor. Could the person please find him the telephone number of a certain individual? This gentle interruption broke up the escalating quarrel.

> *I once entered a store with my friend, Rabbi K.P., only to be met by an angry lady who started screaming and shouting at us in a loud voice. We couldn't imagine what she was angry about, until she said, "And I'm not an anti-Semite. My husband is Jewish."*
>
> *That clued us in to what we were dealing with. I looked at my friend and asked him if he knew her.*
>
> *"I never saw her before in my life," he whispered.*
>
> *I resolved to turn the situation around and get her to respond to us in a friendly manner. I focused on what I could say to interrupt her angry pattern. I noticed that she spoke English with a thick accent. So in the middle of her tirade I asked her, "I notice that you have an accent. Could you please tell me what country you are originally from?"*
>
> *She was puzzled by this non sequitur and replied, "Switzerland."*
>
> *"That's wonderful!" I exclaimed. "I was in Switzerland 22 years ago for my brother-in-law's wedding. What city are you from?"*
>
> *"Zurich," she replied.*
>
> *"That's exactly where we stayed," I said gleefully. "Aren't the Alps beautiful?"*
>
> *"They certainly are," she agreed, and went on to tell us how much she used to like mountain climbing. I asked her if she ever went back to visit and she told us she couldn't afford to.*
>
> *"By the way," I finally said, "What exactly were you upset about before?"*

At first she said that it was nothing. What a contrast to her fury when she first saw us!

"But I would like to know," I persisted.

"It's not that important," she said reluctantly, and went on to explain that the Miami city council had voted to give money to a Jewish organization and she felt that her tax money was being used in a way she didn't approve of. She then offered an apology, and before we left the store, wished us well.

Since then, whenever I am confronted with an angry person, I try to remember the "angry lady in Miami." It was a vivid demonstration of how staying totally calm and interrupting a person's angry pattern with neutral or pleasant conversation can bring him to a more relaxed state of mind, where the issue at hand can be discussed more rationally.

What is this person's pain?

When people are angry, they are in pain. Approach them with compassion. Ask yourself, "What pain is this person in right now?" When someone sees that you have sincere concern for his welfare, even when he is angry he will appreciate your genuine caring.

Ask questions to clarify the exact nature of the situation as he sees it. People tend to exaggerate when they are angry. Keep asking:

- "What exactly happened?"
- "What precisely was said? What were the exact words?"
- "What does this mean to you?"

By giving the person a chance to express himself, he will let off steam and calm down. What frequently happens is that these types of questions enable the person to see more accurately that the situation is not totally the way he was looking at it and this itself decreases, and even eliminates, anger.

After the person calms down, you might be able to ask him, "Did you do or say anything that contributed to this person's becoming angry at you?" When someone is in the midst of anger, he will have a difficult time admitting that he contributed to the person's anger in some way. While even when one is calm this might be difficult, it is still easier to admit one's own part when one is in a better state. It could be what he or she said. It could be the timing. It could be his or her tone of voice. It could be their facial expression. Recognizing one's own part in the total picture is helpful in decreasing anger at the other person.

8. Let the other person have the last word

Most people feel a strong need to get in the final word. In a heated dispute, neither person hears what the other one has to say, nor are they open to giving the other's position an objective evaluation. The arguments and proof presented have no chance of changing their opponent's mind because both of them are probably speaking in a tone of voice conducive to keeping the other person's mind as least as closed, if not more so, as it was when they started. Eventually both get tired of repeating themselves to someone who isn't even listening and the argument dies down, waiting to flare up again with a similar pattern when a new, similar, and often even the same, issue comes up.

When you think in terms of the outcome you wish to reach, you immediately realize that after you've stated your position clearly it's only worthwhile repeating it if the other person is open to listening. When you know that regardless of what you say the other person will just repeat his position, be noble enough to let him have the last word. If this makes him feel good, why not?

One of the most effective approaches to get someone to listen to you when you both want to speak at the same time is to say, "I will listen to you first. When you finish, will you please give me an opportunity to express myself?" Most people will answer in the affirmative. Then, if he keeps interrupting you when you are expressing your position, you can say, "I listened respectfully to you. Please do the same now for me. When I finish, you can raise any objections you wish." This is a highly effective method used by many with great success.

Watching two people in the throes of an argument makes it easy to see the futility of two people repeating their positions over and over again, often to deaf ears. Yet when we ourselves are involved, we feel such a strong urge to repeat our position that we don't stop to question exactly what we are accomplishing. By noticing this no-win pattern when it occurs in others, we will find it easier to recognize it when we do it ourselves.

As you continue to focus more and more on outcome, you will more readily ask yourself, "What outcome do I want? How is what I'm about to say going to achieve that outcome? What alternative approaches can I use to reach my goal?"

C. Know what not to say

When we are calm, we usually have a greater awareness of what is better left unsaid. Anger clouds rational thought. In the midst of a heated encounter or an infuriating situation it is hard to think clearly. At such times, the smart thing to do is to remain silent.

We see a graphic illustration of this truth with the Egyptians' reaction to the plague of frogs. The Egyptians found the invasion of their land by frogs highly distressing. They attempted to rid themselves of the plague by hitting the frogs. Instead of this killing them, though, the blows caused them to multiply. Rational thinking would have made the Egyptians say at this point, "Stop! Why should we continue to hit the frogs when it's only making matters worse?" But their anger made them irrational, and when a person is angry, you can't ask questions! (*Birchas Peretz: Parashas Va'eira*).

This counterproductive pattern is common in people who allow themselves to lash out in anger. They belittle, insult, and berate, but like the Egyptians hitting the frogs, they are the ones to lose out. Words spoken in anger will boomerang. It can take hours, and sometimes years, to repair the damage caused by something said in a moment of rage.

1. Master the art of remaining silent

Often, nothing is the wisest thing to say, especially when we are angry. Remaining silent in such situations is not passive, it is an act of heroism, as our Sages state: "The mighty person is the one who has mastery over his impulses" (Pirkei Avos 4:1).

Mainaining silence when you feel like really letting someone have it full force with all the angry words you can think of takes tremendous will-power. Achieving this silence is as difficult as mountain climbing. When someone manages to reach the top of Mount Everest, he is exhausted but exhilarated. Feel this sense of victory whenever you control your initial reaction and remain silent.

While remaining silent it helps to breath slowly and deeply. Focusing on breathing has a soothing effect, and calms the entire muscular system. Slow and deep breathing will enable you to think more clearly, too. This is such an important habit that you will find it repeatedly suggested throughout this book.

Silence is an art. Angry silence can be seen as a form of aggression, a way of getting back. The silence advocated here is a silence conducive to calming down, so that when communication is resumed it will be in a more respectful manner.

You might want to say, "I'd like to talk to you about this but I need to wait until I gather my thoughts," or, "I need to calm down first before I speak." If this is too difficult when you are angry, just say in a neutral tone of voice, "I'll be back soon."

2. Omit unnecessary words

A general formula for speaking when you are angry is: OMIT UNNECESSARY WORDS.

Especially when you are angry, be concise. Don't go on and on. The more you say, the more likely it is that you will say something you shouldn't have.

Some people have a tendency to give long-winded lectures when they are angry. Put yourself in the other fellow's shoes. How will he feel about having to hear a lecture of condemnation? Will this make him more open to hearing what you have to say?

Telling someone, "I'm not going to tell you what I think about you right now," is similar, and equally ineffective.

The following short statements can be said by anyone, any time they feel anger threatening to push them to speak when they should not. They are neutral statements which let the other person know that you want to abide by the rules of proper speech and expect him to do so as well. These short statements will often have a powerful effect on the other person. Repeating them out loud will make them become part of your spontaneous way of speaking. Eventually, you will find yourself using them when needed.

- "That wasn't helpful."
- "I would appreciate it greatly if you would please not do that again."
- "That wasn't right to do."
- "I found the way you said that painful. Please don't talk to me like that."
- "I am working on controlling my temper. Please help me by being more considerate."
- "Please speak to me courteously."
- "Your sarcasm wasn't appreciated."
- "I think an apology is in order."
- "I treat you with respect, please treat me with respect also."
- "I think that this request is unreasonable."
- "Please try to be more accurate."
- "What would motivate you to treat me better?"

3. Wait until the timing is right

Timing is a major factor in communication. When you try to discuss an issue of major importance with a person when he is angry / tired / hungry / upset / worried, you have a good chance of not being listened to. When you try to outtalk someone who feels an intense need to explain his position to you, you also have a good chance of not being listened to. And when you are so upset that you cannot control your speech, you stand an excellent chance of not being listened to. What does this add up to? Get your timing right.

How long will you have to wait? It all depends, it could take hours or days. And it can be difficult to wait. You feel impatient and want to get it over with. But if your goal in communication is to get your point across, you have no choice but to wait.

Imagine speaking to a person who wears a hearing aid and cannot hear a word without it. His battery has just run down and he won't be able to listen to you until he gets a new one. He has none in the house, and will have to wait until the store opens before buying one. But you feel impatient, and don't want to wait that long. So you start talking. It is quite obvious that you are wasting your time. He can't hear you. He might want to, but until his hearing apparatus is ready, he won't hear you. The same applies in all instances when people have emotional blocks to what you have to say. First you need to overcome those blocks. Be patient and wait, just as you would for new batteries.

Speaking before the other person is ready to hear what you have to say is often not just futile, as in our hearing-aid example, but can exacerbate the situation. When a person is emotionally closed to listening to you, your insistence on discussing the issue is likely to anger him. It's not worth it. Consider any waiting you may have to do as a boost to your expertise in patience.

4. Express yourself without blaming

Some people tend to blame others when anything goes wrong. Blaming others releases some of the frustration felt over the incident, and also frees the blamer from taking any responsibility himself.

When something is over and done with and is not likely to occur again, what positive benefits can there be to pointing the finger of blame? At times, no one is to blame for what happened. Other times, we ourselves may be the guilty party. The next time you feel a need to let off steam, see if you can release your frustration without involving others. Try taking a slow, deep breath. Repeat the words, "calm and relaxed," or, "centered and balanced" on the out breath. If you still feel a need to make a comment to another person, say respectfully, "I realize that this is over and done with now, but I still feel a need to express my disappointment and distress over what happened."

To tone down anger, it helps to remember that there may have been extenuating circumstances of which you are not aware. There is also the possibility that you are making a wrong assumption. The target of your censure may not have said or done what you think he did; or, you might have mis-interpreted his intentions or motivations. Since you may have to eat your words, try to make them as palatable as possible. This is why it is often wise to begin your clarification of the issue at hand by beginning with a qualifier such as, "I was wondering whether or not ..."; or, "I may be wrong, but perhaps ..." Speak in the mildest manner possible, and keep your focus on solutions. Harsh condemnations and resorting to invective will only cause pain without accomplishing anything positive. Especially when the other person already regrets his role in the unpleasantness, there is no benefit in a long tirade.

5. Assign a number to the level of importance

A surgeon once posed the following dilemma: "If I don't react with anger, the rest of the staff won't realize that what

I have to say is urgent. I deal with life and death situations and it's crucial for the people I work with to know how strongly I feel about things."

My suggestion was for him to set up a number system. "Explain to the staff that you would prefer to convey the urgency and importance of matters in a calmer tone of voice. As an experiment, you will assign numbers from one to ten to each request. Ten stands for 'ultra urgent, life or death emergency.' Even seven can mean 'act with full speed.' Tell your staff that you would prefer to speak to them in a balanced tone of voice. If they react to the number system the way they used to react to the sound of anger in your voice, you will continue to use just the number system."

The physician reported back that it was amazing how quickly and effectively the new system worked. The entire staff appreciated not being screamed at and worked as efficiently as possible, so that the surgeon would be motivated to continue using numbers instead of anger.

Everyone can use this system — husbands and wives, parents with children, teachers with students, and employers with employees.

Instead of raising your voice and shouting at someone, you can say, "This is a level 8 issue," or, "It's crucial for you to know that this is close to a 10 for me." You might even say, "Right now this is only a level 3. But if you don't do what you're supposed to be doing, it will go up to a 7."

6. When it pays to look vulnerable

Insults, verbal attacks, browbeating and rudeness can often be stopped in their tracks by a show of vulnerability. Letting the other person know the impact of his words by saying, "I found that remark painful," or, "I felt hurt when you said that," will make a normally kindhearted and sensitive person more careful in the future. By clueing him in to your true feelings you are helping him understand you better so that he can avoid hurting you.

This tactic should not be taken if your attacker is a less sensitive person who is "out to get you." With a person who actually derives pleasure from hurting your feelings or gains a sense of power in being able to cause you distress and pain, it is best not to tell the person that he hurt you. Revealing your vulnerability in such instances might very well draw a callous response of, "You are just acting like a baby," or, "I didn't know you were so sensitive." When dealing with such people it is best to retain an inner balance and say something like, "That's not an appropriate way to talk," or, "It's not right to talk like that."

With people who are very vicious or totally insensitive, it is frequently best to remain silent. Any response to such a person's anger will usually only escalate its intensity.

Motivation

1. We CAN control ourselves

Even though we may get angry, we can still control what we say at that time. People who believe that they can't control what comes out of their mouths often can't. But this comes more from a mistaken belief in their powerlessness than from a lack of ability to gain control. Yes, it does take great effort to control what you say when you are angry. But with the right motivation, it is within everyone's reach.

Imagine that someone does or says something that usually gets you angry. You are highly upset and ready to really let that person have it full force with the strongest language you can think of. What would happen, though, if right at that instant the person pulled out a gun and pointed it straight at you?

Regardless of the intensity of the anger, wouldn't any rational person muster the self-control and self-discipline to keep quiet? And were that same gun-toting person to ask for an apology, none of us would find it that hard to say, "I'm so sorry. I sincerely apologize." Most of the time, we are not afraid of the person we are talking to. And if we remember that our Father, our King, Creator and Sustainer of the universe, is listening to us, it becomes much easier to watch ourselves. The person who is verbally assaulted might not be able to defend himself right now, but his Father and King will eventually make the reckoning. Knowing that there is an eternal tape recorder catching our every word will inspire us to avoid violating the Torah commandment against causing pain with words. Hopefully, too, our strong sense of not wanting to hurt others will motivate us to control what we say. We know too that Hashem wants us to avoid hurting others. Out of love for Him and gratitude for all He does for us we want to try to live up to His expectations.

Even one incident of self-control proves that you can do it. The Wright brothers first plane only had to fly for 12 seconds to prove that it was possible to make a heavier-than-air machine fly. Only one person had to run the four-minute mile to prove that humans can run that fast. So, too, only one instance of success is needed to prove that you do have the ability to control what you say. Try remembering right now those times when you felt like "letting the other person have it," but didn't. By focusing on those successes, and building on them, you will become reassured about your ability to control verbal expressions of your anger.

2. Our speech reveals us

Whatever a person says when he is angry makes a strong statement about his character. Wouldn't we all like it said about ourselves that, "Even when he's angry he still speaks wisely"? Wouldn't it be painful to have it said, "He is usually quite sensible. But what a fool he becomes when anger takes over!" Or, "She is a very kind, compassionate person when she is calm. But watch out when she becomes angry. She is vicious."

Everyone wants to be seen in a positive light, to be thought well of. Some people strive to be seen as knowledgeable and intelligent, others as good and kind. There are those for whom wealth and success are more important, and yet others who see level of spiritual attainment as a measure of a person's worth. While we strive to liberate ourselves from the chains of approval seeking, it is almost an impossibility. Honest introspection will show this to be true. If you feel any different in the presence of other people than when you are by yourself, it is a sign that you care, to some degree, about how others view you. If you are nervous, even to a slight degree, about speaking in public, it shows that you care about what others think of you. Some people will counter that all they want is for others to see them as not caring about how they are viewed — but that very desire itself contradicts their claim!

Since we're pretty much stuck with it anyway, to one degree or another, we can use this need for approval to motivate ourselves to be careful with what we say when we are angry. No one respects or admires people who lash out in anger; it is not a very pretty sight. A sarcastic, frosty, or aggressive tone of voice does not make beautiful music.

Every time we speak, we make a statement about ourselves. What we say when we are angry makes an even bigger statement. Most people are at their worst when they become angry. They reveal things they would be embarrassed to discuss when they are calm. If they were ever to hear what they said and how they sounded when they were "venting" their anger, they would squirm in agony. People tend to deny that they actually said what they did, or to brush it off by saying, "It wasn't that bad." Unfortunately, it often was. If someone gives you feedback about how you sounded and you feel he's exaggerating, keep in mind that the target of the outburst is on the receiving end. If he or she says that what they heard was painful, it most probably was.

Some people demonstrate nobility of spirit when they are angry. They maintain their dignity even under stress, manifesting a lofty elevation. Their compassion for others finds vivid expression when of necessity they must reprimand another. Such people are admired and respected by all.

Make it your goal to make a positive statement about yourself when you become angry.

3. What kind of person will I become?

If you ever feel like giving vent to your anger by insulting someone, first ask yourself two questions, "What kind of person will I become if I insult this person?" and, "What kind of person will I become if I exercise enough self-discipline to refrain from insulting him?"

Every action you take and every word you say creates YOU. Each day is a new page in your autobiography. What do you want said about you? When you reread the book of your life, what key qualities do you want to see expressed? Keeping your ideal in mind makes it easier to act and speak according to that picture.

Regardless of the angry passages in the previous chapters of your life, this very moment, the beginning of the rest of your autobiography, can be a different story.

• *Right now* review past angry statements. If you remember hurting someone in anger and not yet asking and receiving his forgiveness, make up your mind to do so. Take responsibility for your anger and its consequences, because your present actions not only direct your future, but transform your past.

• *Right now* commit yourself to speak respectfully at all times, no matter how you feel.

• *Right now* visualize yourself speaking in more controlled, productive, goal-oriented ways — even when you feel upset or displeased. The more you practice, the more spontaneous your anger-free responses will become.

Step 5

Focus On Finding Solutions That Will Free You From Anger

Step 5:

Focus
On Finding Solutions
That Will Free You
From Anger

A. Anger is a contradiction to finding solutions

In the course of human interaction, conflicts are bound to arise. When they do, we can either turn them into problems, or creatively resolve the issues peacefully.

Our Sages have given us a guiding principle: "Be a student of Aharon — love peace and pursue peace" (*Pirkei Avos* 1:12). Many people mistakenly think that pursuing peace only applies to helping other people end quarrels, but it actually applies to each one of us. We need to make peace with those with whom we are presently angry. And a good way to do this is to think in terms of finding solutions.

One root source of anger is a feeling that our needs are not being met. Finding a way to meet these needs does much to reduce or eliminate anger. When an acceptable solution is found, things often go so smoothly that the interaction is not even considered a problem. People who focus on what they are not getting feel resentful and bitter. This is just the opposite of what they really want. We want our needs met so that we will feel happier. If our main focus creates frequent anger, not only are we not getting what we originally wanted, we are suffering even more because of our dissatisfaction and anger.

This thought is summarized in the Talmud. "When a person becomes angry, he acquires only his anger" (*Kiddushin* 41a). Rabbi Avraham Grodzinsky *zt"l hy"d, mashgiach* of Slobodka Yeshivah prior to the Second World War, commented on this: "There are usually no benefits to becoming angry at others. Your anger does not help you and the subject of your anger usually pays less attention to what you are saying than if you were to have spoken tactfully and patiently. Becoming angry merely causes harm to your health and makes you feel miserable" (*Toras Avraham*, p. 440).

Anger is usually a contradiction to finding solutions. It makes everything worse. When you become angry, your anger creates new problems. Not only are the old problems not solved, but now you have to find a solution to the problems caused by your anger. When you become angry at someone, he is likely to become more entrenched in his position and less likely to see your side. Couples who allow anger to rule find that they need to spend much more time on solving problems than do couples who try calmly to find solutions. Besides the original issue that provoked the anger, angry outbursts will have created more problems that need to be solved.

When a parent screams at a young child, the child usually starts crying. This crying must now be soothed before further steps can be taken. An angry parent creates a nervous child, who will be even more likely to act in ways that arouse anger. The parent might think the child is being provocative, but it is his or her own anger that has made the situation worse.

In a friendship, remarks made in a rage can cause severe damage, sometimes irreparable damage, to the relationship.

Most of us are usually willing to comply with reasonable requests asked politely. Angry demands are likely to be met with firm resistance. It does no good to blame the seemingly obstinate party when it's actually the bossy order-giver who is to blame.

I was considered a very rebellious child. Now that I look back on those years, I realize that I wasn't deliberately rebellious. There is no question in my mind that I would have preferred getting along well with the adults in my life. My problem was that the way things were said to me had a disproportionate effect on how I reacted. If someone asked me to do something in a tone of voice that reflected their respect for me, I was always willing to do what they asked. After all, why not? It wasn't worth the trouble not to. But whenever anyone spoke to me in a tone of voice that I considered to be controlling, patronizing, or condescending, I immediately felt a need to assert myself. I felt I had to prove to whomever it might be that I was an individual with rights and wouldn't tolerate being bossed around or treated like a child.

Now, as an adult, I can see how this response was not to my advantage. But at the time I didn't even think that I had a choice. I just knew I couldn't let anyone get away with speaking to me like that. If my parents, teachers, or other authority figures had realized this, they would have had the key to transform me.

One of the secrets of highly effective people is that they focus on finding solutions. It is hard to remain angry when your mind is occupied with trying to find a solution. Goal-oriented problemsolving creates a very different state of mind than anger does. The *Ralbag* notes the importance of focusing on goals: "Whenever you try to influence others, think first about how you can present the ideas to them so that they will accept what you have to say. It is not sufficient to just make the point. Rather, present what you say in a strategic manner to ensure that the people will listen to you. Even when your goal in communicating a message is totally for the other person's benefit, you should still work on presenting it in a way that will better enable him to accept it.

"Think of different approaches and strategies you can use whenever you need to convince someone to agree to a request you are making of him. The Torah (*Bereishis* 24:10) illustrates this lesson with the following account: When Eliezer, Avraham's servant, went to seek a wife for Yitzchak, he took along 10 of his master's camels laden with expensive gifts. He did this to show that Avraham was wealthy, so that the right family would be willing to allow their daughter to marry Avraham's son. For the same reason, Eliezer gave Rivkah gifts" (*HaDe'os VeHaMiddos, Shaar HaDibbur*, no. 6 *and Shaar HaTachbulah*, no. 2).

Whenever I met with my boss, I felt frustrated and irritated by all the interruptions. He kept taking calls, people kept coming into the room for his signature — it was one thing after another.

I used to leave these meetings with a lot of pent-up resentment. "If he really respected me," I used to tell myself, "he wouldn't allow other people to interrupt my time with him."

Then I thought about it a little more deeply and realized that this was his pattern with everyone and that I shouldn't take it personally. I thought about possible solutions to the problem. I noticed that a co-worker of mine always had short meetings and used to come out in a good mood. I asked him what his meetings were like and how he felt about the constant interruptions. He told me that at first his meetings also lasted a long time and didn't accomplish very much. Then he read about how to prevent such interruptions and followed these steps: Before each meeting he clearly formulated his goals for that particular meeting. During the meeting, he focused on finding solutions and spoke about the problems in the most concise manner possible. This cut down the total time he actually needed. At the outset, he would say to the boss, "I need only 10 minutes (sometimes only five, and sometimes 15). Can you ask the secretary to hold all calls and ask anyone who comes in person to come back in a few minutes?"

What my friend told me made sense. I tried it out and it was amazing how well it worked. This has increased my tendency to look for practical solutions to situations that arouse my resentment.

Some children kept knocking on my front door and then running away. A few minutes later, they would do it again. I didn't consider this a valid form of entertainment and became angry at them. I felt like giving them a strong tongue-lashing, but before I did I analyzed the situation. "Why are they doing this? It's probably not to hurt me, but just to have fun."

I asked myself, "What would be the best approach?" I thought of two possible ideas: One was to politely tell them off. The other was to join their game. I decided on the second approach, and the next time they knocked I waved to them and said with a smile, "Keep it up. Let's see how many times you can keep knocking on the door."

After a few more times, they became bored and stopped on their own. Later on, I approached each child separately and told him, "It's okay to have fun. But it's not right to have fun by causing anyone else pain. You wouldn't want other children to do this to your parents, would you?"

Because I was friendly towards them, they apologized and told me they wouldn't do it again.

B. The three solution-finding questions

The questions you ask yourself at a time of conflict guide your focus. Three questions to keep in mind are:

1. What need of mine is not being met?
2. What is my real goal right now?
3. What can I say or do to find a solution?

Repeat these three questions over and over again until they become automatic.

When you want something from someone and you are not getting it, clarify exactly what you want. Ask yourself, "What need of mine is not being met?"

You might want someone to:

- treat you with more respect
- stop treating you negatively
- do you a favor
- fulfill an obligation
- be fair
- refrain from doing something that is distressful to you
- talk in a more pleasant manner
- speed things up
- do something for his own benefit
- help another person
- be quieter
- return something
- be more careful in the future
- pay for damages
- refund your money
- do some work for you
- act honestly
- apologize

Once you have clarified exactly what you want, step back and take a look at the entire picture. You not only want these specific needs taken care of; you also want to maintain a good relationship with the person with whom you are interacting.

If you have a friend who consistently forgets to return borrowed items and this angers you, your immediate goal may be to get your things back on time. But your larger goal is to keep up a good relationship and perhaps to help your friend realize the importance of responsibility for other people's possessions. Search for a solution based on the entire picture.

If you are a teacher and a student misbehaves in such a way that it arouses your anger, remember that your real goal is not only to handle the immediate situation, but to prevent similar occurrences in the future, and of course, to teach this student more appropriate ways of expressing himself. If you respond only to your inner need at the moment, which may be to release your anger and cower the student into behaving, you will wind up engendering negative attitudes in the student towards you and school in general. The atmosphere in the classroom will also be spoiled (see *Pirkei Avos* 2:6). When a teacher puts aside his own personal needs for the higher goal of educating the student, there is less likely to be a discipline problem with that student. While it can seem easier to reprimand harshly than to build a sincerely caring relationship based on mutual trust, in the long run a teacher's sincere care and concern will have a more lasting effect on the student.

If you are an employer and an employee makes a mistake, ask yourself, "What is my real goal right now?" You want to have a good working relationship with your employee and you also want to prevent similar mistakes from happening in the future. So the solution you are looking for is one that will be respectful of the employee as a person. When an employee feels positive about you, he will do a better job. This is the power of the "One Minute Manager" approach. This is when you make a verbal sandwich. Start off with 20 seconds of praise, then mention the issue you need to comment on for 20 seconds, and then end off with 20 seconds of praise. For example, "I deeply appreciate all the work you do for us. Your integrity and efforts are of the highest caliber. Please make sure to pass on messages more accurately in the future. Again, I feel fortunate to have you working for us."

The praise you say must be genuine and sincere, and this cannot be faked. Trying to sound sincere usually sounds just that: trying to sound sincere. There is a major distinction between a person who does not have an inner feeling of respect for others but tries to sound like he does and someone who truly does have these inner feelings of respect. What is needed is an "*ayin tovah*," a good eye. That is, the ability to see what is right, good, and praiseworthy about other people. When you meet someone who has internalized this quality, you will experience his or her true goodness of spirit. A person with this quality will be slow to anger. He brings out the best in others, and when he expresses a need, others are happy to meet those needs.

C. Be future oriented

The past cannot be changed; what is over is over. The only way to make changes for the better is to keep your main focus on future goals. If you keep thinking about what a person did wrong in the past, it is easy to get angry. People who dwell on the past tend to make statements such as:

"You should have ..."

"Why did you ..."

"Why didn't you ...?"

"You made a mistake the last time ..."

With a future orientation, the focus is kept on what you want to happen: action, not reaction; recommendation not condemnation. Clarify what you are really after. Just blaming someone for what he did in the past is not helpful because what you really want is to encourage positive action for the future. People who have a past orientation repeatedly cause themselves and those they blame unnecessary misery. By having a future orientation you will be able to improve many situations by bringing about constructive changes.

As the Vilna Gaon states, "Even if someone has done something wrong to you, before entering into an argument with him, think of the outcome to which you aspire. If there will be no practical benefit from your argument, avoid it" (*Beur HaGra* to *Mishlei* 3:30).

Some people feel a strong need to resolve issues of the past. It is highly important for this to be done in a solution-oriented atmosphere. If you feel a need to discuss the past, tell the person that your goal is to have a positive relationship in the present and future. But before you feel ready for this, you need to discuss and resolve past issues. If you do this, know your goal! Do you want an apology? Do you want to understand the other person better? Without a clear goal, the other person is likely to feel under attack. This can lead to defensiveness, denial or counterattacks.

D. See the other person's point of view

Try to see things from the other person's point of view. It is only natural that an employer and employee will look at the exact same situation differently, as will a teacher and a student, or a parent and a child. Knowing that differing viewpoints are built into the system makes it easier to depersonalize irritating or infuriating behavior.

When you think about the other person's point of view, take into consideration the question, "Why is this person acting or speaking the way he is?" Try to answer this question in as objective and accurate a manner as possible. When you have a good guess as to why someone is acting a certain way, it is easier to suggest changes that meet both your needs.

Take, for example, a parent who is driving while his or her children are in the back seat. The children are making a lot of noise and the parent finds this distracting. The parent has already repeatedly told the children to be quiet, yet after each reprimand they continue to make noise.

A parent who doesn't think about solutions might get furious at the children. His inner dialogue might sound like this: "They are not listening now. They frequently refuse to listen. They are disobedient and wild. They will probably never learn to obey. I am not only a failure as a parent, but their lack of control could distract me from keeping my attention on the road. We might get into a serious accident if they don't settle down."

By focusing on solutions, a parent will instead ask himself, "What is my real goal right now?" The answer: "I want my children to be quiet so I can drive safely. I love them and want them to be safe."

The next question is: "From their viewpoint, why aren't they quiet?"

The obvious answer: "Most likely it is boring for them, as it would be for most children, to sit quietly without anything to do. They find it hard to be quiet when they are bored."

Having seen the situation from his children's point of view, the solution-oriented parent will then ask himself: "What suggestions can I make to them so that they will be quieter?" The parent will then suggest any one of the many car activities that can keep young children occupied, such as playing a word game, singing a song together, keeping a lookout for cars of a certain color, counting telephone booths, dogs, or anything else that comes to mind, having each child make up a story, or playing a tape, etc. Perhaps he will want to offer a special reward if they are able to be patient until the destination is reached. The parent's own patience will serve as a positive role model.

When adults argue, each side usually feels that he is right and the other side is 100 percent wrong. There seem to be no two ways about it. This is a common misperception of reality. Don't fall into this trap. Don't let anger create a heated dispute with the potential of developing into a long-lasting feud. Start off by trying to see the issue from the other person's point of view. In many instances you will be able to see that if you were in his situation, you would feel exactly the same way he does now.

Some arguments are over personal tastes. But others fall into situations where there is a clear Torah perspective on the matter. Present the disagreement to a recognized *halachic* authority to find out what the correct Torah approach would be in this specific situation. Whenever possible, it is important to define this as a clarification of *halachah*, rather than as a din Torah, taking someone to court, which is more of a legal battle between two adversaries. When clarification is the goal, it will be easier to find a solution that will enable both parties to feel good about doing what is right.

> *As owner of a medium-sized store, I had a constant feeling that people would try to take advantage of me financially if I didn't show them I was tough. I would argue with customers when they tried to bargain with me, and I later found out that many of them felt uncomfortable with my attitude. Every time someone asked me to charge less for a given item, I saw it as their trying to cheat me out of money that was rightfully mine. Didn't they realize how hard I worked? Didn't they realize all the expenses I had? Didn't they realize how hard I was struggling to make a go of it financially?*

One day it dawned on me that, no, they didn't realize any of this. The only thing on their mind was their own pocketbook and the motto that it's always worth a try to get someone down on price. Where I grew up, prices were fixed and no one would think of bargaining — it just wasn't done. But now I know that for some people bargaining is one of their greatest pleasures in life.

Since I began seeing it from their point of view, I have become more patient with people who try to bargain. While I don't always agree to lower my prices, I weigh each situation more carefully. With steady customers who love to bargain, I am willing to give slight reductions so that their need to bargain is met and they continue to shop in my store. Some customers waste too much of my time, so I maintain a friendly smile but refuse to lower the price. If they go somewhere else, it's okay with me.

I now actually enjoy watching the various approaches people use when they try to bargain. Recently I bought a new car and saved a lot of money using some of the bargaining techniques I learned from my own customers!

E. Calm an angry person before seeking a solution

Remember that a person has to be in a fairly calm state to negotiate. When you need to find a solution to a problem with someone who is angry, allow the person to calm down before discussing the issue at hand. Listen to him express his thoughts and feelings until you feel you understand his point of view. Try to understand why he feels the way he does. By listening carefully you will hear points that you may not have thought of, points which you can later use in your negotiations. Avoid the temptation to immediately rush to your own defense. After he has let off steam, he will feel calmer and will be more open to discuss a workable solution. When you are both able to discuss the matter rationally, you are more likely to find an acceptable solution.

When two people are working through an issue, it is common for both parties to want to speak at the same time. Each feels that unless the other person hears him, he doesn't want to listen to what the other person has to say. Take the initiative. Tell the person that you will let him go first.

Be aware of what is not helpful to say. For example, telling someone who is angry, "I can't understand why you are angry," or, "You shouldn't be angry," will rarely bring out a response of, "Yes, you are right, I'll calm down right away."

If there is some justification for the other person's anger, the sooner you acknowledge your mistake and apologize the sooner he will calm down. A person cannot stay angry for very long at a person who says, "You're right. I was wrong." This is such an important sentence to learn to say that I would advise you to repeat it over and over until you find it relatively easy to say to others when appropriate. Again: "You're right. I was wrong." Even if at first you cannot put your whole heart into it, after trying it a few times in various situations and seeing the magical effect it has on the angry party, you will want to use it more frequently.

Once your opponent has calmed down, it is a good time to say, "I'm sorry I caused you distress. I apologize." After he accepts your apology, you can then say, "Let's work this out together in a mutually acceptable manner."

When a person is angry over something you have said or done, an apology is much more powerful and effective for calming him than repeated defensive denials of responsibility. Often, once he has heard an apology he will be willing to listen to your defense.

F. Influence and motivate with positive approaches

The more proficient you are at influencing and motivating other people, the more your needs will be met, the less frustration you will experience, and the less angry you will get. The question to keep in mind is, "What would motivate this specific person?"

You can only use this approach if you are willing to momentarily let go of your way of seeing things, and put yourself in his shoes. Keep his needs, wants, values, and personality in mind. Then ask yourself, "What would make this person want to do what I want him to do?"

Focus on the questions:

"What is important to this person?"

"What would this person like to have or gain that I can help him with?"

"What aspects of this person's self-image could I appeal to?"

For example, a person who sees himself as compassionate will be willing to do things if he can see how they would be a help to someone who is suffering. Since many of the people we come into contact with daily are basically good-natured, it is often effective to start off a request by saying, "I have a problem. Can you please help me?" This often brings out the best in people.

If possible, try to find out what, if anything, motivated the person to do something similar in the past. This will reveal to you what to focus on in your presentation. At times it is simpler to ask openly, "What might make you willing to do this?" When someone is open to telling you what would motivate him, you don't need to guess. In many win-win situations people will be happy to tell you what will motivate them since both of you stand to gain. If someone doesn't want to do something that you would like him to do, you might ask him, "What is the key factor that stops you from doing it?" Knowing what stops the person might make it possible to search for ways to overcome that obstacle. For example, a person might tell you that he can't go with you because he is too busy. You might easily be able to help him take care of a few tasks, and then the obstacle will be removed.

At times a person has certain fears preventing him from reaching a mutually agreeable solution. Initially, he might not feel comfortable sharing those fears. He might fear that you would look down at him, even if you never explicitly say so. About this the *Ralbag* comments, "Try to figure out what specifically is holding this individual back from doing what you would like him to do. What fears might he have? What obstacles might he be focusing on that would make it difficult for him? Then show the person why he has no reason to be afraid and that the potential obstacles will not be a problem." (*HaDe'os VeHaMiddos, Shaar Ahavas Rayim,* no. 12)

As mentioned in STEP 1, six key terms for motivating and influencing anyone are: right, wrong, gain, loss, pleasure, pain. When you want someone to do something, show him that it is the right thing to do, that it is wrong not to do it, that he will gain by doing it, that he will lose out by not doing it, that he will have pleasure doing it, and that he will have pain if he doesn't do it. In most instances, you won't be able to use all of these factors, but these are the factors to focus on.

With certain people in certain situations all you need to do is to show the person that something is the right thing to do and he will follow through. At other times, it is more effective to show him how he will gain greatly by doing what you are requesting or suggesting. When you want someone to stop doing something, show him that it is right to stop, that it is wrong to do it, that he will gain by stopping, and that he will lose by doing it.

Anger is a poor motivator. It tackles only one of these six key motivators: avoidance of pain. Most people don't like the pain they feel when they are shouted at in anger, and therefore some people are motivated to do what you ask them to do so as to avoid your anger. Helping people gain is preferable to causing pain. If someone's typical motivating strategy is anger, it is wrong and he will eventually suffer in many ways. This is a good reason to stop trying to motivate others with anger.

Correcting other people

A lot of the anger in the world arises from situations where there is a real need to correct another person. The more effective we are in correcting others by using a positive approach, the less anger there will be.

Before attempting to influence another person or rebuke him, make sure your perception of the situation is correct and that your motives are pure. You must not only be positive that what the other person is doing is objectively wrong, but you must also be sincerely concerned with his welfare before offering any criticism.

Whenever you need to correct someone, you always have the choice of doing so in a way that will make him feel better about himself, or in a way that will cause him pain and distress. So before you begin, clarify in your own mind the approach that will not only be most effective in getting the change you feel is necessary, but the one which will be least hurtful. Getting angry might work temporarily; out of fear, the person will listen to you right now. But an educational approach is needed to have a long-term positive effect on children, students, employees, and anyone else you want to correct.

Your motivation for correcting others is in order to promote positive change. By using a harsh approach, you are working against your own goal. What happens when you try to correct people in a harsh manner? They usually become defensive. Instead of giving you a fair hearing, they are more likely to argue with you. You'll hear statements such as:

"I didn't do it."

"It wasn't my fault."

"I'm not to blame."

Be specific when you try to correct someone. General statements such as "You need to make some important changes"; "Improve your middos"; or, "Learn to do things the right way" will not be very effective. A more specific and more effective approach would be: "I found your sarcastic remarks about my intelligence very inappropriate. I hope that you will refrain from such remarks in the future."

Remember this rule: Keep the main thrust of your comments on what the person can do to improve, not on what he did wrong. For example: "If you talk to me in a softer tone of voice, it will make it easier for me to meet your requests." Or, "When I ask you to do something important, please write it down so you will remember to do it."

When you speak in a kind and friendly manner, others will be able to hear and accept your corrections much more easily than if they feel attacked. Sincere concern is a key ingredient in overcoming resistance.

Be prepared for a defensive reaction even when you do speak in a calm and reasonable manner. Some people are very sensitive to any implication that they are less than perfect and may even get angry at you and verbally attack you for bothering them. By anticipating such a possible reaction, you will be able to remain calm and focused on your goal — getting your message across — despite any negative reactions you might encounter.

G. Look for win-win solutions

When conflicts arise it is easy to get embroiled in a heated quarrel. If not handled properly, disputes can degenerate into a war of insults. A wise person will master the art of finding peaceful solutions that leave both parties of the conflict feeling like winners.

The first step is to clarify openly the wishes of each side by having both clearly state what would be for them an ideal outcome. Once the two goals are out in the open it may be discovered that the gap is not as wide as had been thought. Even if there still remains quite a distance to bridge, knowing exactly where each party stands will facilitate creating a win-win solution where both sides feel they gained. During the negotiations keep the question, "What does each of us really want?" foremost in mind.

A simple example of a conflict of interest is two children quarreling over the same toy. (Since many adults act like children when they get angry, the illustration is helpful for all ages.) When asked what they want, both children will say that they want to play with that particular toy. But the underlying, real reason that they want to play with the toy is because they want to enjoy themselves. If an alternative source of pleasure can be found for either one of them, he will give up the toy to the other child. If children are taught to understand how this works, you will hear them saying to a sibling or friend, "If I can show you how you can have more fun doing something else, will you let me play with this now?" The answer will usually be yes. The first child can then offer a different toy, game, or activity that is more desirable to the second child. This way, they both gain.

Suppose two people argue because they both want use of the family car at the same time. Were they to ask themselves, "What does each of us really want?" they would discover that what they need is not really this specific car, but a mode of transportation. Finding an alternative means of transportation for either person will keep both sides happy.

When conflicts of interest arise, keep your focus on the real issues and avoid getting sidetracked into a power struggle, where the focus is on making sure the other person doesn't get what he wants. When that happens, everyone is a loser. Disrespectful remarks are a good way of getting both sides involved in defending their egos rather than in searching for mutually acceptable solutions. It takes strength of character not to answer an insult with another insult, but by saying, "Let's both speak respectfully to each other so that it will be easier for us to work this out," you have a better chance of coming up with a win-win solution.

H. Apply the power of unconditional love

When people like us they are more willing to listen to what we have to say. If we find qualities to admire in the people we meet and feel truly concerned for their welfare, they will respond in kind.

When you want to influence or motivate others, what is the most powerful ingredient for success? Sincere, unconditional love. You can know all the strategies, techniques, approaches, and tools, but if the other person doesn't feel that he can trust you, he won't buy what you say. If he doesn't feel that you care about him, he will doubt that you have his best interests in mind. If we don't feel that someone is genuinely trying to help us, all the tools and techniques to get us to move in a certain direction can appear very manipulative.

Before trying to influence or motivate someone, increase your positive feelings for him. Focus on his positive qualities. Think about what you respect or admire about him. Think of a person you greatly respect and then treat this person the way you would treat the person you respect.

Think about the difference in your own willingness to do what someone asks you to do. Picture a person you highly respect and who you know cares about you very much asking you to do something for him. Now picture someone else, a stranger or someone who you think has only his own best interests at heart asking you to do something for him. Awareness of the difference you feel in both cases can help you be more aware of how others whom you are trying to influence and motivate are likely to feel.

I. Apply the power of calm persistence

Remember these two powerful words: "calm persistence." Calm persistence is much more effective than anger, and learning how to do it is easy. All it entails is repeating your request as many times as necessary while remaining calm. It's sometimes called "the broken record."

Calm persistence can take a few minutes, but anger can waste hours and even days, causing untold havoc. Our spiritual, physical, and emotional health is so valuable that even if calm persistence seems to take more time, it is actually shorter in the long run. Studies have shown that many people who live exceptionally long lives are those who are able to remain calm at all times, even in situations which would upset others.

Some parents repeat things two or three times and then blow up at their children for not listening to them. Some people who feel that another person has treated them unfairly and try to straighten out the matter give up trying if the other person doesn't accept their point of view right away. They then feel strong resentment. This is needless defeat.

Practice repeating a request into a tape recorder until you feel confident about your ability to repeat yourself over and over again calmly. After you see that you can do this when you are by yourself, imagine that you need to interact this way with another person. Realize that if you are able to do this when you are by yourself, it means that your brain has the ability to do this even when you are in the presence of others.

Anger that comes from having to repeat ourselves comes because we are telling ourselves, "I shouldn't have to repeat myself." It is more productive to keep the focus on how a calm repetition of the message is developing the character trait of patience; this will make it easier to remain calm. You might want to repeat to yourself, "Every repetition is giving me a greater amount of serene empowerment."

There are many times when I've heard people say, "There is absolutely no solution to this." And then a solution was found. Not everything is solvable. But without calm persistence you will never know if there really wasn't a solution to the problem. It's very possible that a solution could have been found — you just didn't persist. It is not uncommon to hear the "stubborn" party say later, "I would have given in if he had kept on asking. The fact that he stopped made me think that it wasn't that important to him." Don't let this be said about you.

> *An internationally renowned businessman said that the biggest mistake people make in negotiating is that they give up too easily. He has participated in hundreds of deals and found that it is those people and teams who are willing to calmly persist that are the most successful. Years ago a mentor had told him that everything is negotiable and that as long as you are willing to spend as much time as it takes you will frequently get what you want. Will you always be successful? Of course not. But a wise negotiator will be able to gauge when it is worthwhile to spend a lot of time on pursuing the matter.*
>
> *He ended by saying, "As soon as you lose your cool, you've lost. When the person on the other side sees that you are getting frustrated and angry, he knows that he's got you. You will make errors and he will take advantage of that."*

J. Apply the power of strategic submissiveness

Rabbi Chaim Zaitchyk explains that "there is a very powerful tool that will enable you to overcome many potential quarrels. This is the art of knowing how to act strategically with submissiveness when a needless quarrel might arise. By being willing to forego illusory honor, and speaking to someone from a humble position, you will often be able to soften even a heart made of stone. Your adversary's heart will melt in the face of your warmth when you act in a submissive manner. The form of submissiveness that is being referred to is only a loss of what might seem to some as honor, yet actually the person who acts submissively in this manner loses absolutely nothing in a spiritual sense. It is an outward compliance with the wishes of another person, but inwardly you and your spiritual level are not affected" (*Maayanai HaChaim,* vol. 3, pp. 64-5).

It is not necessary to lose yourself in your submissiveness. Never give up your sense of worth and identity. Never needlessly empower someone else by giving up your own inner sense of empowerment. Always maintain an inner awareness of your immense value for being created in the Creator's image, and feel your importance in being a child of the Creator and Sustainer of the universe. At the same time, there will be situations when it is pragmatic to talk and act humbly and submissively in order to avoid a fight or argument. At times you might need to act with more humility than you actually feel to clerks or bureaucrats holding various levels of authority. If you lose your sense of self-respect, you make yourself vulnerable to feeling belittled and inferior. This can easily lead to anger, if not immediately, then soon afterwards. A person who has an internalized sense of intrinsic, eternal value, enjoys being flexible and practical. He will be grateful to the A–mighty for giving him the wisdom to use strategic submissiveness to avoid problems and achieve his goals more effectively.

> *I used to get into many needless arguments that created so much animosity that, in the end, the people I argued with refused to help me out. One time I was at the airport checking in, close to take-off time. The baggage checker said that my luggage was overweight and that I would have to pay extra. I felt that I didn't need to pay and told him so loudly, in no uncertain terms. I threatened to report him to his*

supervisor. His face hardened as he coldly told me that there was nothing he could do about it and that if I missed the plane it would be my own fault. I demanded to see his supervisor but he claimed that the supervisor wasn't around. The angrier I became, the slower he moved. Believe it or not, I missed the plane.

An elderly gentleman who had witnessed the scene came over to me and politely asked me if he could tell me something. This is what he said:

"When I was around your age I used to react the same way," he opened with a smile. "But then someone told me that the best way to handle situations such as the one you were just in is to speak in a soft voice full of humility and apologize for the request you are making. He also suggested that I get into the habit of saying, 'I realize that what I am asking you is beyond the call of duty, but you seem like a kind person. I'm in a predicament. Could I please ask you for a special favor?'

"I was skeptical," the stranger continued, "but since I was not having too much success with my method, I decided to experiment and see what would happen. I found that the new approach worked like a charm. Someone did me a great favor by sharing this with me, and now I am passing it on. If it works for you, please pass it on to others who might benefit from it."

I tried it out and was amazed to see how well it worked. I now feel it's a great act of chesed to pass this on to others.

K. Don't just protest injustice — do something constructive

When there is a need to protest injustice, we have the choice to just vent angry feelings or to take corrective action. Many people who just explode and let off steam are left emotionally depleted after the release of frustration. They then don't have the necessary energy and clarity of thought to do what it takes to make a real difference.

Learn from people who take action. Solutions can take time, and many major problems and issues can only be resolved by planning long-term strategies. What is needed is strong determination and perseverance. Be resolved to channel angry feelings into constructive action. Angry feelings over injustice can be valid and serve as a powerful energy mobilizer. But be very careful not to do or say things impulsively. As long as there is not an immediate emergency, you gain much more by being patient and thinking through the entire situation thoroughly than by prematurely saying or doing something that will not provide a real solution.

L. Remove the source of continuous irritation

"Continuous irritation can provoke even the most patient person to become angry" (*The Wisdom of Mishlei*, p. 191). If someone's behavior is irritating you and you just remain silent, there is a possibility that you might blow up at that person. Therefore either:

(1) Develop a positive attitude towards what the person is doing. Find positive reframes. It can be viewed as an exciting challenge. You might be able to think of pleasant associations for the sounds that annoy you, such as foot tapping, knuckle cracking, finger snapping, and anything similar. What positive scenes can these sounds evoke?

(2) Politely ask him to stop the behavior you find irritating. Often, the person will stop when you speak in a normal tone of voice and you will not need to resort to an angry tone of voice to motivate the person. Most people don't overcome long-standing habits with just one or two reminders. So be patient. Realize that every time you politely repeat to the person to stop, you are conditioning his mind, and eventually his brain will spontaneously remember to stop these annoying habits.

If someone does something spitefully to annoy you, speak with greater determination and have a sense of authority in your voice. Don't shout an insult, just speak with a total sense of empowerment.

(3) Leave the room. Rather than get into an avoidable angry exchange, it is often preferable to walk out of the room.

> *There are a large number of minor habits of others that bother me. I hate it when someone keeps clearing his throat, when someone claps his hands, when someone whistles under his breath, when someone drums his fingers on a table, and a number of other similar annoying things. I used to view anyone who did such things as totally insensitive. I thought that almost everybody was annoyed as I was. I never became too aggressive, but when I told people to stop doing these types of things, my voice would always sound highly annoyed. If after I told someone to stop, he would continue, this would increase my annoyance. After the third reminder I would make sarcastic and critical remarks.*
>
> *Someone once asked me why these habits bothered me so much. Most people don't react to them as*

strongly as I do, he told me. I started to monitor my thoughts and became aware that I said to myself, "This person knows I can't stand what he is doing, and he's doing this just to bother me. I recalled hearing someone say years ago that all such behaviors are just sneaky ways in which people can express their aggression.

Now I realize that the vast majority of people with these types of habits aren't always aware that they are doing them. And even when they do try to stop, it is difficult. Nervous habits take a lot of effort to change. It is foolish on my part to think that anyone would be deliberately trying to annoy me with one of these habits, and it is certainly unrealistic of me to expect them to change overnight.

M. Be especially careful when in a rush

Some people lose their usual equanimity when they are running late. Their nervousness makes them snap at family members, employees, clients, or anyone who "gets in their way."

If you notice that too tight a schedule or an unbalanced one are the cause of some of your anger, make it a priority to improve your time management. Think of practical solutions to eliminate the factors that keep you from being on time. It may be not putting things away in their proper place, it may be an overly optimistic estimation of the amount of time it takes to get things done, or it may be nervousness itself. If your efforts to stick to a schedule and be on time meet with failure, at least decide that no matter what, you will keep calm. Of course, in life or death situations even a little late can be too late. But in most daily interactions any problems caused by being late will never be as serious as those caused by anger. It is usually better to be late and arrive in a positive state of mind than to arrive on time having left a trail of upset and anger.

If you deal on a regular basis with someone who is frequently late, cool your irritation and anger by thinking of constructive things to do with your waiting time. Of course, if you can motivate him to be more punctual, do so. When you do have to wait, realize that by remaining calm and patiently waiting for another person, you are utilizing your time fulfilling the mitzvah of emulating the A–mighty's ways by being *erech apayim*, slow to anger. Time spent on developing your character traits is time well spent.

N. Deal efficiently with inefficiency

When faced with other people's inefficiency, be careful not to allow your frustration to control what you say. Think about your goal, which is that he become more efficient. This can be achieved in ways that are neither insulting nor offensive. When a person himself realizes that his inefficiency has caused a loss, he will be especially grateful to you for being considerate of his feelings. Keep asking yourself, "What positive approaches can I use to help this person become more efficient?"

One business executive whose office has several secretaries found a face-saving way to handle inefficiency and other slip-ups. Whenever a mistake is made, he will go to the person involved and say something to the effect of, "This letter was returned because someone forgot to put on the street address. Please find out who mailed it and remind the person to be more careful in the future."

O. Use the salesman's approach

One of the top sales consultants advises salesmen to mention any fears they may have right at the beginning of a sales pitch. He stresses that this technique is especially effective in preventing people from becoming angry. For instance, if you need to discuss an issue, you can start off by saying, "There is something I would like to say but I'm afraid you might get angry at me." The other person will usually assure you that he won't get angry.

And it is likely that he won't.

P. Improve service effectively

Some people get furious when faced with service they feel is less than adequate. Their ire is aroused by a slow-moving line in the bank, a salesman not paying attention to them, a waiter who is slow in bringing the order, etc., etc. Because they overreact, they frequently insult and humiliate people who are not even at fault. And even when incompetence is to blame, it is no excuse to insult another human being. Finding ways to improve service without causing pain shows greater maturity. Remember, clerks and waiters have feelings too, just like you. The fact that they are paid for their services does not entitle the customer to insult them.

> I went out with someone several times and was seriously considering him as a marriage partner, for he had many of the qualities I was looking for. But one evening he did something that made me end the relationship.
>
> We went to an exclusive restaurant and were looking forward to a pleasant evening. We placed our orders, but they were a long time in coming. When the waiter finally arrived, the young man I was with

began an angry tirade. "What's the matter with you people?" he said in a loud voice. "You don't have the faintest idea what good service is all about. It's absolutely disgusting how slow you are."

I felt that the way he spoke to the waiter was horrible. Even though he was polite to me, I refused to see him again.

Overreaction to trivial inconvenience comes from a "center of the universe" complex, which includes a lack of awareness of other people and their needs. Instead of realizing that they may be wrong, or that there may be extenuating circumstances of which they are unaware, such self-centered people take everything personally. By becoming more humble and patient, and acquiring skills at problem solving, they can learn to shift focus to eliminate anger.

If slow service will bother you, try to let the clerk or waiter know in advance that you would appreciate fast service. One positive approach would be to say, "I'm in a bit of a rush today, so I'd appreciate it if you'd speed things up if you can." An even more patient approach is to tell the overworked person, "I see that you are overextended right now. Please take care of the other people first. When you get a chance to catch your breath, I'll be waiting for you patiently." Often this will win you the royal carpet treatment. Yet even if it does not, it will certainly develop your character, a gain far more important than getting better service.

Q. How to ask

Some people have a very giving approach to helping others. They feel so happy about being able to help people that whenever they have an opportunity to do a *chesed* for another person, they will try their best to do it. This level of behavior is called *ahavas chesed*, love of kindness, and the Chofetz Chaim has written an entire book on the subject. Naturally, we all have limitations of time, energy, and resources. But people who love helping others find that even if they cannot fulfill the request, they feel no annoyance for having been asked. In fact, they would love to do everything for everyone, and it is only human limitation which stops them.

Other people have not yet developed this degree of loving to do acts of kindness. At times they will agree to do what someone requests, and at other times they seem to have no compunctions about refusing. A large number of people who fit into this category find that when someone tries to order them into doing something, they immediately balk. They value their independence and feelings of freedom to such a degree that at times they can do things that are self-defeating and counterproductive solely because someone has made a demand on them.

When speaking to someone with this type of personality, more will be accomplished by making subtle suggestions than by speaking with force and power. Make presentations based on reason and logic. State the facts in a matter-of-fact way. This will enable the person to weigh the situation objectively. Show him how he will gain by following your suggestions, and how he will lose by failing to do so.

Tools and Techniques to Prevent and Control Anger

Step 6

Tools and Techniques to Prevent and Control Anger

There are many tools and techniques that will either prevent anger in the first place or will enable you to calm down after you have become angry. Different techniques work best for different people. Also, you might find that at times one technique works best for you, while at another time you need a different approach. This part of the program presents a selection of known, effective tools. Familiarize yourself with them and experiment to see what works best for you. Be creative and create your own variations.

1. What has worked in the past?

First of all, think of what has worked for you in the past. When you have been able to overcome anger quickly, how did you do it? Even if it took you a long time to overcome your anger, when you finally let it go, how did you do it? Some people eventually tell themselves, "This anger is just harming me and wasting my time. It isn't worth it." Then they are able to mentally move on. If you can do this, then practice giving yourself this message earlier on. Some people tell this to themselves after just a few moments of anger, and you can too.

Keep a journal of self-mastery. Every time you successfully handle a difficult situation write down how you handled it. Writing down successes will remind you of what you can do.

2. Learn from everyone

A wise person learns from everyone (*Pirkei Avos* 4:1). Learn from people who are able to remain calm in situations that get you angry; learn from people who are able to let go of their anger easily. Ask them how they do it.

Ask them questions such as:

- "What made you able to stay so calm? How did you view the situation?"
- "How did you handle this so well?"
- "What approaches or techniques have you found helpful?"
- Most people will be glad to share any strategies they have found helpful.

3. Count from one to ten

The classic way to give anger a chance to subside before speaking is to count from one to ten. Some people count from one to 20 and some need to get all the way up to 50. This can be even more beneficial when the words "more and more relaxed" are repeated after each number. Or, you might find that repeating the words "centered and balanced" or, "patience and humility" or, "serenity and compassion," between each number will have a calming effect. By practicing when you are not angry, this technique will have a more relaxing effect when you need it.

It is almost guaranteed that any anger will have cooled somewhat by the end of the counting. This makes it easier to rationally decide on the right move. At times remaining silent and letting the issue pass is the wisest choice; at other times it is preferable to speak. The clearer your mind, the better chance you have of making a wise choice.

4. Breathe slowly and deeply

Breathe slowly and deeply to access calming states and release stress and anger. As soon as you notice that you are feeling angry, breathe slowly and deeply. Exhale slowly. As you exhale, feel all the anger, frustration, and stress being blown out.

When you breathe in slowly and deeply, feel the fresh oxygen energizing you and giving you greater feelings of serenity. Feel grateful for being alive and for each breath of air. If your mind wanders, calmly bring it back to watching your breathing. One try is all it takes to prove how highly effective this technique is. Be patient. Some people take only four or five breaths and claim it doesn't work. Be willing to keep this up for 10 to 20 minutes in instances of strong anger. As you practice this form of breathing, it works faster.

5. Keep a journal

In trying to reduce anger it is very helpful to keep a list of every time you get angry. Write down the situation, the person involved, and what the subject of the anger was (such as poor service, insults, nagging, lack of consideration, unfairness, etc.). Note the time of day, place, and your general state before the incident (tired, rushed, or under stress, etc.). By doing this you are likely to find patterns. See STEP 2 for various patterns with which you might identify.

Ask yourself what was going through your mind at the time you felt angry. How were you viewing what happened? Then challenge those statements. See STEP 3 for ways to reframe. The habit of writing down incidents along with your challenges of the attitudes that caused the anger will enable you to gain greater control.

Don't forget to write down your victories, too. Keep a list of times when you didn't become angry in situations that could have been very anger provoking.

Some people find that if they keep a journal of their anger, it tends to increase their anger. If this is true for you, only keep a positive trait journal.

6. Give up blaming and faultfinding

Make a conscious decision to give up the detrimental habits of blaming and faulfinding. Learn to see things from the other person's point of view. Make it routine to ask yourself, "How does this person view what he or she has said or done?"

Learn to judge people favorably. This will eliminate much anger. Ask yourself, "How can I judge this person favorably?" Perhaps he is not even at fault. Often, too, understanding why a person acts the way he does will decrease and possibly remove all anger towards him.

View other people's anger as a message that they are in pain. Ask yourself, "What pain is this person experiencing?" and, "What is most helpful to say right now?"

The Chazon Ish wrote: "A wise man will not get angry at an insane person who wrongs him. This should be our attitude towards someone who wrongs us because of a lack of spiritual sensitivity and lack of good character. There is really no difference between a person who lacks sanity and a person who behaves improperly" (*Chazon Ish, Shabbos* 56:4).

A great deal of the anger in the world is over trivialities. Realize that most situations are so trivial that it is not worth the harm to your emotional, physical, and spiritual well-being to get angry. When you feel angry, ask yourself, "Am I angry about a triviality?"

7. Go to the opposite extreme

The *Rambam* wrote: "Behave in a manner that is at the opposite extreme of your fault until you are able to behave in the middle path. If you have a bad temper, completely ignore all insults until you no longer feel anger when insulted. If you are arrogant, behave in an extremely humble manner until you no longer feel conceited. Then you can behave in a moderate manner which is the good path on which to go" (Hilchos De'*os* 2:2).

8. Silence, low voice, and don't look

Orchos Tzadikim (ch. 12) gives three practical ideas for dealing with anger:

A. Learn to remain silent until you feel calmer.

B. Practice speaking in a low tone of voice. This prevents your anger from increasing and also has a calming effect on your emotions.

C. When you are angry at someone, don't look at him straight in the face because this can increase your anger. By speaking to him without looking at his face, your anger will subside.

9. Decide to release anger

When you feel yourself becoming angry, at first just silently experience it. Feel the sensations of anger in your muscle system. Mentally, check each limb, from head to toe. Then ask yourself, "Am I ready to release my anger now?"

If you can say, "Yes," then follow this by saying, "I now release my anger." Feel your anger being released from every limb of your body. To see how this works, right now make a fist with one hand. Tighten it. Now tell yourself to release those muscles, and allow your hand to relax. This shows that you do have the ability to release stress and tension at will.

If you are not yet ready to release your anger, say to yourself, "I choose to hold onto my anger for one more minute." After one minute ask yourself again, "Am I ready now to release my anger?"

Repeat this process each minute until you allow yourself to release your anger. Realizing that holding onto anger is your choice makes it easier to let it go.

10. Take a sip of water

Some people have a habit of taking a sip of water and holding it in their mouth for three to five minutes until their anger subsides. This prevents them from saying something in anger that they will later regret. The effort to keep from swallowing the water has a calming effect.

Other people drink a glass of water to reduce anger. The blessing they make before drinking reminds them of their Creator. This in turn reminds them that everything that happens is only through His will. This helps them calm down.

11. Let off steam by walking, dancing, gardening

Seek healthy ways to let off steam when you become angry. Physical exercise releases anger. Take a brisk walk, run, dance, or engage in other exercises such as jumping with a rope or on a mini-trampoline. This will dissolve stress, frustration, and anger.

One Torah scholar even said that dancing to release anger can be termed "rikud shel mitzvah," a form of dance that is a mitzvah!

For some people, gardening releases stress and anger. Attacking weeds is much better than attacking people.

12. Go to the balcony

If you are in a situation that could easily get you angry, mentally go to the balcony. That is, imagine that you are watching the scene from a distant balcony. This will enable you to emotionally dissociate yourself from what is happening. You are able to observe the entire scene as an outside observer and will therefore find it much easier to remain calm. Some people even imagine that they are in a balcony watching themselves in the audience watching themselves on stage. This is a double dissociation and if you try it you will see that it allows you to observe an otherwise anger-provoking scene as if you were watching the entire scene in a play. From this perspective you will be able to think much more clearly and rationally.

When you are not involved emotionally, you can coolly observe the other person's words and pattern of thought as if he were talking to someone else. This is a skill that many professional negotiators use to remain objective in difficult negotiations. When you master the ability to become an objective observer, you will even be able to enjoy watching yourself in a scene that used to get you angry.

A good example of when to use this is during discussions with someone who is very mistrustful and tends to be suspicious that the other person is trying to cheat or deceive him. When we are accused of ulterior motives, most people feel hurt and often angry. But by going up to the balcony and watching the other person as if he were an actor on stage it becomes easy to ask, "What is this person's pattern?" When we are aware that someone's brain constantly warns him, "Danger, someone might be cheating you," we won't take his accusations personally. Even though we won't necessarily like what he is saying, we will have the freedom to take a more objective look at the situation and choose our strategy.

Right now think of how "going to the balcony" will be helpful to you. Think of someone who easily provokes your anger. Visualize yourself using this tool and remaining calm as you interact with that person.

13. Stay out in the car and send in an actor playing psychiatrist

A highly successful sales consultant with a sense of humor gives the following advice to anyone wanting to be more effective when trying to influence others:

"Stay in your car. Don't go out 'yourself' to meet someone who might be hostile or intimidating. While 'you' are sitting calmly in the car, send in 'an actor playing psychiatrist.' A psychiatrist doesn't get offended or thrown off balance by what anyone says. Since you are only an actor playing a psychiatrist, you are even more emotionally safe. Your feelings of safety are increased by the consciousness that the 'real you' is sitting peacefully in the car."

Look forward to the next time you will need to interact with someone who might possibly provoke your anger, and experiment with this approach. It's amazingly effective for anyone who has a basic knowledge of how to interact well with others, but whose fear or anger prevents that knowledge from being accessed. Seeing yourself as an "actor playing psychiatrist" lets you access more of your knowledge.

14. Find a partner or coach

If possible, find a partner, coach, or mentor who will help you work on your anger. When you report back to someone about your progress, it is easier to stay motivated.

Tell family members that you are working on anger and that if they see you becoming angry, they should remind you of your resolution to control your anger.

Rabbi Avraham Yellin (*Erech Apayim*) suggests that parents can even ask their children to help remind them to conquer anger. Children must be careful to speak to parents in a way consistent with the obligation to honor parents. A child can be given permission by a parent to say something to the effect of, "You asked me to remind you to stay calm."

15. Focus on your body's inner reactions

An experiential technique that is effective for overcoming feelings of anger is to focus on your body's inner reactions when you are angry. Stop thinking for a moment about the topic of your anger and focus totally on what is going on inside of you. Focus on your shoulder muscles, stomach muscles, face and forehead muscles, arms, and any other muscle tension. Mentally travel up and down your muscle system. Many people find that this alone releases their muscle tension. If not, then practice tensing and relaxing each muscle group. When you yourself tense your muscles, it is easier to let them go. As you let your muscles go, say, "Relax." After enough practice, just saying the word "relax" will cause your muscles to let go and relax.

16. Torah meditations

A meditative approach is to repeat either of the following two verses over and over again as you breathe slowly and deeply.

A. "*Ein od milvado* — There is nothing else besides Him" (*Devarim* 4:35). Rabbi Chaim of Volozhin wrote that there is tremendous power in repeating this verse as a meditation. Reflecting on the profound concept of this verse causes anger to disappear.

B. "*Yehi ohr* — Let there be light" (*Bereishis* 1:3). As you repeat this verse think about how the entire planet was in total darkness until these two words were said by the Creator. Feel the Creator's light entering you and calming your muscles and cells from head to toe. Visualizing this light will have a wonderful effect on your nervous system, and will melt anger.

17. Watch yourself in a mirror, or listen to yourself

One cure for anger is to see and hear yourself as others see and hear you when you are angry. Decide that the next time you get angry you will go to look at yourself in a mirror. There is an ugliness to anger, and especially if you contrast it with the way you look when you smile, it will strongly motivate you to do whatever you can to conquer anger.

You might want to ask someone in your family or office to record you the next time you lose your temper. Give them permission in advance to tape you surreptitiously so that you can later hear exactly how you sound to others. When you are calm, listen to the tape.

18. Envision your role model

Think of a role model who is able to react with calm certitude in every situation. The next time someone does or says something that used to get you angry, pretend that you are the calm role model and react the way that person would.

19. Role playing / Two-chair method

If you are afraid you might say the wrong things to a person you are angry at, or alternatively, when it is impossible to speak to someone, role-play a dialogue with him. Imagine that he is in the room, and tell him out loud why you are angry. Since he isn't present, you can express yourself more freely than if he were there.

Then role-play the other person and state his defense as best you can. This technique will help you understand him better and will make it easier for you to overcome your resentment.

The two-chair method can add to the effectiveness of role-playing. Use two chairs. When you are in one chair, speak as yourself. Then sit in the second chair and role-play the other person. Respond to yourself as if you were that person. This will frequently be helpful in trying to gain a better understanding of that person's position.

20. Write a letter ... but don't send it

Write an angry letter without sending it. Write down all your angry thoughts in a letter addressed to the person you are angry at. Since you are not going to send the letter, you can express yourself more spontaneously and less tactfully. Then make certain to tear the letter up into little pieces. Make absolutely certain that no one else will see the letter you have written. Expressing yourself in writing will release some of your pent-up anger in a harmless way.

Important note: Even if you haven't finished writing all that you wanted to say, tear up the letter if you have to leave the room. You can always repeat yourself in the next imaginary letter. The harm caused by someone else mistakenly seeing words written to alleviate your own pain can be grievous. So is the harm of expressing angry thoughts and words that are not filtered with tact and a focus on your goal.

21. Focus on good qualities

If someone has done something to you that you feel angry about, focus on some good quality of that person. That person might have done you favors in the past, he might have done much good for other people, or he might have certain virtues that you respect. Even though you don't appreciate the way he interacts with you, you can still respect him for the positive things he has done in his life (*Tomer Devorah*, ch. 1).

When you are angry at someone, your focus is limited to what he said or did that got you angry. By focusing on what is positive about this person, you will have a more balanced perspective and will find it easier to say things to resolve the issue at hand.

22. What would you advise someone else?

When you become angry, ask yourself, "What would I advise another person in a similar situation?"

It is much easier to tell other people reasons why they needn't be angry. Viewing the situation as if you were talking to another person might help you find a better way of looking at it.

A similar idea is to ask yourself, "What would a wise person tell me right now?" You might think of a particular wise person you know or have read about. Imagine what he or she would tell you. This will help you access knowledge that you already have stored in the wondrous data base in your brain but might not have thought of without this approach.

23. Imagine a large crowd

If you are angry at someone, imagine a tremendously large crowd cheering you for your self-mastery as you courageously remain silent until you feel calmer. Since you are creating this crowd in your mind, you have the ability to create a crowd of millions cheering for you with intense enthusiasm. Some people increase the effects of this imagery by playing a tape with a crowd cheering and mentally imagining that they are shouting words of encouragement. Imagine what it would be like to win a trophy for self-mastery.

24. Develop perspective

Develop a sense of proportion. When something is about to get you angry, ask yourself, "How important is this in my life?"

Other questions that will help you get a more accurate sense of proportion are:

- "What is my actual loss?"
- "Why is what happened not really so awful?"
- "How will I look at this in a week from now?" "In a year from now?" "In ten years from now?"
- "How will I look at this after 120 years?"
- "How could this be worse?"
- "Compared with what people went through in the Holocaust, how terrible is this?"

And the final question:

- "In the scheme of the entire universe how important is this?"

25. Choose a better state of mind

You can't be in two incongruent states of mind at the same time. Therefore whenever you feel angry, ask yourself, "What state of mind would I prefer to be in right now?" It might be a state of patience, a state of joy and enthusiasm, a state of serenity and tranquility; it might be centered and balanced, it might be calm persistence, serene empowerment, love and compassion, or it might be self-mastery.

Then act as if you were in that state. How would you talk if you were in that state? What would your posture be in that state? What would your facial expression be if you were in that state?

Remember a time in the past when you were in the state of your choice. Imagine it vividly. How did you feel then? What was your posture and facial expression? How did you breathe? What did you tell yourself?

Think of what it would be like to be in such a state in the future. Imagine a situation in which you would naturally be in that state.

Think of a role model who personifies the state of your choice. Imagine for a few minutes that you are that person. Think, talk, and act like that person would.

Imagine having an inner part of you that is serenely empowered, joyous, patient, centered and balanced, calmly persistent, or loving and compassionate. When you begin to feel angry, allow that part of your choice to take over for a while. Some people find that thinking in terms of parts makes it much easier for them to enter a specific state.

Practice accessing your favorite state. It might help to practice in front of a mirror for instant feedback. A small mirror is one of the most accessible and inexpensive biofeedback machines available.

Some people find it helpful to write the states they want to master on cards that they carry with them, or they attach the cards to a wall where they will frequently see them.

26. Imagine a relaxing or cooling scene

If you start becoming angry, focus your thoughts on another scene. Start off by visualizing peaceful and relaxing scenes such as waterfalls, gardens, forests, mountains, and lakes. You might think of places that you actually visited in the past, or you can even imagine being in a place that you have only seen in photographs.

It can be useful to imagine yourself in the snow in a freezing climate. Anger makes a person hot. Seeing yourself in freezing snow has the ability to cool you off. Either remember a specific cold winter snow scene that you once experienced, or imagine what it would be like to be in the North or South Pole, or high up on Mount Everest or the Alps.

If these images don't work for you, imagine yourself standing in the middle of a cemetery. This has the ability to give you a different perspective on the situation and will help you calm down. It is a way of reminding yourself of the brevity of life and what a shame it would be to waste precious time and energy on anger (see *Chochmah U'Mussar*, vol. 1, p. 69).

27. Replace anger with humor

Laughter is totally incongruous with anger. When we laugh, our brain produces chemicals which give us a good feeling. Every time you recall times when you laughed or giggled, you are momentarily returning to that state of being. Research has shown that laughter can be a powerful painkiller. The endorphins produced by laughter coat the nerve synapses, reducing the pain message they are able to transmit.

From now on, every time you laugh make a mental note of the entire scene. Then, whenever you feel yourself starting to get angry, replay your laughing scene. If you haven't yet mastered the ability to laugh at will, imagine what it would be like if you could. When you are by yourself, practice making faces at yourself in a mirror to see how quickly you can start laughing. If it's appropriate right now, see if you can say something to yourself or visualize a scene that will make you laugh.

28. Accept in advance

Before asking someone for a favor, realize that he may not grant you the favor. Although you can use strategy to try to influence him to help you, learn to accept a "no" with grace. Even before you ask him for the favor, think how you can judge him positively if he does not help you (see *Mivchar HaPeninim, Sha'ar HaTikvah*).

29. Create new associations ("Anchors")

Much anger comes from associations, or by what is known as "anchors." Any stimulus that elicits a specific response is called an anchor. That is, the brain links a certain image or sound with anger. The most famous example of an anchor is the Pavlovian bell which at first signaled that food was going to be offered to dogs and eventually triggered their anticipation of food automatically. Unfortunately, many people associate classical conditioning with dogs and fail to see how pervasive and powerful anchors are in our daily lives. We all have thousands of anchors. Sounds, words, and music all automatically evoke memories of the other times you have heard them. Pictures and images remind you of those times when you have seen them or similar ones. Touch, taste, and smell create similar associations. This gives us a powerful tool for conquering anger. You can reassociate any anchor and therefore even anchors that previously provoked anger can now provoke joy, courage and confidence, humor, and even a calm, relaxed feeling. Some people have flexible natures and can do this fairly quickly. Others do not; it will take them more time and effort to reprogram their associations, but it is a worthwhile investment since it will free them from a great deal of anger.

If a person has a certain facial expression that until now has provoked your anger, reassociate that facial expression with feelings of joy. Repeat to yourself, "Every time this person makes that face I will feel more joy." As you say this, remember a time when you felt totally joyous. Vividly remember details of that moment. Experience it as if it were happening now. As you feel those feelings of joy, visualize this person making that face. You might want to associate the facial expression that used to get you angry with a funny Purim scene. Visualize someone with a clown outfit. Then associate that with the facial expression. As this takes effect you will find yourself smiling or laughing in situations that previously evoked your ire.

If it is a certain tone of voice that gets you angry, repeat to yourself, "From now on, this tone of voice will give me a sense of being serenely empowered." Or, practice associating this tone of voice with a humorous scene. Mentally visualize something you find funny. See the scene in vivid color and detail. Then mentally replay that person's tone of voice and respond to it with your new attitude.

Think back to a specific time when you felt totally calm and relaxed. It could have been on a vacation, or it could have been some time many years ago when you were a young child. As you remember vivid details of a specific scene, you will experience relaxed feelings in the present. Now think of something that triggers anger in the present, yet continue to feel as if you are in the safe, relaxing place you envision.

30. Set an alarm

Set an alarm on a watch, clock, or electronic organizer that will remind you to remain centered and balanced. If you are having an encounter with someone who is likely to provoke your anger, you can set this alarm to go off during the time you will be meeting. With electronic organizers you can type in a message to yourself: "Stay calm" or, "Think before you speak."

31. Prepare with visualizations

Right now in the present you can mentally prepare yourself with visualizations to program your brain to remain calm in future stressful situations. If you anticipate being in a situation that is likely to get you angry, such as another person challenging, berating, or trying to manipulate you, mentally picture the situation in advance. Visualize yourself handling it well (*Reishis Chochmah: Shaar HaAnavah*, ch. 5).

Rabbi Eliyahu Eliezer Dessler also suggested using visualization: "There is a powerful tool that will help you cope with even the most difficult situations. Mentally picture yourself coming across difficult life tests and see yourself coping well with them. Repeat this over and over again in your mind. Formulate for yourself all the concepts and arguments you can use to overcome the difficulty. See yourself feeling great joy in mastering your impulses. When you do this, it will be easier for you to cope in reality with the difficulties that arise. This tool has proven itself many times to be powerfully effective.

"We find that Rabbi Akiva used this technique in order to master feeling so much love for the A–mighty that when he recited *Shema Yisrael* he could see himself sacrificing his life for this love. When, in his old age, the Romans tortured him to death, he was able to calmly recite the *Shema* with complete serenity. His use of mental imagery in advance had so prepared him for this eventuality that for Rabbi Akiva this was not a new experience, but a repetition of something he had done many times before" (*Michtav MeEliyahu*, vol. 4, pp. 252-3).

See yourself feeling serenely empowered regardless of what anyone else says or does. You can visualize worse-case scenarios in which a person acts much worse towards you than he actually would in reality. See yourself remaining calm and relaxed no matter what the person says or does. See and hear yourself talking and acting in ways that are self-respecting and respectful of others.

Rerun the scene a number of times until you feel confident that you can act this way in reality. Since brains work extremely fast, in just a few minutes you can mentally repeat a new pattern hundreds of times. The more repetitions, the more intensely your new reaction will be recorded in your brain cells and the more likely it is that in the future you will react in the new way. The great *ba'alei mussar* would repeat a verse enthusiastically, hundreds, even thousand of times, to internalize and integrate it.

If possible, role play the scene with someone. Ask someone to challenge or insult you in a way that usually provokes your anger. Practice remaining calm and responding in the way you would wish.

32. Focus on your own faults

If you start to become angry at someone for his shortcomings, switch the focus to your own. Think of all the areas in which you need to improve and how far you have to go to utilize your full potential. When the emphasis is on correcting our own faults, those of other people pale in significance (Rabbi Yisrael Salanter; *Tenuas HaMussar*, vol. 1, p. 339).

Keep in mind that we have a natural tendency to notice the same faults in others that we have ourselves. When another person's faults infuriate you, take it as a sign that you may need to correct that very same flaw in yourself.

Since strengths and weaknesses are usually in the same areas of character, you can also ask yourself, "What good qualities does this person have that might be the other side of the coin of these faults?" This will enable you to keep your major focus on what is positive about other people. Do the same with yourself. This will also give you the encouragement to continue to develop your own strengths.

33. Fine yourself

A good way to cure anger is to fine yourself whenever you get angry. The fine might be monetary, or it might be denying yourself some treat. This method is sure to make anyone think twice before becoming angry (*Reishis Chochmah: Shaar HaAnavah*, ch. 3).

The fine might be to buy an expensive gift for the person at whom you became angry. One person overcame his anger at others by inviting his victim to dinner at an expensive restaurant. Some people sleep on the floor for one night, or do something for someone else that they don't feel like doing. You might resolve to write 100 times, "I will remain centered and balanced regardless of what anyone else says and does"; or, "I will speak with self-respect and respect for others at all times."

34. Listen to anger's message

Some people find the following approach very helpful: Speak to your anger. Your anger has a message for you. Listen to what that message is. You can ask, "Anger, what are you trying to tell me?" Listen carefully.

Some of the answers anger can give are:

"I want you to ask this person to speak to you with more respect."

"I want you to figure out a way to get your child to listen to you."

"I want you to be treated fairly."

"I want you to stop injustice."

When you know what your anger is telling you, it will be easier to find effective ways to have your needs met, and then your anger can hibernate quietly and peacefully.

35. Prepare sentences to read

There was once a righteous king who had one major fault: He became angry very easily. To overcome this harmful trait, he wrote three lines on a piece of paper and appointed one of his servants to show it to him whenever he started to become angry. The first line said, "Remember that you are a being who has been created and you are not the Creator." The second line said, "Remember that you are flesh and blood and will eventually be eaten by worms." The third line said, "Remember that there will be no mercy on you in the future if you do not have mercy on others" (*Sefer HaMiddos L'HaMeiri*, p. 239).

Think of some words or sentences you can write for yourself that will help you to calm down or remain silent when challenges arise. Put the message in a place where you will easily be able to reach for it if you become angry.

36. Sing a song

Think of a humorous or inspiring song that you can sing as soon as you start to feel angry. Sing that song the next time you begin to feel angry and see what happens to the anger.

37. Make funny faces in a mirror

When you begin to get angry, run straight to a mirror and start making funny faces at yourself. If this seems silly, which of course it is, realize that it is still a lot healthier than getting angry.

38. Imagine a candid camera

When you are angry, imagine that there is a person standing near you with a candid camera recording all that you say and do. Wouldn't it be much easier to have self-mastery if you knew that what you say and do would be broadcast worldwide? This will give us a greater awareness of the self-mastery that will be ours when we strengthen our awareness of the Divine camera recording all we do and say.

39. Imagine large amounts of money

What if you were to receive a million dollars for talking and acting with nobility and tact even when you are angry? How would you talk and act then?

If you become angry, ask yourself, "How would I talk and act if I were being paid a large amount to speak and act nobly?" If a million dollars isn't enough for you, imagine the amount that would influence you to speak and act nobly. This teaches you the power you have for self-mastery when you are strongly motivated. Keep in mind that emotional self-mastery is worth more than any amount of financial wealth.

This tool can help you cope well with insults. If someone insults you, ask yourself, "If someone were to pay me a million dollars today in case anyone insulted me, how would I feel right now?"

The mashgiach of a major yeshivah related to me how 30 years before he had reframed an insult.

Someone had said something to belittle him and this hurt a lot. He immediately visualized the other person giving him a crisp $100 bill. He made such a strong mental image of this, that when he recalled the incident years later, he remembered only the imagery of that $100 bill. He couldn't remember anything the other person had said.

Isn't this a more pleasant memory than replaying the insult?

40. Imagine a glowing light

When you feel angry, try imagining a glowing white light that soothes and heals flowing through you from head to toe. Feel the white light relaxing each muscle and each cell. Some people prefer the light to be yellow or blue; any color is fine.

41. Visualize a pool of light and energy

Mentally visualize a special pool of shining light and energy that sparkles and shines. See yourself swimming back and forth in this pool of radiant light, feeling calm and relaxed. See yourself becoming more and more energized and invigorated. Take an imaginary swim in this pool whenever you feel stressed or frustrated, and feel yourself becoming infused with new energy.

After practicing a number of times, even 30 seconds of mentally swimming in this pool can be enough to help you feel refreshed. Both before and after difficult encounters visit this magical pool which is accessible wherever you are.

42. Imagine colors

If someone speaks to you in a way that provokes your anger, imagine different colors surrounding the person. The color can be any one you choose: blue, yellow, green, red, pink, brown, violet. See the colors changing from one to another. Find the color or variations of colors that are most effective for you. This frequently makes a difference in the way you feel towards what the person says.

43. Imagine clowns, funny music, a robot

If someone purposely insults you or is saying or doing something spiteful to make you angry, imagine 100 clowns jumping up and down on the person's head. Imagine funny music playing loud and clear. Imagine 50 sparrows singing in harmony on this person's head.

Imagine the person who is getting you angry as a tiny infant, either sleeping peacefully in a crib, or crying tearfully. Or you might want to imagine the person as a robot, or wind-up toy. After doing this, it will be difficult to allow yourself to feel hurt by what he says.

44. Imagine a special bubble

A tool that is helpful for deflecting insults is imagining yourself totally covered by a special plastic protective bubble. This is a bubble that it is impossible for any words to penetrate. Visualize any negative energy coming your way bouncing off.

A similar tool is to imagine that you have a magical shield. Visualize verbal barbs as arrows that bounce off rather than pierce the shield.

A note of caution: These dissociative tools are meant only as techniques to be used in emergencies. They are not meant to be used as a general way of being. As mentioned in previous steps, the goal is to have a positive self-image and to find negotiating approaches to work issues out. If, however, an individual is not open to reason, these techniques can be helpful. Use with moderation.

45. Look at a photograph of yourself

Prepare a photograph of yourself taken at a joyous moment. It can be a picture of you dancing or at a celebration, or perhaps a picture taken during a happy moment. When you look at yourself in that picture, remember as many details as you can in order to re-experience the same feelings you originally felt.

46. Imagine a friend agreeing

When a person is angry, he often calms down right away when a friend takes his side and says, "Yes, you were right and that person was wrong. If I had been in your place I would have been angry too." Try picturing yourself telling someone you respect your version of what happened and hear him agree with you.

Doing this with a real live person can present problems. The details you want to relate may be considered *lashon hara*; you are only relating your version of what happened, so of course it is biased. When it is necessary to consult a third person for practical advice or for his mediating a solution, it could be permissible since the goal is for peace. Consult a *halachic* authority when questions arise.

47. Make an anti-anger tape

Make a first-aid anti-anger tape for yourself to play if you become angry. Some of the things that you might want to add to your tape would be: a pep talk or calming message to yourself; music that puts you in the states you would like to be in; stories or jokes that make you laugh; segments of inspiring talks. You might be able to record a few friends or teachers giving you words of encouragement. Play your tape as soon as you begin to feel angry.

You might want to make two tapes: one to prepare yourself in advance for a potentially difficult encounter, and another that will enable you to release anger and change your frame of mind if you have already become angry.

48. Prayer

Pray for the A–lmighty's help. You can do this formally in *Shemoneh Esrei* and you can do this any time you think about it. Whenever you are in a situation that might provoke your anger, ask your loving Father and powerful King for His guidance and help.

49. Hall of Fame list

Keep a "Hall of Fame" list. I suggest three lists. One, a list of stories of greatness you have heard about others who didn't become angry in difficult situations. The second would be a list of your own personal victories over anger. Remember past victories and keep adding to your list in the present.

The third list is your own virtual reality list. That is, think of potentially ultra-challenging situations and vividly visualize yourself conquering anger in those situations. Perhaps you would see yourself celebrating your magnificent handling of such situations.

Here is one person's first Hall of Fame list:

1. A father bought a new laptop computer. The first day it was in the house, his four-year-old son got curious and tried to carry it to his room. The computer fell and was badly

damaged. The father said right away to his son, "You are more precious to me than this computer."

2. Someone stayed up almost an entire night with a friend in the hospital emergency room. After only two hours of sleep, she woke up just 10 minutes later than usual and was told by someone who didn't know about her kindness, "You are lazy." She smilingly replied, "I guess if I wouldn't have even a drop of laziness in me, I would have woken up earlier."

3. Someone was wearing a new suit at a Shabbos meal. Another person spilled his chicken soup and a good portion of it landed on the new suit. "No problem," said the victim. "The soup has cooled off enough that it didn't burn me. While I didn't get to eat it, it is chicken soup for my soul."

4. A storekeeper in a busy store patiently told two potential customers to take their time after they had changed their minds 12 times about what color to choose.

5. A medical expert was told by someone who didn't realize he was a leader in the field, "I don't think you really know what you're talking about." The expert replied, "Yes, I know enough about this to know that as much as I know, I've just barely begun to scratch the surface."

6. Someone broke off an engagement a week before the wedding. The other party calmly and sincerely said, "I would only want you to marry me if you really wanted to. I wish you much success in finding someone you feel is appropriate for you."

7. Someone advised a friend to invest a large amount of money in a certain stock. The value of that stock plunged and almost the entire investment was lost. The next time the investor met his friend, he said, "Thank you for giving me the advice you thought best. The financial loss got me in touch with how being joyous about being alive is the only secure way of guaranteeing consistent happiness."

Developing the Traits That Will Free You From Anger

Step 7

Develop the Traits That Will Free You From Anger

Whatever we pay attention to tends to become reinforced. It is wise, therefore, to keep our major focus not on anger, but on developing the positive qualities that are incompatible with anger. If we work at increasing our patience, feeling unconditional love and compassion, being centered and balanced, gaining self-mastery, acquiring humility, achieving serenity, developing calm persistence, living with joy and enthusiasm, growing in serene empowerment, and feeling self-respect and respect for others — we will keep anger at bay.

Some people and situations seem to bring out the best in us, others don't. As long as we can act according to a positive trait *even once,* and even if only for a limited period of time, this serves as proof that we have within ourselves the ability to act that way. We may not always be able to maintain our loftiest standards in all situations, but if we concentrate on increasing the number of times we do, we will find it increasingly easy.

To access a computer file, we enter the name of that file and the file appears on our computer screen. Our brains operate in a similar manner. By thinking or saying a certain word we automatically call up our mental files associated with that word. We can use this information about how the brain works to consciously create mental files of the character traits to which we want easy access. When we act in a way consistent with a positive trait we wish to develop, we can say the name of that trait. That way, our action will be "filed" under the heading of that word. Then the next time we want to access that trait, we can say the word and call up our past experiences and emotions at will.

A good way to internalize the positive qualities highlighted in this chapter is to first read the entire chapter, and then to reread one section a day for ten days. Repeat this cycle at least five times. At the same time, get into the habit of repeating the names of the character traits mentioned here. You might want to do this as a song, or as a form of autosuggestion or meditation. Particularly when you feel yourself beginning to get angry, repeat these names. You will find your state changing to a more positive one, and, over time, the admirable traits will become more and more a part of you. After a while, just by mentioning these qualities you will be able to enter that specific frame of mind.

1. Patience

The first quality is patience. Impatience is a prime cause of anger, and patience is the solution. What is patience? It is waiting peacefully and calmly. In a way, learning patience is like learning how to float. You need to learn to do nothing. You let go of tension and just wait. At times you might need the patience to repeat something again and again; at other times, you need patience to wait before you speak. Each act of patience makes you a more patient person.

R' Shlomo Wolbe, one of the great *mussar* personalities of our time, wrote that he advises students who work on anger to work on increasing their patience and acceptance. He cites Rabbi Simchah Zissel of Kelm who said that the trait of "*savlanut*" is the root of all positive qualities. Patience and acceptance are the foundations of good interpersonal relationships. Without patience and acceptance, angry interchanges are bound to arise. As Rabbi Wolbe says, "When people share the same room and lack "*savlanut*" the room will be Gehinnom. People who eat at the same table and lack this trait, will need to flee from the table" (*Alai Shur*, vol. 2, pp. 213-24).

R' Wolbe also tells students that they need to be patient and accepting towards themselves as well. Self-improvement requires patience. Without patience for ourselves, we easily become discouraged and give up. We must remind ourselves that we are only responsible for doing what is in our power to do. Of course, it is wrong to allow patience with oneself to turn into laziness or apathy. One must continue working on himself and continue to strengthen himself, and then he will be successful (ibid., pp. 216-7).

The Chofetz Chaim elaborated on how patience, which comes from accepting the A-mighty's will, frees a person from feeling a need to speak against others (*Shemiras HaLashon: Shaar HaTevunah*, ch. 8).

When other people are too slow, when they interrupt again and again or ask endless questions, when someone keeps us waiting — in the absence of patience, all these provoke anger. With patience, they are elevating challenges. The A-mighty sends us many opportunities throughout each day to help us continue developing our patience.

It might be very hard to wait for someone. But what if the reward were a week's salary for every hour waited? Or more. Moshe's sister Miriam waited patiently for her infant brother and received a reward many times greater than the amount of time she waited, when years later in the Wilderness the entire Jewish people waited for her for an entire week. The lesson we learn from Miriam is that it pays to wait. If you wait for another human being, your Father, your King, will be the One to reward you.

> I used to be very impatient, which led to a lot of frustration and anger. Then one day I had to interact with two very wealthy people. The first one was extremely impatient and kept repeating, "Time is money." He couldn't sit still and was annoyed: that he didn't get his coffee fast enough; that the computer was down for a few minutes; that a telephone number was busy; that he couldn't get the exact flight he wanted right then and would have to call back to see if there was a cancellation. He told me that since he deals with large amounts of money, he has a valid reason for constantly being so impatient. In my opinion, his money seemed to be causing him more irritation than pleasure.
>
> A few hours later, I met another equally wealthy person. He was totally calm and patient. He kept saying, "Being calm is worth more to me than anything

money can buy." No matter what went wrong, he worked patiently at finding solutions. He was pleasantly relaxed with all of his staff members and I could see and feel how much they enjoyed working for him. He told me that since he deals with large amounts of money, he has a valid reason for being calm. He also said that a loss here or there doesn't really make any practical difference in his life. Moreover, he feels that being patient saves him a lot of money in the long run.

Seeing these opposite types, both in the same financial bracket, helped me to see that being patient or impatient has nothing to do with external factors. I realized that people can use anything to justify their impatience. From then on I decided to use the patient person as my model.

When my children were not moving as fast as I would have liked them to, I used to feel impatient. I felt that I was wasting my time. Now I realize that this waiting time is time well spent, because I am building up my patience and creating a better personality.

I once watched a worker at an information booth at a trade fair. Throughout the morning, hundreds of people asked him how to get from one exhibit to another. Again and again, he calmly repeated himself. I decided to ask him how he remained so calm.

He told me, "Each time I give someone instructions, I am doing him a favor. There is no difference between doing hundreds of different acts of kindness or doing the same thing over and over again. Each time I can help someone I feel good about it."

When I told this to someone who becomes impatient after repeating instructions only a few times, he said, "That may very well be, but that person gets paid to repeat himself."

"You're right," I agreed. "It's all a question of motivation. The person who gets impatient isn't motivated."

2. Unconditional love and compassion

The quality of unconditional love and compassion enables us to overlook trivial errors and mistakes. It also enables us to see the situation from the other person's point of view, even if we don't agree with him.

How do we develop this unconditional love for other people? By having a good eye, "*ayin tovah*" which means seeing their positive qualities and virtues. In this way we follow in the ways of our forefather Avraham (*Pirkei Avos*, ch. 5), keeping the positive traits, accomplishments, and good deeds of the people with whom we interact uppermost in our mind. Of course, everyone has faults. But when we make it a top priority to see the good in people, searching for their strong points, we automatically feel more admiration and respect for them, and this in turn eliminates anger.

"When someone feels an inner hatred towards another person," explains the Vilna Gaon, "even a minor offense can arouse feelings of animosity. Even though what has actually occurred right now could be trivial, the previous negative feelings create quarrels. But when someone feels love for another person, he is able to forgive whatever the other person does" (*Beur HaGra* to *Mishlei* 10:12).

Most people would love to be able to win friends and influence people, and there have been many books written on the subject and much advice given. Yet a single statement by Shlomo HaMelech says it all: "Just as water reflects a face, so too does the heart of one person reflect that of another" (*Mishlei* 27:19). When we feel positively towards people, they reciprocate. We then live in a pleasanter world and feel less provocation for anger. This is not merely a tool, but a major approach to relating to others. Not only will unconditional love towards others prevent anger, but it will enhance every interaction we have. It is one of the most important skills to master.

Rabbi Yeruchom Levovitz speaks of another dimension of love for our fellow man:

> The root cause of all negative behavior towards others is *sinas chinam,* feelings of dislike towards others. If you violate the prohibition against hating others in your heart, you can end up harming people in many ways. Someone who hates another person carries within himself the cause that can ultimately even lead to murder.
>
> For this reason it is so important to develop the attribute of feeling love for other people, since this generates all forms of positive actions and behaviors. When you plant a small seed, a giant tree bearing delicious fruit will grow. The seed of love for other people is a cause whose effect is the everlasting bliss of the afterlife. Our forefather Avraham lived with this reality and therefore felt this state of bliss whenever he did acts of *chesed* for others (*Da'as Chochmah U'Mussar,* vol. 1, pp. 236-7).

The Chazon Ish writes about love and anger:

> A person who constantly works on himself and has reached a proper level of love for other people will

not feel hurt or angered by what others say to him, for love has the ability to cancel all wrongdoing. Although he personally will be meticulously careful to show respect to everyone, he realizes that the majority of people have not perfected their character traits and he does not have excessive expectations of others. Such an elevated person will not have to constrain himself not to feel anger, for he is in a constant state of happiness (*Emunah U'Bitachon* 1:11 and 15).

When you have unconditional love and compassion for someone, you think of what you can say or do that would help him, and you avoid saying and doing things that would harm that person or cause pain and distress. Since anger causes so much pain to others, you do all you can to conquer it.

Viewing the actions of others with compassion prevents much anger. Instead of being angry at someone for not acting the way he should, you feel compassionate care and concern. When you speak to someone about making changes, your motivation is compassion and your approach will be guided by what would be the most compassionate thing to say or do.

Whenever we have compassion for someone, we emulate our Creator: "Just as G-d is merciful and compassionate, we too should be merciful and compassionate" (Shabbos 133b). Our compassion towards other people merits that measure for measure, our Father, our King, will be compassionate towards us. The more difficult it is for us to be compassionate, the greater we become for talking and acting in ways that are consistent with this quality.

Rabbi Naftali Amsterdam once asked his teacher Rabbi Yisrael Salanter, "What is the antidote for anger?" Rabbi

Yisrael Salanter replied, "When a person works on mastering the quality of constantly doing acts of kindness for others, this will free him from anger" (*MiMayanosos HaNetzach, Pirkei Avos*, p. 270).

Rabbi Eliyahu Dessler also commented on this concept:

> Love comes from giving to someone. When you do altruistic acts of kindness, you are giving the other person part of yourself and will therefore feel love for the recipient of your acts of kindness because you will find yourself included in his being. You will feel love for him since you identify with him. Just as you love yourself, so too will you love him.
>
> The ultimate level to strive for is to do so many acts of kindness that even if someone wrongs you, you will view it as if your right hand accidentally cut your left hand (see *Yerushalmi, Nedarim* 9:4). Although you will try to prevent this from happening, you will not take revenge on your own hand. This is the love we should have for our fellow man: the same level of love as we have for ourselves (*Michtav MeEliyahu,* vol. 3, pp. 89-90).

Even when we do need to confront someone, there is a major difference between confronting that person with love and compassion, and confronting him with anger. Your sincere feelings of love and concern will be reflected back to you, which will, in turn, give you less cause for anger.

Rabbi Avraham Yellin (*Erech Apayim*) wrote that he frequently held himself back from reacting with anger when he was wronged. He made a special effort to be kind and friendly to those people who had wronged him. Because he acted friendly to them, they responded in kind and became close friends. Eventually they rectified the harm they had caused. He wrote: "If I would not have reacted with patience, I would have lost all the acts of kindness those persons later did for me.

A butcher once became enraged at Rabbi Chaim of Volozhin for declaring his meat *treif.* In his anger, he devised a scheme to murder the Rabbi. On a pretext, he had the Rabbi travel with him on a lonely road. In the middle of the way, the butcher took out his sharp knife and made a motion to kill the Rabbi.

At first the Rabbi pleaded with the butcher to have compassion on him. But his pleas were to no avail. When the Rabbi saw that nothing he could say would make a difference, he started to mentally focus on all of the positive qualities and attributes of the butcher. Suddenly there was an amazing transformation. In the middle of the Rabbi's thinking about the virtues of the butcher, the butcher changed his mind. With a strong feeling of love and with tears in his eyes, the butcher kissed the Rabbi and begged his forgiveness (Rabbi Chaim Zaitchyk, *Maayanai HaChaim*, vol. 3, p. 191).

A man who has been married for 10 years explains how developing compassion has enabled him to overcome a pattern of many years of frustration.

My wife would ask me for my opinion on things and then would change her mind. She would waver back and forth and this used to infuriate me. Then I was advised to view the pattern compassionately from my wife's point of view.

She suffered a lot of distress from her difficulty in making decisions. When she was indecisive, she felt confused. She grew up with fear of making mistakes.

I decided to be compassionate and understanding. I now realize that it's pretty common to go back and forth before coming to a conclusion. I notice that I do it myself, too. Now I am able to say, "I realize that you have mixed emotions about this. It's okay for you to take the time to sort them out."

3. Centered and balanced

Being centered and balanced means that your mind is clear and you are in an emotionally balanced state. Your center is right in front of you and you are in control over what you say and do.

A person who gets angry allows external factors to control him. When anger takes over, what you say and do will not come from a balanced place.

Picture in your mind what you will be like when you are centered and balanced. See yourself talking and acting centered and balanced. Whenever you feel that you are losing control, repeat to yourself, "centered and balanced," and feel yourself gaining greater control over your thoughts and emotions.

Visualize yourself being centered and balanced in the future. Think of specific situations that are likely to arise in the future and mentally picture yourself being centered and balanced in those situations. Hear the way you will talk and see the way you will look. Be prepared to remain centered and balanced regardless of what anyone says to you.

Think of situations in the past when being centered and balanced would have helped you handle them better. Think of what tone of voice or what kinds of statements have thrown you off balance before. Mentally rerun those scenes seeing yourself being centered and balanced. This will now be a resource for the future.

Think of a person who can serve as a role model for being "centered and balanced." Mirror or model that person and feel yourself becoming more and more centered and balanced.

As you repeat the words, "centered and balanced," feel yourself becoming more centered and balanced. Repeat this throughout the day.

> *When I first heard about the state of being centered and balanced, I found it difficult to understand. What exactly was I supposed to do? I thought about this for a while and realized that this was not a concept or an idea that one can verbally explain. Rather, it was a certain feeling that I could experience. I began to be aware of the times when I started to feel off-balance. I repeated the words, "centered and balanced," and felt myself like a ship in the ocean. When the ship was blown to the right or left and was ready to topple over, being centered and balanced brought it back to the middle. This metaphor has been very helpful for me.*

4. Self-mastery

"The powerful person is one who has mastery over his impulses" (*Pirkei Avos* 4:1). Our Sages have told us that each one of us is obligated to say, "When will my deeds reach the deeds of my forefathers, Avraham, Yitzchak, and Yaakov?" This shows that we have the ability to reach greatness (*Michtav MeEliyahu*, vol. 4, p. 23). All greatness is achieved through self-mastery — control over actions, words, and thought. A person who holds the reins to his own impulses will steer clear of anger and avoid its pitfalls, especially when he knows there are smoother, faster routes to get him where he wants to go.

> When I kept thinking about how often I said things I shouldn't have said and took actions I shouldn't have taken, I became discouraged. Then I started to keep a self-mastery journal. Every time I refrained from doing something that I felt an impulse to do, I wrote it down. Every time I did something I knew I should do but I didn't feel like doing, I added the incident to my self-mastery journal. Seeing the victory list adding up gave me the motivation to increase my self-control and self-discipline.

5. Humility

Humility is the awareness that everything we have is a gift from the Creator. It is also the awareness of the vastness of the universe and human limitations. Humility is the awareness that we are fallible and can make mistakes. Humility is the awareness that there are other people on the planet and that we must take their needs and feelings into consideration.

"Arrogance springs from blindness," writes Rabbi Moshe Chaim Luzzatto. "The only way a person can be arrogant is for him to be unaware of his faults and shortcomings. If he takes an honest look at himself, he will automatically overcome inner conceit and all of its many consequences" (Mesillas Yesharim, ch. 11).

Humility is freedom. Humility frees us from all the problems caused by conceit and arrogance. Humility enables us to have self-esteem that is independent of what anyone else says, does, or thinks. Humility frees us from the demand to control others. Humility frees us from anger. "Humility eliminates many of life's problems. A humble person will not be bothered by life's circumstances and will not envy others for what they have. It is very pleasant to be in the presence of a humble person, therefore people will invariably like him. He will not become angry nor quarrel with others. All of his interactions with other people will be serene and tranquil. Fortunate is the person who has acquired this attribute ...

"True humility must come from an inner attitude of humility; otherwise it is not humility. Someone who only tries to act as if he were humble without truly feeling that way, will have a false humility. Instead of being a virtue, this is a fault" (*Mesillas Yesharim*, ch. 22).

Think of a great person you have met, heard of, or read about who is the personification of greatness and humility combined. Let that person serve as a role model for you.

> *I am a doctor in a busy hospital. I used to be impatient with both staff and patients. What I was doing was so important that I did not feel I needed to worry about other people's feelings. If someone's life needed to be saved, I was there — and that's much more important than worrying about how you speak to people.*
>
> *But then I had a heart attack while traveling in a foreign country. The people in the hospital there didn't know me and treated me like everyone else. It was a very humbling experience. I felt weak and helpless. I saw who reacted to my requests with patience, and who didn't. I realized that I was a frail mortal like every other human being. When I recovered and returned to my practice, I was a different person. I learned humility the hard way.*

Anytime someone didn't treat me with the honor I felt I deserved, I got very angry. Even when someone did show me respect, if I didn't think it was sufficient, I felt long-lasting resentment. I never dreamed of telling anyone that they should treat me with greater honor, since that would be perceived as arrogance.

Once when I was fuming over a certain slight to my honor, it hit me that I was needlessly causing myself an excessive amount of pain. I saw that I was guilty of a form of idolatry. In a way, I wanted people to worship me. I began thinking about Hashem and His creation. This gave me a sense both of awe and humility. I realized that viewing myself as created in the Creator's image would give me true good feelings about myself and I didn't need the honor of anyone else to feel important.

I used to get angry whenever someone would tell me something that I felt was obvious or simple. I tried to figure out the root cause of this anger. When thinking about how humility frees us from anger, I realized that because of a lack of humility I didn't want anyone to think for a moment that I didn't already know what they were telling me. I now utilize such incidents as an opportunity to increase my humility. I also realize that most people are not thinking that I don't know something and am therefore stupid. They are either trying to be helpful or this is their standard pattern of explaining things.

6. Serenity

Inner serenity is one of the most valuable qualities that a person can master. A serene person is free from stress, tension, anxiety, and anger (*Da'as Chochmah U'Mussar*, vol. 3, p. 169). When we are serene, our mind is clearer. This helps us think of the best thing to say or do in any given situation. In a serene state, it becomes easier to remain silent when silence is called for.

On a day we would call serene, the atmosphere is clear. The sky is blue and everyone feels their best. The inner state of serenity is the mental equivalent of a serene day. When you are serene, you are totally calm and your mind is clear, like an infant whose needs have been met.

When you experience serenity regularly, you have peace of mind. Rabbi Simchah Zissel of Kelm said, "Peace of mind is one of the greatest pleasures a person can have. Conversely, lack of peace of mind can make one's life constant torture" (*Chochmah UMussar*, vol. 1, p. 255). In the words of Rabbi Shlomo Wolbe, "A person who has gained peace of mind has gained everything. To obtain peace of mind you need to be at peace with the people in your environment. You need to be at peace with yourself, with your emotions and desires. Furthermore, you need to be at peace with your Creator" (*Alai Shur*, vol. 1, p. 195).

Appreciate each moment of peace of mind; it is a great treasure. By experiencing this for a short time, you will be able to learn to increase it. Practice peace of mind when you have to wait in a line, when you have to wait for another person, when you are traveling and when you are walking. Much of the time that is spent on learning how to be an expert worrier can be used more profitably in learning how to be an expert at peace of mind and serenity.

Bitachon, total trust in the love and power of our Father, our King, equals serenity. When we experience a sense of inner bitachon, we feel that our needs are taken care of (see *Chovos HaLevavos: Shaar HaBitachon*). For this reason, prayer, when we are closest to Hashem, is the best time to increase our level of serenity.

Total acceptance of the A-mighty's will leads to a life of serenity (*Chovos HaLevavos*, ibid.). As Rabbi Mordechai of Lechovitz used to say: "If things don't go the way you wish, wish them to go the way they are" (*MiGedolai HaTorah VeHaChassidus*, vol. 20, p. 107)

> Having *bitachon*, which will bring you peace of mind, should not be confused with a fatalistic attitude towards life. It does not mean you should sit back and refrain from taking action for your welfare. Rather, it means that even when you do take action, you realize that the ultimate outcome of what you do is up to the A-mighty, and you accept His will. Therefore, you have peace of mind regardless of the outcome. Moreover, while you take action, you will not panic. You do what is necessary under the circumstances, but you do not react with desperation (*Da'as Chochmah U'Mussar*, vol. 1, p. 10).
>
> The essence of Shabbos is peace of mind and serenity (*Da'as Chochmah U'Mussar*, vol. 2, p. 204). The rest we have on Shabbos is not merely rest from work on that day alone. Rather, Shabbos has the ability to give us peace of mind every day of the week (Rabbi Eliyahu Meir Bloch; *Shiurei Da'as*, p. 109).

> *Whenever I used to hear the word "serenity," I thought that only rare individuals could really feel serene. I have to travel a lot and interact with many people. How is it possible for someone like me to be serene? Then I saw someone who worked in the complaint department of a large company. People would come in*

angry and although he wasn't to blame, many would
scream, yell, and insult him. He remained calm and
relaxed regardless of what anyone said to him.

I asked him how he was able to stay so calm. He
was one of the most serene people I ever met. This is
what he told me.

"When I took this job, I knew that I would be the
brunt of people's anger. I decided that I wouldn't take
it personally. The people that come in are frequently
very frustrated. By staying calm and giving everyone
a fair hearing, I see how the people who walk in
eventually calm down. I really enjoy this job since I
view what I do as an act of kindness. If someone
comes in very angry, I view him as if he were speak-
ing on a distant screen and I stay calm."

7. Calm persistence

What is the probability of encountering obstacles, hur-
dles, and interruptions when you are on your way to meet
an important goal? Usually, the chances are 100 percent.
There will always be obstacles. Some people give up; others
persist — but they get angry.

Calm persistence is the ability to keep going until you
reach your goal — and to do this calmly. Being persistent
means not giving up too early. It means being willing to
repeat the same message over and over again as many times
as necessary.

A person who is calmly persistent demonstrates that he
will keep on trying until he succeeds. His calmness shows
that he is serious about his intentions and will not allow
himself to be sidetracked.

A person who gets angry shows that he doesn't have
patience. An adversary can easily use this to his advantage.

When you persist calmly, your voice stays calm whether you need to repeat your position five times or 50 times. You might need to find different approaches each time. But when you have mastered calm persistence, you will keep on going until you reach your goal or decide that for the moment it is better to change your goal.

> *I was visiting a friend who told his son to stop playing and take a bath. The boy was in the middle of a game and wasn't in a rush. The father patiently repeated to his son, "It's time to take a bath now." Finally after a number of repetitions, the son said, "All right. I'm going." In many homes this could have been an angry scene. But I witnessed the success of calm persistence.*

> *Hearing about calm persistence has benefited me greatly. I used to make a request once or twice and if the person didn't meet my request, I gave up. I would frequently feel very angry when I felt that what I had asked for was reasonable and the person didn't have a valid reason for not doing it. I resolved to experiment with calm persistence. In situations that in the past would have seen me throwing up my hands in frustration, I now calmly and patiently repeated my request. Although I still wasn't always successful, I frequently was. Moreover, acting in this way made me feel better even when I didn't get the outcome I wanted.*

8. Joy and enthusiasm

A person who is sincerely joyous and enthusiastic about life won't lose his temper as frequently as someone who isn't. The more joyous and enthusiastic you are, the less anger you will experience. A person who is joyous and enthusiastic about mitzvos will intensely appreciate the Torah he learns, the *chesed* he does, and his ability to communicate with his Creator through prayer. He will feel joy that he is working on the mitzvah of walking in the A–mighty's ways, which is the mitzvah to develop our character traits. All efforts to conquer anger are part of this mitzvah and its joy.

How does a person master joy and enthusiasm?

Rabbi Simchah Zissel of Kelm advised his students: "Internalize the awareness that the life the Creator has bestowed upon you is a magnificent present. This in itself will make you feel great joy" (*Chochmah U'Mussar,* vol. 1, p. 192). When you master the ability to feel joy for being alive, you will realize that most things that create anger are minor and trivial (see *Eichah* 3:39; *Kiddushin* 80b).

The Vilna Gaon comments that "the person with a 'good heart' is like a person who is constantly having parties ... When a person is at a party and his spirits are elevated from drinking wine, he feels even better off than a wealthy king. After the effects of the wine wear off, however, he is no longer in that same happy frame of mind. But a person who has mastered the attribute of appreciating what he has, is constantly in as emotionally elevated a state as an inebriated person during the height of a party" (*Beur HaGra* to *Mishlei* 15:15).

Become a master at finding positive reframes for the events and situations that used to provoke your anger. Ask yourself, "What is positive about what is happening? How can I develop my *middos* because of what is happening?"

Every situation that used to provoke your anger will either teach you that you still need to devote more time and effort into conquering anger or else that you are making progress.

Either feel joy that you are improving or feel joy that you have gained the awareness that you need to improve even more. By loving this criticism (no. 35 of the "48 Tools To Acquire Torah" listed in *Pirkei Avos,* ch. 6) you will either feel joy now or feel joy when you see your progress.

The *Mesillas Yesharim* (chs. 7 and 23) states an important principle about how we can increase our enthusiasm even when we don't spontaneously feel enthusiastic: Act externally as if you were enthusiastic, and you will experience enthusiasm.

> *I heard a story that changed my life. Someone told me about a man who worked in a toll booth in San Francisco. This man used to play loud music, sing and dance while he worked. Whenever someone would ask him what he was doing, he would reply, "I am having a party. And I'm even getting paid for it."*
>
> *After hearing this story, I began to notice other people, people whose lives seemed no different from mine, yet who allowed themselves to experience joy regularly. I now sing happy songs to myself and find that my entire way of relating to other people has improved.*

> *I used to complain a lot about things not being the way I wanted them. Then I heard about a person who went through great deprivation in childhood. This person told me that as long as she has food, clothing, and a pleasant place to live, she feels like a queen in a palace. I've decided to adopt this attitude and make it mine.*

I met a person who received training in the U.S. Marines. He had an instructor who would repeat the word "enthusiasm" over and over again with great fervor. This would fill the entire room with enthusiasm as the recruits carried out tasks not necessarily associated with enthusiasm.

As the person told me the story, he told it to me with great enthusiasm. I repeated the story and noticed that whenever I said it over, I felt tremendous enthusiasm. Now I see that I have the ability to turn on enthusiasm at will. My prayers have become much more enthusiastic ever since I realized this.

I used to blame other people for my unhappiness. "If only they would be more considerate of me and my feelings and needs, then I would be happy," I'd tell myself. When I shared my thoughts with an older person, he told me, "How can you blame others for not making you happy, when you are not making yourself happy?! Be resolved to be your own best friend. Increase your level of appreciation and gratitude. Throughout the day you have hundreds of opportunities to experience this. Consciously practice and in a relatively short time you will find your normal state one of happiness."

What he said to me made sense. I made an effort to repeat, "I am grateful for ..." "I appreciate ..." "I like ..." This has made a major impact on my life.

9. Serene empowerment

Feeling a sense of helplessness leads to frustration and anger. On the other hand, a person who aggressively tries to get people to do what he wants will be met with resistance. This will make him mad and infuriate the person with whom he interacts. Serene empowerment avoids both helplessness and aggression. It is a calm, peaceful feeling of inner strength. Serenity alone is a quieter state, while serene empowerment is necessary when we need to take action. When we want to negotiate, influence, or motivate another person, being in a state of serene empowerment enables us to think, talk, and act at our best. The approaches we use when we are in this state will be more acceptable to the people with whom we interact. When we feel serenely empowered, our tone of voice reflects both an inner calm and at the same time conveys confidence and determination.

A person who feels serene empowerment focuses on reaching his or her goals, but remains serene even if there are many obstacles.

> *I mistakenly thought that if I showed others I was angry I was giving a message of power. After hearing about "serene empowerment," I realized that anger is a message of weakness and expresses loss of control. Just repeating the words "serene empowerment" gives me a feeling of self-control. Recently I was told by people whom I had previously tried to intimidate with anger that they now take me more seriously than they did before. Whenever I became angry, they knew I would feel guilty about losing my temper and this gave them an advantage over me. When I feel serenely empowered, I feel an inner strength independent of how others respond. Now I have a double advantage: I am listened to more frequently and when I am not, I still have an empowered feeling.*

10. Self-Respect and respect for others

True self-respect is when we respect ourselves so much that nothing anyone says or does can take this away. Getting angry at someone for not treating us with respect demonstrates weak self-respect; we still need the respect of other people to feel good about ourselves. Total self-respect means that you respect yourself too much to allow anger to control you. Talking and acting with anger is not acting in a way that is self-respecting.

"Just as a person needs to believe in the Creator," writes Rabbi Tzadok HaKohen, "so too does he need to believe in himself" (*Tzidkas HaTzadik,* no. 154). That is, we need to believe that our soul comes from the Creator and that He cares about what we do. Part of this belief in ourselves is the belief that we have the ability to elevate ourselves through the life situations that are sent our way.

The other half of this is having respect for others. Increase your awareness that each and every person you speak to is created in the image of our Father, our King. Even if someone is angry, he will speak to a powerful King with respect. He will also speak to the King's children in the King's presence with respect. When you feel sincere respect for others, most people reciprocate and appreciate you. This will eliminate many of the things they say and do that lead to your becoming angry.

> I used to react with angry rages when others didn't listen to me. I started to think about why I became so angry and realized it was because their failure to listen to me made me feel inferior. I wanted respect, and not being listened to was disrespectful to me. When I viewed my anger objectively, I realized that my acting like a wild man was more disrespectful to myself than

anything anyone else could do to me. I resolved that if I wanted respect from others, my focus would have to be in first respecting myself. This gave me the strength to have greater control and eventually I did gain more respect from others than I had before.

I heard the story of how Rabbi Nosson Tzvi Finkel, Rosh Yeshivah of the Slobodka Yeshivah, wouldn't stick out his tongue even if a doctor asked him to. He just couldn't treat another human being without respect. Another story I heard is how Rabbi Aharon Kotler, the Rosh Yeshivah of Lakewood, would tell drivers who took him past toll booths on highways always to go to a toll booth with a human being rather than one with a machine. It wasn't respect to humanity to pass up a human for a machine. While I realized that both stories reflected the greatness of these Torah giants and that for a regular person like myself they were beyond my level, I still became more committed to be very careful about how I spoke to anyone when I felt frustrated or angry. I realized that the more difficult it was for me to speak with respect, the greater respect I was showing to my Father, my King, by being respectful to His children.

Summary

Keep your main focus on mastering the traits, qualities, and states that you want. When you think about not being angry, immediately think of what state you would prefer to be in. Increase your level of joy, patience, unconditional love, being centered and balanced, being serenely empowered and any other trait or state that will enhance your life. The ultimate trait and state to master is ahavas Hashem, love of our Father, our King. When you are full of ahavas Hashem, you will be free from anger. Reflect on what your life will be like as you continually develop this attribute, raising yourself spiritually and connecting with your Creator.

Step 8

Condition Your Mind

Step 8

Condition Your Mind

There are two particular times of day when our minds are especially receptive: in the morning when we wake up, and right before we go to sleep. We can use these times to gain greater control over anger, or any other trait.

This chapter of the book is divided into two sections: a morning conditioning pattern, and a pre-sleep conditioning pattern. Both are reviews of the ideas offered in this book, presented as instructions for conditioning the brain, because just knowing the ideas is not sufficient for overcoming strong feelings of anger. What you read below are instructions for reconditioning your brain. Every repetition of these concepts strengthens the neural pathways and makes these ideas more of an integral part of you. By reading these sections regularly for 30 days, you will find that you automatically have greater control over anger. You may want to record these sections and listen to the tape repeatedly.

The effectiveness of this method comes from daily repetition. In the beginning, just read the words without worrying about how much you are internalizing what you read. Consistent repetition will enable your brain to spontaneously integrate the messages that you are reading.

Some people constantly scrutinize themselves as they read, measuring what they have read against their present reality. While this is often a good way to read, it is not appropriate for this section because it can create tension. Try to read these programs in a calm tone of voice; they will be more effective that way. The more relaxed you are, the deeper these ideas will penetrate your subconscious. However, just reading them over and over again will be helpful even if you aren't as relaxed yet as you would like to be.

You might not have the time to read the entire morning program each morning. Someone who loses his temper frequently should make this such a high priority that he will be able to find the time. The amount of time it takes to read this daily will be much less of an investment than the time lost because of anger. You will end up gaining more time by conquering anger. You may even extend your life.

If, nevertheless, it isn't possible to read this in the morning, then do so in the afternoon or evening. You might find it beneficial to divide the material and read for two or three minutes every hour. After reading this enough times, just glancing over it will be sufficient.

Find the paragraphs that speak to you the most and read them regularly. Even reading a small part of this each day will have a positive effect. The main thing is to consistently condition your brain.

A. Part One: Before-sleep program

Right before going to sleep is a wonderfully effective time for integrating and internalizing ideas. As you sleep, these ideas will reverberate in your subconscious mind.

Read this program before you fall asleep each night for at least 30 days. You will find that you are calmer and more relaxed by day.

Right now allow yourself to relax. Imagine what it would feel like to be pleasantly sleepy and tired. Imagine what it would feel like to let go of all anger, frustration, tension, and stress. Let yourself release these feelings and in their place feel calmer and more relaxed.

Say to yourself, "I now release all stress, tension, and anger. I allow myself to feel more and more relaxed with each breath I take."

As you continue to breathe now, continue to allow all tension and stress to leave every muscle and every cell of your body. Each time you breathe, you take in life-giving oxygen. Together with this, you are clearing your mind and are more ready to listen to ideas that will enhance your life.

Keep breathing slowly and deeply, feeling more and more relaxed with each breath.

Hear an inner voice telling you, "It's all right now to let go and become deeply and profoundly relaxed." Repeat it until you feel it.

Imagine being in the most restful place on earth. Imagine in vivid detail what the entire scene would look like. Imagine what it would feel like being there. Imagine the most soothing and pleasant music playing in the background as you are becoming more and more relaxed every time you breathe.

If you don't yet imagine that you are in a restful place, pretend that you could imagine being there and allow yourself to relax more and more every time you breathe.

The quality of your life is dependent on the states that you experience each and every day. Tomorrow allow yourself to be free from the un-resourceful state of anger by creating a magnificent inner world.

Imagine what your life will be like when on an ongoing basis you experience patience, joy and enthusiasm for life, serenity, serene empowerment, calm persistence, being centered and balanced, unconditional love and compassion, humility, self-mastery, self-respect and respect for others.

Visualize yourself talking and acting in ways that are consistent with these qualities.

Think of role models you have met or heard of for each quality. As you sleep tonight, your brain will access memories of these role models and this will make it easier for you to mirror and model those qualities tomorrow and in the future.

Feel patience becoming more and more a part of you. Every time you have ever been patient, it has been stored in the vast library of your brain. As you sleep, your brain will remember times and moments when you were patient. Knowing what it is like to be patient, tomorrow you will find it easier to remain patient for longer amounts of time. Allow yourself to become deeper and deeper relaxed with each breath.

Feel unconditional love and compassion becoming more and more a part of you. Feeling unconditional love for others will free you from anger. Every time you have ever experienced love and compassion it has been stored in the vast library of your brain. Tomorrow you will find it easier to access the state of unconditional love and compassion. Imagine how your relationships with others will be enhanced by your interacting with love and compassion. Allow yourself to become deeper and deeper relaxed with each breath.

Feel humility becoming more and more a part of you. Experience all of your positive qualities as gifts from the Creator. Appreciate them and at the same time view them with humility. This will free you from anger and from all the problems caused by arrogance and conceit. Allow yourself to become deeper and deeper relaxed with each breath.

As you are feeling more and more relaxed, imagine that your brain has suddenly been given special powers. Your brain has been given the ability to put you into the state of your choice at any given time.

Imagine yourself handling difficulties, arguments, and conflicts in a calm and relaxed manner. See yourself remaining in a peaceful state regardless of what anyone says to you.

Tomorrow, you will have a greater ability to be an objective observer if someone says or does things that used to get you angry. By being an objective observer you will be able to remain centered and balanced while you observe the words and actions of any person you encounter. This will enable you to think more clearly about the best course of action in any situation.

See yourself remaining silent, when remaining silent is the wisest thing to do. See yourself feeling wonderfully serene and peaceful as you are able to remain silent. See yourself feeling totally empowered by your inner strength to remain silent.

As you are becoming even more relaxed with each breath you take, become aware of the type of situations that used to get you angry, and now see yourself remaining in a state of tranquility, a state of inner harmony and peace as you see yourself talking and acting calmly and serenely.

As you make pictures in your mind about how you wish to act tomorrow, those pictures will become more and more of your everyday reality. In your brain, create new realities for yourself. And tomorrow you will be able to speak and talk with greater amounts of patience, joy and enthusiasm for life, serene empowerment, and calm persistence.

See yourself talking with self-respect and respect for others to someone you used to find difficult. See yourself radiating with inner joy as you feel the great success in handling difficult situations with ease. It is your mind, and since it's yours, you can create the world you wish for yourself.

See yourself being cheerful and friendly to others. See others appreciating your cheerfulness and friendliness and responding to you in ways that you appreciate.

Right now you can mentally create a large crowd cheering for you and showing their intense admiration for your victory over your anger. The crowd cheering you enables you to have greater and greater amounts of self-mastery. Since it's your mind, the crowd can be a few cherished friends, or it can even be thousands and millions of people.

Tomorrow when you wake up, feel the enthusiastic energy of this large crowd giving you more enthusiasm for life.

Tonight, allow yourself to sleep well. When you wake up tomorrow, allow yourself to feel fully alive and energized. Feel more and more enthusiasm for life and for the good that you will do.

While you sleep tonight, your subconscious mind that keeps you alive by knowing how and when to breathe and by delivering oxygen and all other nutrients to the right cells, will be able to resolve many issues for you. Your subconscious mind knows exactly why you become angry. It has a storehouse of all the times you became angry in the past, and it can figure out the patterns of your anger. Regardless of what the pattern is, you can learn new reactions to those same situations.

Your subconscious mind has thousands of role models to choose from. Every person you ever met and every person you ever heard is recorded in the vast storehouse of your brain. Tonight while you sleep, your subconscious mind will be aware of the role models from whom it is worthwhile for you to learn. Your mind will then replay old situations with a new script. Your subconscious mind will have you thinking clearly and calmly in situations that previously got you angry.

• Tomorrow, you will be able to respond with love and compassion when before you responded with anger.

• Tomorrow, you will be patient when before you were impatient.

• Tomorrow, you will be centered and balanced when before you acted out of control.

• Tomorrow, you will be able to enjoy what previously you found frustrating.

• Tomorrow, you will speak respectfully to each person you encounter.

Just as your subconscious mind creates dreams every night, tonight the part of your mind that creates dreams will create new and better ways of talking and acting in old scenarios. As these images and sounds come to the forefront of your mind, they will become more and more a part of your ongoing reality tomorrow and in the future.

Your mind will now be open to finding solutions to situations for which you have not yet found solutions. As you sleep, your subconscious mind will gently find solutions that you have not thought of before. The creative part of your being will dream of creative solutions. Even if you don't remember those dreams when you wake up, you will spontaneously find solutions that you haven't thought of before. This will help you in all areas of your life. Thinking about this will help you become more and more relaxed right now. Calm feelings will be permeating your entire being. You are more and more relaxed with each and every breath.

When you think of any situation in the past that used to get you angry, you will now be able to view the situation from a different perspective. Find ways you can benefit and grow from the situation. Find humor in what you took too seriously. Mentally add enjoyable music to those scenes.

See yourself radiating with an inner joy that comes from knowing you are transforming your character. See yourself being so emotionally independent that you can easily ignore anything said to you that is not an expression of respect and sensitivity. See yourself feeling greater and greater joy that you have the inner confidence and strength to be the master of your reactions and responses. Right now allow yourself to become more and more relaxed with every breath you take.

As you continue breathing slowly and deeply, allow yourself to see a beautiful relaxing scene. Everything about this scene will give you a deeper and deeper sense of profound relaxation. The feelings of calm and relaxation are becoming more and more a part of you and will enable you to be calmer and more relaxed tomorrow.

As you become even more and more relaxed with each breath you take, you will have more confidence in your ability to create an inner world of serenity and joy. As you sleep, the messages presented here will be repeated over and over again in your subconscious mind. Your mind will calmly and serenely repeat the words: patience, serenity, joy, centered and balanced, inner peace and harmony. This will be repeated thousands and thousands of times and will travel from cell to cell in your brain adding serenity and joy to your past memories and to the future.

Now as you are about to fall asleep, see yourself as you wish to be tomorrow. Allow yourself to feel wonderful with the knowledge that you are creating yourself in the direction that you wish.

Have a pleasant and relaxing night's sleep which will help you have a more joyous day tomorrow.

B. Part Two: Morning program

Good morning. Welcome to another day of your life. Each day you create another page in your autobiography. Enjoy today's page. Speak and act in ways that enhance your life and the lives of everyone you encounter.

Today, allow yourself to create the inner world you truly desire.

Celebrate the wonderful and magnificent gift your Father, your King, has given you today: the gift of life.

Today, become closer to your Father, your King. Allow yourself to appreciate His entire creation. And you and everyone you meet are part of that creation.

Today, say each blessing with inner feelings of gratitude.

As you breathe, appreciate each breath and feel fully energized and alive as you continue breathing throughout the day. Feel grateful to your Father, your King, for each breath. The oxygen you are taking into your system is giving you life. Feel yourself becoming more and more alive with each breath you take.

Any time today, if you begin to feel tense, frustrated, or angry, slow down your breathing. Breathe slowly and deeply and feel yourself becoming calmer and more relaxed. Feel yourself becoming calmer and more relaxed right now.

Right now, ask your Father, your King, for the ability to be free of anger today. "My Father, my King, allow me to serve You with love and joy. Free me from anger. Give me the ability to speak to all of Your children with respect and love at all times. Give me the strength to walk in Your ways and continually develop my *middos* (character traits)."

Today, think about what you say and do in a way that will give you greater self-mastery.

Today, perceive every difficulty as a challenge, opportunity, and adventure. Every difficult situation with another person will enable you to develop your character.

Right now, be resolved to gain greater mastery over your emotional states. Look forward to today as a day in which you increase: patience, unconditional love and compassion, self-mastery, serenity, joy and enthusiasm, serene empowerment, and self-respect and respect for others.

People who allow what others say and do to get them angry, are giving over control of themselves to others. This isn't the wisest move. Fortunately for you, your goal is self-mastery. You will be gaining greater control over your states each and every day.

Think of the states you would like to experience today.

Imagine for a moment what your day will be like today as you experience: patience, joy and enthusiasm, serenity, serene empowerment, calm persistence, being centered and balanced, unconditional love and respect for others.

All of these states will enable you to accomplish more in your life and raise your emotional standard of living. And all of these states are incompatible with anger.

As you talk and act today in ways that are consistent with these states, they will become a greater part of your spontaneous personality.

> Just as you breathe and the breath flows to every cell in your body,
> and just as you eat and the nutrients flow to every cell in your body,
> so, too, allow these states to flow from your brain to every cell in your body.

Enhance the next exercise by making a motion with your hands that represents for you a flow of these qualities from head to toe.

Right now, allow the quality of patience to permeate your entire being. Feel yourself becoming more and more patient all the time. Repeat the word "patience." Each time you feel patient, say the word "patient." Throughout the day, repeat the word "patience" and allow yourself to experience this quality.

Right now, allow the quality of joy and enthusiasm to permeate your entire being. Feel yourself becoming more joyous and enthusiastic about life. As you talk and act with enthusiastic joy, you will radiate with positive energy. Repeat the words, "joy and enthusiasm." Throughout the day, repeat these words frequently. Whenever you feel joyous or enthusiastic, repeat these words a few times and their power will become stronger.

Right now, allow the quality of serene empowerment to permeate your entire being. Feel yourself radiating with serene empowerment. Imagine what it would feel like to experience serenity today. Your sense of empowerment which increases each day will allow you to use your inner strengths and positive qualities to pray, study, work, and interact with others in wonderful ways. Serene empowerment will enable you to accomplish things in a calm and serene manner. Repeat the words "serene empowerment."

Right now, allow the quality of calm persistence to permeate your entire being. Whenever you need to persist, be resolved to do so calmly. Feel yourself being able to be calmly persistent as long as it takes. Repeat the words "calm persistence."

Right now, allow the quality of unconditional love and compassion to permeate your entire being. As you feel increased amounts of unconditional love and compassion, you will judge people favorably and will be free from anger. See yourself as a loving and compassionate person. See yourself interacting with love and compassion even when you find this difficult. Repeat the words "unconditional love and compassion."

Right now, allow the quality of humility to permeate your entire being. Increase your awareness that all you have is a gift from your Father, your King. Increase your awareness of the immensity of the universe with all its billions and billions of galaxies, and feel awe for the Creator of it all. Think about eternity and the One Who is eternal. Feel yourself experiencing the emotional freedom of sincere humility. Repeat the word "humility." Throughout the day, your Father, your King, will send you many opportunities to increase humility. Appreciate those opportunities.

Right now, allow yourself to feel centered and balanced. Feel yourself being able to remain centered and balanced regardless of what anyone else says or does. If something does take you off your center, calmly bring yourself back to being centered and balanced. Repeat the words "centered and balanced."

Right now, feel a greater sense of self-mastery. Feel yourself gaining more and more mastery over your emotional states. Feel yourself gaining more and more mastery over all that you say and do. Today and every day, each act of self-discipline will give you a greater awareness of your power for self-mastery. Repeat the word "self-mastery." Throughout the day as you repeat the word "self-mastery," feel this quality becoming a greater part of you.

Right now, feel a greater sense of self-respect and respect for others. This will be reflected in how you speak and how you act. Repeat the words "self-respect and respect for others."

Today, allow yourself to feel tremendous joy for the self-mastery of refraining from saying anything that is a product of anger.

Feel intense empowerment as you have the strength to remain silent when silence is the wisest course of action. Your silence will not be passive, but an active silence that comes from self-mastery. As you remain silent, hear an inner cheer. Your silence is as great as any skillful move that anyone can make in a sports championship. It is a victory that deserves a standing ovation. Hear an inner voice saying to you, "I'm proud of you for the self-mastery to remain silent." Your silence is the silence of a true champion.

And when you are ready to speak, feel intense joy and self-mastery as you select your words carefully. Feel the joy of winning a great prize for your careful editing as you omit unnecessary words and say only words that will enable you to express yourself with self-respect and respect for others.

Today, see yourself transforming difficulties into triumphs. The more difficult the situation, the greater the victory.

Realize that just as you are working on greater mastery today, so are many other people. This gives you greater power, because you are a member of the group.

Since you are part of the planet, and also part of the entire universe, by your making yourself a more joyous and serene person, our planet and the entire universe is automatically a more joyous and serene place. By your reacting in an elevated manner, the world has become a better place. Let this thought empower you. This will broaden your concept of where you are living and the importance of what you say and do.

Crown yourself. Right now, mentally put a crown on your head. Don't make yourself a slave to anger — you be the ruler. Make your sense of royalty independent of how anyone else views you. When you view yourself from a viewpoint of royalty and this is an inner consciousness for you, no one can ever take it away. Maintaining an inner sense of royalty will give you greater mastery in all areas of your life.

True power is power over yourself. This is the power tha you will increase today. Feel a sense of serene empowerment permeating your entire being from head to toe. Feel every muscle and every cell radiating with serene empowerment. As you walk, feel the power you have and use to take every step. As you talk, feel the power you have and use to choose every word. As you think, think of the power you have and use to choose every thought.

You choose what you say and what you don't say. To prove this to yourself, say right now, "I choose what I say and don't say." Either you just said this, or your didn't say it. Either way you chose what you actually did. Throughout the day feel joyous that you have the free will to speak or to remain silent. Make the choices that your Father, your King, would want you to make.

Today, if anyone says or does something that used to anger you, feel the choice of saying, "I would like to get along well with you. Let's speak to each other in ways we both find acceptable."

Will everyone say in return, "That makes sense. Let's enhance each other's lives"? There is no way to know in advance. But regardless of their choice, you still have the choice of speaking in a way that is elevating.

Keep asking yourself today, "What is the best way for me to speak right now?"

Each moment you choose what to focus on and how to evaluate things. Because of these two choices, you ultimately create the world you live in. Today, be totally committed to choose thoughts that are consistent with joy, serenity, and unconditional love and compassion. Create an emotional world for yourself that will enhance your life and the lives of those with whom you interact.

If difficulties with someone arise today, think of possible solutions. Clarify your goal and ask yourself, "What is the best thing for me to say or do right now to reach my goal?" and, "What creative solution can I think of right now?" or, "What solution would a wise person suggest to me?"

Every hour on the hour create an inner mental cheer for being alive. Hear an inner enthusiastic voice shouting, "It's great to be alive!" See and hear an immense crowd cheering for your being alive. Your being alive enables you to serve and praise your Father, your King. See and hear the same immense crowd cheering you for conquering your anger.

Every time you hear a telephone ringing, hear a joyous inner cheer, "I am alive." Every time you hear a horn or bell, hear a joyous inner cheer, "I am alive." Every time you hear something that used to get you irritated or frustrated, allow yourself to hear a joyous inner cheer, "I am alive."

Today, be resolved to view potentially frustrating situations in a humorous way. If something trivial goes wrong, just laugh.

Find fascination instead of frustration. Today be resolved to be fascinated with what other people say and do. Be fascinated with the reactions of other people. At a zoo, notice how people are fascinated with animals. People are infinitely more fascinating. Each person is different. Each person has different reactions. People are absolutely fascinating. A person who is filled with fascination doesn't get angry. He gets fascinated. This fascination will help you understand other people better. Even if you disagree with someone, you can still be fascinated.

Become a greater expert at reframing. View situations and occurrences in a way that enriches your life. Find enjoyment and good feelings where others find distress and irritation.

Today ask yourself about situations, "What is good about this?"

If you begin to find something irritating, repeat to yourself, "This is getting me more and more relaxed."

Today, be committed to seeing the good in other people. When you think positively about other people, they will feel more positively about you in return. When people like you, they will be much more careful not to do things that get you angry. When there is mutual positive feelings and respect, it's easier to find solutions if difficulties arise.

Train your brain to think about the good and praiseworthy in people. Keep asking yourself, "What do I like and respect about this person?"

Today, view every person you find difficult as your partner in character development. View every encounter as an opportunity to develop your positive qualities. Today, be resolved to keep developing patience, creativity, emotional independence, confidence, courage, humor, serene empowerment, calm persistence, self-mastery, unconditional love and compassion.

Today, when you need to influence or motivate someone, use a positive approach. Keep asking yourself, "What positive motivation can I think of now?" See the situation from the point of view of the person you want to influence or motivate. Be calmly persistent. Persistence is powerful.

Learn from positive role models. Every person you meet today will have positive qualities, habits, and strengths that you can learn from. Learn from role models who handle difficult situations calmly and effectively.

Today, don't allow any setbacks to cause you to become discouraged. Learn from each experience. Every new day you are better prepared than the day before.

Think of any difficult situations that are likely to arise. Mentally prepare yourself right now to handle them with clear thinking.

Today, you won't react impulsively. Slow down and think carefully about how you will respond.

Right now, allow yourself to feel energized and fully alive. Be prepared to experience the joy of being alive throughout the day.

Live today as if it were the first day of the rest of your life, because that is exactly what it is. Have a great day!

Step 9

Take Mental Vacations to Release Stress

Step 9

Take Mental Vacations to Release Stress

T ension and stress are a major cause of anger. Consequently, learning to let go of stress and replace tense nerves with calm and peaceful feelings can free a person from a major source of anger. As you increase your coping skills, you will decrease stress and consequently experience less anger.

Taking a "mental vacation" is one excellent way to reduce stress. Even if you are not the type of person who has a vivid imagination, you will find it helpful to practice this simple technique which has proven itself many times over. The benefit of a vacation is the effect it has on your mind and state. You leave your regular environment for a while and go to a place where you give yourself permission to feel calm and relaxed.

After reading through, or having read to you, the following mental vacation scenario several times, you will probably find yourself able to visualize a calm, relaxing scene by just saying one word, such as, "waterfall," "garden," "mountain," "forest," or "palace." Whenever you feel especially calm and relaxed, add that scene to your list of mental vacations. Giving a scene a name is like giving a file name to a computer file. The file name enables you to access it. The same rule applies to your mind's magnificent data bank of words, ideas, and images.

If you do not visualize easily, the next time you see an actual picture of anything that reminds you of the scenes described here, look at the picture as if to take a mental photograph of the scene. This will help you collect a data bank of relaxing scenes that you can later call up at will.

There are many wonderful vacation spots on our planet: botanical gardens, rain forests, the Grand Canyon, the Sahara, Mount Everest, tropical islands, spectacular caverns, the Alps, national parks. There are many countries to visit and many cities to see. Just thinking about these places will change your frame of mind as you imagine what it would be like to experience each and every special place. As you visit any of these places, you can leave your anger behind and replace it with feelings of inner calm and tranquility.

Right now you are about to take a mental vacation. The benefit of a mental vacation is that even a few minutes can refresh you and give you renewed energy. A mental vacation is something that everyone can take. And if you have to return in the middle, you can always go again as soon as the opportunity presents itself. And right now you can read this entire section and take the full vacation. Or, if you wish, you can go on part of this trip and gain the benefits of a shorter mental rest. Whenever you decide to come back to the here and now, you will be able to do so and you will feel refreshed and re-energized. Your mind is powerful. Any scene you've ever seen in real life or in pictures is in your mind. You can think of the most relaxing and serene places that exist and mentally go there. Your mind is full of spectacular scenery that you can recall whenever you wish as long as you know it's there.

In your mind you can even go to a place that doesn't exist and feel the calm and relaxed feelings of being there. Almost everyone can do this by watching a film. You are about to do this in your mind. Each time you read this you will gain more insights and deeper understandings.

A mental vacation

Right now you are about to take a mental vacation that will release stress and tension. Make yourself comfortable, whether sitting in a chair or lying in bed. Give your muscles permission to relax. Tell them to "let go." Take a few slow, deep breaths and feel all your muscles relaxing.

Allow yourself to breathe slowly and deeply, taking the air in as if you are smelling a fragrant flower, and letting it go out in a whisper. Feel all your anger, frustration, tension, and stress drifting out along with each breath. Watch the gauge on your inner tension level go down as you release more and more tension with each breath out.

Feel your body get heavy and warm as it sinks down, pulled by the weight of gravity. Stretch gently and lightly, and feel the tension and stress melting away.

Now you are traveling to a beautiful waterfall. See the water flowing and falling. Hear the soothing noise of the running water. Feel how wonderful it is to be at such a magnificent waterfall. As you watch the water tumble down, feel all your stress and tension being washed away. In their place is a very peaceful feeling. You feel your mind becoming clearer and clearer, as clear as fresh water. Enjoy the waterfall and the peaceful feeling.

Seeing the waterfall reminds you of a piece of wisdom that will help you conquer anger. This piece of wisdom might be clear now or it might become clearer later on. Just allow yourself to relax and feel a greater sense of inner peace right now as your unconscious mind is gaining greater ability to conquer anger. When you see any water falling from a faucet, your mind will take you back to the waterfall. Appreciate the water that is within reach. And as you think of a waterfall, feel more centered and balanced.

Now you travel to an enchanted garden, a garden with the most beautiful flowers. Picture them in your mind: red, yellow, orange, pink, blue, violet — a panorama without beginning or end.

As you walk along this special garden and see your favorite flowers, you will be transported into a different world, a vibrant world full of life and freshness. As you walk, you feel renewed and invigorated. Allow yourself to feel a unique calm feeling as you gaze at the flowers. Each moment among these flowers calms and relaxes your mind. And as you smell the flowers and feel the warmth of the healing sun, you are reminded of the best smells you have ever experienced. Each breath among the flowers increases your profound sense of well-being and renewal. As you feel more and more relaxed, you feel your mind becoming crystal clear. You see how each flower is unique, just like you. Each and every moment you gain a greater sense of your uniqueness and cherish it — for only you are you.

Later, when you have returned from this vacation, every flower you see will remind you of this experience. Each flower will be more beautiful and more meaningful. You will appreciate your own uniqueness and beauty as you gain a profound sense of the value of all life. You will remember the special garden and realize that other people are the flowers in your garden, and must be appreciated and cared for.

Now you leave the garden and drift to a serene lake. The water is clear and peaceful. This is one of the most pleasant places you can imagine. Everything about the entire vista increases your feelings of tranquility and inner harmony. Savor the quiet.

As you look out at the horizon beyond the lake, feel a deep sense of relaxation. Look into the lake. The face reflected back to you looks calm and serene. You wish you could be this serene more often, and you begin to realize that you can. Looking out over the lake, become aware of how deep your own mind is, endlessly deep.

And as you look deeper into the lake, you see fish of all shapes and colors swimming gracefully back and forth. You are fascinated, and feel that you could watch the fish for hours and hours. And as you watch the fish, you feel slightly mesmerized, and are reminded of other times you felt this way. This feeling allows you to think of an inner quality that you want very much for yourself, a quality that you admire and respect in others. And as you think of that quality, you can imagine yourself gaining greater mastery over it. In the future, whenever you see or think of fish, they will remind you of the quality that you admire and respect.

Now lift your eyes from the lake to the majestic mountain in the distance. Looking at the mountain in all its grandeur and magnificence fills you with awe.

You approach the mountain and begin to climb. Every step up makes you feel lighter and lighter. Lighter and lighter. Each step gives you more inner strength. Feel the inner strength spreading from head to toe. Feel a powerful sense of confidence that no one can take away. As you reach the top of the mountain, look at the breathtaking scenery and feel a sense of awe permeating your entire being.

This mountain is a perfect place to introspect and think about the purpose of your life. As you stand on the top of the mountain, you feel exhilarated. You feel totally alive and energized as you gain a greater appreciation for the entire Creation. Now think about anger. View conquering anger with the same drive and intensification of will that a mountain climber views climbing a mountain. Just as you climbed this mountain, so too you can meet the challenge of anger and overcome it.

And now travel to a glorious palace filled with royal splendor that is always a part of your inner mind. As you wander from room to room, the entire experience — the intricate tapestries, the incredibly designed artwork, the luxurious multicolored carpets — has an expansive effect on you. You feel that this palace belongs to you and that you are truly royal.

As you walk through the splendor, you come upon a special painting covering an entire wall. You find this painting elevating and inspiring. You sense that this is a painting that will teach you something important, that the lesson you learn from the painting will help you on your journey through life. It might take some time until the full implications of this lesson are understood. And that is okay. You can always come back to this painting and it will change in ways that make the message relevant to the specific moment when you see it.

You leave the palace to go on a special safari. It is a trip to a safe and secure jungle that stretches for miles and miles. You appreciate the richness of life that flourishes here — lions, elephants, tigers, leopards, monkeys, pumas, butterflies, kangaroos, antelope, parrots, giraffes, and zebras. You feel a sense of fascination and wonder at the many animals your Creator created. You feel at one with the entire Creation and your inner sense of harmony gets stronger.

The many animals you see have an awareness of how special you are. And as these animals come close, you feel a bond with them as they give you the greatest amount of respect. This respect is reflected in their eyes. This increases your own self-respect and a shining light radiates from you. Each step you take in this extraordinary world increases a feeling of serene empowerment. Each animal symbolizes a part of you, and you are master of all the parts. And after the vacation you will experience greater self-mastery each and every day.

Now you go to a special marketplace in a city that you would love to visit. In the marketplace are many spices, and the aroma creates a profound sense of inner paradise. All around you is fruit from every corner of the world. There are special herbs that heal and strengthen. Thinking of them is healing and strengthening for you. Just looking around gives you an awareness of the inner potential within you. And you have greater confidence in your ability to conquer anger.

This is a happy marketplace where people are grateful for the good in their lives. Wherever you go, people smile at you with sincere friendliness and wish you well, just as you wish only good for them. Each person you see is different and each one can teach you something. You feel open to learn from the strengths and positive qualities of every person you have met in the past and will meet in the future. And wherever you are and wherever you go, as you sincerely wish others well, they will wish you well.

After you leave the marketplace, you go to a small house. It is a plain house with just the barest of furniture. You have heard of the wise person who lives here and feel fortunate for being able to gain from someone with great wisdom and insight. This wise person reminds you of someone who has inspired you in the past, and whispers an important message in your ear. You smile as you hear the message, for it is a message that has much meaning for you. Either the message is clear now or it will become clearer later on. Remember an inspiring moment in your life and feel some of that inspiration right now, as you have greater inner resolve to conquer anger.

And now you enter a gigantic library full of rows and rows of books. Walking in this special library reminds you of the great library in your brain, a library that consists of all that you have read, heard, and experienced. As you pass by the rows and rows of books, you begin to remember more and more of all that you have read and heard in your life.

And now you walk over to a book on a stand which is open to a specific page. As you look at this page, you read of an idea that will be highly beneficial for you. It might be an idea you heard before or it might be an idea you will hear today, tomorrow, or some time in the future. As you come across an idea that is important for you, you will remember it and it will serve as a guide.

Now you travel to a special forest. It is a safe and secure place that is peaceful and serene. The gigantic trees all around give you a sense of inner peace and tranquility. Each tree is a wonder, and all the trees together are awe-inspiring. As you walk among the towering trees, you feel better and better with each step. The trees keep growing just as you keep growing in the important areas of your life. As you look around, you appreciate the inner strength you feel as you are more in touch with all of your inner resources. You feel a greater sense of courage and confidence, a wise courage and confidence that enables you to take action when action is called for, and to have the courage to remain silent, just as the trees are silent, when silence might be difficult but wise. After your vacation, whenever you pass a tree, it will be a subtle reminder that you are alive, and as long as you are alive you will continue to grow and develop your character.

As you are about to leave the forest, you see a beautiful, graceful bird that reminds you of yourself. For a little while, you become this bird. As the bird begins to fly, you feel lighter and lighter. Every moment of flying gives you more inner strength and a sense of renewal. You fly over many fields of life-giving grains: wheat, barely, oats, rice. You fly over acres and acres of colorful orchards, over green pastures with cows grazing peacefully, over rich meadows, over horse farms, over parks with children playing, over rushing rivers.

As you continue flying, you feel exhilarated and peaceful. You feel a sense of inner freedom and you become aware of how many of your limitations are imaginary. Just as the wings of birds enable them to fly, so too the wings of your imagination will enable you to visualize yourself overcoming limitations. See yourself talking and acting in ways that you have always wanted to talk and act. As you continue to mentally fly, you are slowly but steadily integrating a way of being that overcomes imaginary limitations. Becoming aware of a specific limitation that is holding you back, you will be able to see yourself overcoming that specific limitation. And at the thought of being able to do this, you will have an inner sense of joy.

Each bird you see flying after your vacation will remind you of the power of your inner imagination to see yourself be and become the kind of person you've always wanted to be. You will have much greater mastery over the way you feel at any given moment, and this will make you much more centered and balanced, just as a bird in flight is perfectly balanced.

And now you can go to an inner sanctuary that is yours alone. This is a quiet and peaceful place where you can come for renewal and inner strength whenever you feel a need for it. Since your inner sanctuary is yours alone, you can design it any way you wish. As soon as you come here, your inner brain accesses your best moments. You remember how you are when you are at your best. Even a way of being that was yours for only a few seconds is yours again and again, forever.

And now you become more aware of what way of being will be best for you today, and you remember a moment when you were that way, or even a time when you pretended to be that way. Because if you can pretend to be joyous, patient, confident, compassionate, full of life and energy, centered and balanced, than you can practice thinking the thoughts and taking the actions that will enable you to internalize these qualities. So now allow yourself to be more joyous, patient, confident, compassionate, full of life and energy, centered and balanced. And now take your insights and inner strengths and utilize them for the greatest good for yourself and those you encounter today and every day in the future.

As you return from your mental vacation, you feel that you have been enriched, that your mind has expanded. You have more awareness of what to say and do in each situation that arises — and also of what not to say and do.

And now, as you feel a greater appreciation for being alive, you will have greater access to all of your inner resources. You will be more centered and balanced whenever you see anything that reminds you of your mental vacation.

Now, when you think of how wonderful it feels to be calm and relaxed, you will have a greater sense of commitment to internalize and integrate the attitudes and images that will make your entire life much calmer and more relaxed. Your mental vacations will teach you that much of the stress and tension that people experience is unnecessary. Wherever you are and whatever you do, you can create the emotional environment in your own mind that is best for you.

This will help you grow spiritually. You will connect on a deeper level with the Creator and Sustainer of the universe, your Father, your King. You will now be able to interact with His children in a more elevated way: full of wonderful feelings and free from anger, ready to do the will of your Creator with joy in your heart.

Appendix

Learn to Identify Anger

Appendix

Learn to Identify Anger

The following list of possible anger-provoking situations is by no means complete. Its purpose is to arouse awareness of everyday situations that can elicit anger. Some of the scenes, and the accompanying tension they evoke, will be instantly recognizable. Others may not seem irritating to you at all. That others find them so reflects the large subjective component of our anger.

The first time you read this list mark those situations in which you might very well get angry. The next time you read this list think about which of the reframes suggested in STEP **3** would help you deal with them.

Go over the list again, this time thinking of people who would remain calm in the very situations that you find so challenging. Ask yourself, "What is So-and-so telling himself about such a situation? How does he reframe it to prevent anger?" You might want to ask other people: "How do you view this situation?" Hearing the effective reframes of others will build up your own ability to reframe situations.

This list can be used for "reframing parties" with a group of friends. In a reframe party, difficult situations are mentioned. The participants suggest different ways to reframe those situations so that they don't cause anger or distress. The members think of ways that a person can gain spiritually, emotionally, and financially in these situations.

At a reframe party, all the participants applaud and cheer every suggestion. This creates an enjoyable atmosphere which is conducive to creativity. You will remember the enjoyment and laughter at such parties, and it will be much easier to reframe those troublesome situations in the future.

This list can also be used to desensitize yourself to irritations. Find a comfortable chair and sink into a deep state of relaxation. Breathe slowly and deeply and imagine that you are in a very soothing environment. You might want to listen to relaxing music. As you read the list, visualize yourself remaining calm and relaxed in each situation. Spend a longer time on those situations that have elicited strong reactions in the past. Repeating this exercise a number of times will enable you to be calmer in the future whenever these situations arise.

You can do the same thing with humor. Read this list and see yourself laughing. This trains your brain to find humor in situations that could cause irritation. Everyone will admit that laughing is a lot healthier and more fun than becoming annoyed or angry.

1. When someone is angry at you.
2. When a clerk gives you a difficult time.
3. When someone doesn't follow your instructions.
4. When someone tries to cheat you.
5. When someone asks you questions:
    a) that he should know the answers to himself.
    b) that seem silly or stupid.
    c) over and over again.
    d) after others have asked you the same questions many times.
    e) to challenge you.
    f) that are personal.
    g) in the "wrong tone of voice."
    h) when you are busy.
6. When someone tells you that you should have acted differently after it is too late to do anything.
7. When someone is going too slowly.
8. When someone makes too much noise.
9. When someone bumps into you.
10. When someone wastes your money.
11. When your children don't listen to you.
12. When your children fight with each other.
13. When your parents ask you to do things you don't want to do.
14. When someone insults you.
15. When someone offers you constructive criticism.
16. When someone prevents you from falling asleep or wakes you up in the middle of the night.
17. When someone violates an important principle or value.
18. When someone boasts.
19. When someone exaggerates.
20. When someone damages your property.
21. When someone is careless with your belongings.
22. When someone wastes food.

23. When someone doesn't let you finish what you have to say.
24. When someone quotes you wrongly or out of context.
25. When someone disagrees with you.
26. When someone doesn't pay you on time.
27. When someone doesn't come to visit you or neglects to show up at your celebration.
28. When someone doesn't invite you to his home or celebration.
29. When someone is ungrateful for what you have done for him.
30. When someone is needlessly nervous or afraid.
31. When someone is joyous and you aren't.
32. When someone doesn't respect a person whom you respect greatly.
33. When someone doesn't follow your advice.
34. When someone praises a competitor of yours.
35. When someone belittles your achievements.
36. When someone doesn't pay attention to you.
37. When someone doesn't validate your feelings.
38. When someone makes you feel guilty.
39. When someone claims you are making a mistake or an error.
40. When someone doesn't hire you.
41. When you are paid less than you think you are worth.
42. When an employee doesn't seem to be working as efficiently as he should.
43. When someone writes an evaluation of you which is less expansive in its praise than you would like.
44. When someone doesn't reciprocate a favor.
45. When someone is inconsistent.
46. When someone's praise lacks real feeling.
47. When someone praises you in a condescending manner.
48. When someone repeats personal information about you.

49. When someone speaks to you sarcastically.
50. When someone comes late.
51. When someone wastes your time.
52. When someone wastes his or her own time.
53. When someone asks you for a favor that you do not feel in a position to do.
54. When someone refuses to listen to you.
55. When someone interrupts you.
56. When someone embarrasses you.
57. When someone plays a practical joke on you.
58. When someone accuses you of doing something you didn't do.
59. When someone doesn't wait for you.
60. When someone deceives you.
61. When someone won't share personal information about himself.
62. When someone doesn't answer your questions.
63. When someone misunderstands or doesn't follow your instructions correctly.
64. When you are not given the honor or respect you feel you deserve.
65. When someone talks to you rudely.
66. When someone uses your belongings without permission.
67. When someone refuses to lend you something.
68. When someone misplaces your belongings.
69. When someone returns something later than promised.
70. When someone keeps changing instructions.
71. When someone gives you too many instructions too fast.
72. When someone doesn't clean up after himself and you have to do it for him.
73. When someone does something that is dangerous to himself or others.

74. When someone shouts at you.
75. When someone keeps you waiting.
76. When someone is impatient.
77. When someone puts you down for being overly emotional.
78. When someone accuses you wrongly of being angry.
79. When a salesperson tries to sell you something you don't want.
80. When someone is more stringent than you in religious practices.
81. When someone criticizes an organization with which you are affiliated.
82. When someone tells you that you are overreacting.
83. When someone ignores you.
84. When someone makes fun of your accent.
85. When someone tries to rush you.
86. When someone complains in a self-pitying manner.
87. When someone cries.
88. When someone speaks to you patronizingly.
89. When someone gives you a gift you don't like.
90. When someone doesn't thank you enough.
91. When someone acts immaturely.
92. When you ask someone not to do something, and he does it anyway.
93. When someone gives you unsolicited advice.
94. When someone claims more credit for help rendered than you think reasonable.
95. When someone demands gratitude.
96. When someone complains about you to others.
97. When someone repeats the same mistake over and over again.
98. When someone keeps asking you to repeat what you have told them.

99. When someone acts towards you in a passive-aggressive manner.
100. When someone doesn't take what you have to say seriously.
101. When someone doesn't believe you.
102. When someone belittles your professional competency.
103. When someone doesn't return your telephone calls.
104. When someone needs constant reassurance.
105. When someone fails to pick up from you something he asked to borrow.
106. When someone else takes credit for something you did.
107. When someone who is supposed to fix something for you procrastinates.
108. When someone gives you investment advice that results in a loss.
109. When someone name-drops to make himself seem important.
110. When someone lies to you.
111. When someone tells you how much better things were in the "old days."
112. When someone blames you for his mistakes.
113. When someone tells you that you are abusive even though you only raised your voice a little.
114. When someone denies your charge that he is abusive.
115. When someone acts like an expert and isn't.
116. When you are trying to look at the situation positively, and someone tells you, "You're talking yourself into it."
117. When someone celebrates while you are suffering.
118. When a salesperson is not sufficiently responsive.
119. When you do someone a favor and he criticizes the way you did it.
120. When your computer breaks down.
121. When someone blames a computer for his own error.
122. When someone keeps asking you for the time.

123. When you feel that your spouse is too hard or too soft with the children.
124. When you feel that your parents are too hard or too soft with you or your siblings.
125. When someone doesn't give enough charity.
126. When someone doesn't take care of himself.
127. When someone drives poorly.
128. When someone is critical of your driving.
129. When someone criticizes your cooking or won't eat food you prepared.
130. When someone praises others but not you, and you feel that you are as deserving as the one praised.
131. When someone shows off.
132. When someone is not friendly.
133. When someone is too friendly.
134. When someone is not neat.
135. When someone complains that you are not neat.
136. When someone acts or speaks in a bigoted fashion.
137. When someone distorts reality.
138. When someone gets his facts wrong.
139. When someone minimizes your difficulties or troubles.
140. When someone exaggerates his difficulties or troubles.
141. When you feel you are doing more than your share.
142. When someone tells you to stop singing.
143. When someone continues singing after you told him that his singing bothers you.
144. When someone keeps misplacing things.
145. When someone refuses to seek help for his problems.
146. When someone walks on a still wet floor you have just washed.
147. When someone won't stop talking about his health problems.

148. When you are accused by someone of criticizing him even though you were only trying to explain why you acted as you did.
149. When someone speaks too low for you to hear, even after requests to speak louder.
150. When someone keeps changing his mind about what he wants from you.
151. When you are talking on the telephone, and someone who only hears your side of the conversation interrupts you with irrelevant comments.
152. When someone expresses pleasure over your distress.
153. When someone tells you, "I told you so."
154. When someone uses up something that you wanted to use.
155. When someone "spaces out" every time you ask him to do something.
156. When someone you are working with is too slow.
157. When someone tells you that what you said was simplistic.
158. When you feel that someone is making a simple thing too complex.
159. When someone laughs at you.
160 When someone encroaches on your space.
161. When you were not told to reorder a needed item in time.
162. When someone repeatedly misses deadlines.
163. When someone pressures you to meet deadlines.
164. When you are searching for something, and someone tells you that you should be more careful where you put things.
165. When someone doesn't wake you up on time.
166. When someone keeps trying to wake you up.
167. When someone tells you that you overpaid.

168. When someone tells you that something which is difficult for you is easy.
169. When someone takes too long in the shower.
170. When someone rushes you when you are in the shower.
171. When you make a charitable donation and the recipient asks for more.
172. When someone asks for charity that you feel he doesn't need.
173. When you are asked a difficult question on a test.
174. When someone doesn't study sufficiently and then complains that the tests you write are too difficult.
175. When someone takes your seat.
176. When you see someone fail to help another person struggling with a heavy load.
177. When someone reacts defensively to your rebuke.
178. When you try to correct someone, and he tells you, "It's your issue."
179. When someone spills something on you.
180. When someone talks during prayers.
181. When someone doesn't visit you when you are ill.
182. When someone forgets your name.
183. When someone complains that you forgot his name.
184. When someone is too interested in the news.
185. When someone has no interest in the news.
186. When someone tells you that your jokes aren't funny.
187. When someone tells you stupid jokes.
188. When someone doesn't give you vital information.
189. When someone you care about doesn't eat properly.
190. When someone comments on your weight.
191. When someone makes jokes about your height.
192. When someone speaks negatively about others in your presence.

193. When someone stops you from speaking about others.
194. When someone reminds you of past mistakes.
195. When someone says, "You always," or "You never."
196. When you tell someone that you are in a rush, and he keep talking.
197. When someone questions your motivations for doing good.
198. When someone puts down your accomplishments as overcompensating for your weaknesses.
199. When someone keeps tapping his toes, snapping his fingers, or whistling after you've asked him to stop.
200. When someone questions your intelligence.
201. When someone makes fun of what you are wearing.
202. When someone points at you.
203. When someone doesn't allow you to be yourself.
204. When someone goes shopping and forgets to buy what you asked for.
205. When someone accuses you of ingratitude.
206. When someone refuses to answer your questions or answers evasively.
207. When a person builds himself up by making you look bad.
208. When someone is excessively pessimistic.
209. When someone is excessively optimistic.
210. When you are accused of being excessively pessimistic or optimistic.
211. When someone wrongly claims you aren't taking him seriously.
212. When someone keeps telling you, "You don't understand."
213. When someone is unfair.
214. When someone accuses you of being unfair.
215. When someone is apathetic about the suffering of others.

216. When someone denigrates others for faults which he himself possesses.
217. When someone doesn't congratulate you on a praise-worthy accomplishment.
218. When someone is too extroverted.
219. When someone is too introverted.
220. When someone belittles your dreams or aspirations.
221. When someone doesn't greet you properly.
222. When someone disregards your feelings.
223. When someone tries to humiliate you.
224. When someone is too zealous or not zealous enough.
225. When someone acts in a wimpy manner.
226. When someone reacts aggressively.
227. When someone is too abrupt.
228. When someone speaks sharply or bluntly.
229. When someone is absentminded.
230. When someone is too certain of himself.
231. When you feel left out.
232. When you see someone running after honor.
233. When someone is inconsiderate.
234. When someone refuses to conform.
235. When someone does not give you the encouragement you need or expect.
236. When someone offers platitudes in place of solid advice.
237. When someone close to you goes to a competitor of yours.
238. When someone doesn't give you the permission you sought.
239. When someone tries to flatter you.
240. When someone tries to flatter others.
241. When someone keeps arguing with what you say.
242. When someone doesn't keep his commitments or promises.

243. When someone doesn't give you your messages.
244. When someone tells you, "It's all in your mind."
245. When someone mimics you.
246. When someone speaks to you insolently.
247. When someone remains calm while you are upset.
248. When someone is highly judgmental.
249. When someone is insincere.
250. When authority figures don't meet your expectations.
251. When authority figures try to tell you what to do.
252. When someone calls you by a nickname.
253. When a messenger tells you bad news.
254. When someone tries to break into a line.
255. When someone is gullible.
256. When someone is cynical.
257. When someone refuses to accept your help.
258. When someone spends money ostentatiously.
259. When someone belittles a friend of yours.
260. When someone blocks you from getting ahead.
261. When someone claims to have accomplished more than he actually has.
262. When someone doesn't respect your boundaries.
263. When someone gives you the wrong directions.
264. When someone brings out the worst in you.
265. When someone doesn't stick to a budget.
266. When someone acts like a bully.
267. When someone overburdens you with work.
268. When someone keeps challenging you.
269. When it takes someone a long time to make a decision.
270. When someone acts coldly towards you.
271. When you suspect someone of malingering.
272. When someone is too conscientious or not conscientious enough.
273. When someone lacks flexibility.

274. When someone is deliberately annoying you.
275. When someone disobeys you.
276. When someone makes you look foolish.
277. When someone refuses to forgive you after you apologize.
278. When someone thinks that he can get away with distressing you by asking forgiveness.
279. When someone disturbs you during meals.
280. When someone disturbs you while you are studying.
281. When someone doesn't give you a letter of recommendation.
282. When someone makes a commitment for you that you feel obligated to honor.
283. When someone denies that he said or did something which you know he did.
284. When someone asks you for your opinion and advice and then rejects it.
285. When someone changes his plans and doesn't inform you.
286. When a person asks you questions for the purpose of trapping you.
287. When someone is clearly angry but denies it.
288. When you reach an agreement and the other party tries to change the deal at the last moment.
289. When someone tries to imitate somebody else rather than being himself.
290. When someone belittles you for modeling yourself after someone else's positive points.
291. When someone tells you that you need psychological help.
292. When someone is rigid.
293. When someone tells you he is giving you a bargain and you find out he didn't.

294. When someone is eating and doesn't offer you any food.
295. When someone expects you to offer him food whenever you eat in his presence.
296. When someone disagrees with your political views.
297. When someone accuses you of philosophizing when you try to talk about something that is important to you.
298. When someone makes trivial matters more important than they really are.
299. When someone denies your physical or emotional suffering.
300. When someone is a hypochondriac.
301. When you offer valid criticism to someone, and he reacts angrily.
302. When someone calls you out of the blue after not having spoken to you for a long time.
303. When you need to speak to someone, and he engages himself in irrelevancies.
304. When someone tells you not to take an umbrella and it rains.
305. When someone packs your suitcases and forgets to put something in.
306. When someone ignores your advice on how to save money.
307. When someone insults you and then accuses you of acting like a baby for feeling hurt.
308. When you try your hardest, and you are accused of not trying hard enough.
309. When someone causes you unnecessary extra work.
310. When someone insults your parents, children, or grandchildren.
311. When you work hard on a task or project, and instead of focusing on what you did, all a person does is focus on a minor point not to his liking.

312. When someone speaks against you to others.

313. When someone keeps talking about irrelevant topics.

314. When someone talks you into buying something you didn't really need or want.

315. When someone doesn't let you talk.

316. When someone requests that you do something and then makes a contradictory request. ("Put this here. No, put it there. No, put it in the first place.")

317. When someone asks you for your opinion, and then accuses you of being controlling when you offer your opinion.

318. When someone insults your intelligence.

319. When someone breaks an agreement.

320. When someone deleted your backup files and you no longer have the originals.

321. When someone keeps asking you for favors.

322. When someone sets a verbal trap for you to see how you will respond.

323. When someone purposely gets you angry and then asks you, "What did your anger teach you?"

324. When someone gets you angry and then says, "I thought you were working on overcoming anger."

NOTES

NOTES

NOTES

NOTES

NOTES

NOTES

NOTES

This volume is part of
THE ARTSCROLLSERIES®
an ongoing project of
translations, commentaries and expositions
on Scripture, Mishnah, Talmud, Halachah,
liturgy, history, the classic Rabbinic writings,
biographies, and thought.

For a brochure of current publications
visit your local Hebrew bookseller
or contact the publisher:

Mesorah Publications, ltd.

4401 Second Avenue
Brooklyn, New York 11232
(718) 921-9000